Acknowledgements

Thank you to my divine family and friends who have supported me over the years. I thank those who may not be related by blood but are related by love. A special thanks to my supremely, beloved daughter; my beloved, divine parents and my divinely, beloved siblings. I give thanks for every connection I have experienced. I give thanks to my ancestors and the supreme force!!!

Dedication

I dedicate this book to the love within us all. To Yemaya the Yoruba Orisha who is known as the goddess of living ocean. She is water. Water is essential to us all. We come from it when we are in our mothers womb. We are made up of it. I give thanks to and for my ancestors, who live through us as us. I give thanks to Zuri, who is a seed that has been utilized to show me who I am. I give thanks to my divine family, those who are not only related by blood but those who are related by Love. This has been a dream since I was a child to become a published author. It took me a while to realize that I have been an author for a very long time by what I say, what I do and how I think. Yes, I have been an author and so are you. What will your story be? Last but not least thank you to anyone who is reading this, you are reading my heart. I share with courage, love and peace with the will to continuously create.

Printed in the United States of America
ISBN 978-0-692-91091-7

~ FOREWORD ~

There is much to be gained as ordinary acquaintances become treasured friends. I met Dannie nearly two decades ago when we attended the same place of worship. What I remember the most is how her smile and the intensity in her eyes were always honest. She was assertive and confident. She was imaginative and inspiring, and easily became a role model for young ladies in our organization. I admired her artistry as she danced and sang. At that time, I had no way of knowing the depth of her creativity and the many gifts she had not yet allowed to be revealed.

A few years ago, after time and space had amassed between us, we subsequently crossed paths again after finding ourselves back in the same small town where we became acquainted as teenagers. In the time that passed, Dannie had become a mother and educator. She began to seek the truths that resonated with her about Spirit, and that had provided clarity on the woman she was, is, and is becoming. She was on a journey to find her own rhythm and her own voice, and as a result, she was more in tune with her higher Self than ever before. Again, I admired her. The intensity in her eyes was all too familiar, and I felt as if she could see through me. I needed a friend who could see through me. Reconnecting with Dannie has been a blessing the Universe knew I needed. She is empathetic and supportive, genuine and trustworthy. She is a dreamer and a visionary. She is a listener and an encourager who consistently challenges the people she loves to seek and become their best Self. She shares herself and her experiences with others altruistically. She is no longer merely a friend to me; she is my sister.

I have eagerly awaited the unveiling of Eyes as Bright as the Moon since Dannie communicated her desire to write and publish a book. We have shared many late-night conversations about life, light, and love. We have shared ideas and discussed our goals and plans for the future. I only hope that throughout this process, I have reciprocated a portion of the positivity that she projects on me as I pursue my dreams. Eyes as Bright as the Moon and narratives like it are necessary, and I trust that each reader will revel in the sensory descriptions and emotional details in the same way I did while reading an excerpt from the book. I am beyond delighted to accompany Dannie on this part of her journey, and I look forward to every divine moment that occurs in her life and the lives of those she touches through her gift of writing.

Dr. Dramona Page ~ 'Dr. DeeP'

About The Author

I am so mysterious; I am unexplainable even to myself at certain moments yet it always makes sense in hindsight.

Some call them psychics; others call them prophets, seers or those with intuitiveness and or insight. She heard a conversation one night through the gift of intuitiveness. The question she heard was, "What did you see in her?" and her reply while in deep thought within after hearing the question asked so clear: "What he saw was more than, having nothing to do with the physical; for what he saw could never be erased. For what he saw was within. It just so happened to shine in the midst of adversity as she traveled on a soul's journey."

She began to see, love and experience the love within. As she accepted this truth, her life would forever change. He helped her to see beyond. Not so much in those moments but it would be many years before she would be ready to accept love so deep within. It wasn't him. It was love, a soul's journey; eyes as bright as the moon, sol light shining through.

At one time all of the philosophies, teachings, and truths that were unveiling and being revealed had her head spinning. If it were not for those things she was remembering and learning, she would not have seen the inward path. Those philosophies, teachings and/or truths, revealed levels of an innate awareness of unique sequences and tailored patterns that connect ever-evolving truths that are for a specific trip ~~ the journey she was on.

She was on a path to discovering and rediscovering. Where soul traveled would be exactly where she needed to be in order to accept her truest self. Through heartache and love she realizes now that she gained a higher level of awareness. What she imagined actually turned out to be real. Eyes as bright as the moon, sol light shining through.

Chapter 1

My name is James Reginald Fletcher III. My birth date is July 12, 1940. Everyone called me Fletch, well; everyone except for Ma and Sadie. They called me James Reginald most of the time. Sadie is extra short. She is just under 5 feet and I am 6'3". She made me feel what I intuitively have always felt. She made me feel special, loved and protected. Sadie instantly became a major influential person in my life.

My childhood was full of lessons that revealed love. From early on I can remember many sleepless nights; and not because I could not sleep, but because I was up comforting my Ma as she cried many tears. I would say, " Ma, it's ok. It's ok Ma." I would hold on to her tight. My love for her was and is as pure as a 3-year-old's love could be. I never really knew why my Ma would be up crying in the wee hours of the night, until one day in 1954 (eleven years later). I'm not too sure about the month, but it was very hot. So I'm certain it was in the summer when my Ma decided to take my two sisters and myself downtown in Wilmington, Delaware. My sister Ruby was 13, my sister Lois was age 12 and I was 14. Ma didn't really take us out much. She always seemed as though she was watching or waiting for something and at the time I didn't know what, until that day in 1954.

My sisters and I were so excited to be out and about with Ma. All three of us rode in the back seat while Ma drove. I loved Ma so much. She is the color of sand with long golden brown hair that she typically wore in a bun but for some reason on this day, it was out. Her hair reminded me of an ocean's waves. Ma adored both of her parents, big Daddy Joe and big Mama Ruby. She looked nothing like big Daddy Joe and there was a slight resemblance of big Mama Ruby there. Anyway, when we went out with Ma we always went downtown. We would order lunch at a Mom-and-Pop diner, and felt so happy. For me, I was just happy that Ma seemed to be happy. My sister Lois worshiped the ground Ma walked on, the toilet she sat on, the fork she ate off of, the tissue she blew her snot on. Ruby, on the other hand, was a different story. I think that Ruby resented the fact Ma seemed to favor Lois. Ruby was also the sassy one and still is to this day, Ma didn't care for that very much.

We arrived at Ma's favorite kitchen diner. We had ordered our food and began to give thanks then began eating and it was so good. We all ordered the same thing every time. I had the fish and chips. Ruby ordered fried chicken and potato salad. Lois ordered a tuna sandwich with fries on the side and salad. Ma ordered a root beer float, chicken thigh and a biscuit. I always finished first. I only had a few more bites left when I just happened to glance up at Ma. She was staring out of the window that was directly in front of our booth. Her eyes were as bright as the moon. She asked for the check and told us to hurry. She quickly got up from the table and spoke with the waitress. Ma came back and said, "Finish up and when I come out of the ladies room we will be leaving; now come on, go on and finish up!" So my sisters and I did just that. Ma seemed anxious and even though I really did not know exactly what she was anxious for I could see it on her face and I surely felt it. My sisters were finished eating; I on the other hand, was trying to slurp down the rest of my root beer, because we did not drink things like root beer at home.

Ma quickly paid for our meals and left a tip after returning from the ladies room and began walking so fast to not be in a hurry but not too fast as if it were an emergency. It was as if she knew how much time she had to get to wherever she needed to go.

We arrived in front of a tall building not too far from the diner. Ma parked the car and she just sat there staring at this building. No one asked her why we were sitting. My sisters started hitting one another and I slid up with my face in both hands staring at the building with Ma. It was as if my sisters were in the background for a moment until Lois started crying. Ma was so focused that she had not even noticed until Lois said, "Ma, Ruby pinched me!" still whimpering and Ma finally said, "Ruby if you don't leave your sister alone I'm going to give you something to cry for and I don't want to hear no back talk and I will give wind of this to your Pop, do you hear me?" A tear fell from Ruby's eye as she looked out the window and quietly responded, "Yes Ma." We all knew Ma was not going to spank Ruby. She told us she didn't like spankings. I think Ruby cried because she thought that Ma believed Lois could do no wrong. The thing about it was Lois had started the hitting and was always teasing but it really did seem as though Lois could do no wrong in Ma's eyes and Ruby resented Ma for that, however; Ruby loved Lois so much.

Ruby looked a lot like Pop. She is the color of coffee and long coal black hair. Lois, well; she looked very different. Lois is very light, almost pale looking, she was lighter than Ma. Her eye color are a greenish brown. I look like Ma and Pop. My skin tone is the color of almond which is also the shape of my eyes. All three of us have deep dimples on each cheek and one on the chin just like... Well, at the time I did not know who. Until this very tall man came outside of the tall building we had been watching for quite some time. In that moment it seemed to be the most silent it had ever been. The time was still. The moment turned into the longest breath I had ever held. The man stood there looking directly at Ma and then walked towards the car. I was in the back seat, but I was sitting so close up to the front I saw a tear fall from Ma's eye. He stood by the drivers side for a moment and then bent down to look in the back seat. He smiled having the most brilliant smile, nodded his head and tipped his hat. We stared; still holding our breath. He went inside his jacket and pulled out an envelope and Ma rolled down the window to take the envelope; but they held hands for what seemed to be longer than a moment for an exchange of a white envelope. I remember thinking how Lois looked just like the man's twin. He was a distinguished looking man. He was about 6'4" with dimples, brown hair, and almond shaped greenish brown eyes, like Lois's eye color.

My sisters and I were still in silence. He took out a cigar as he turned slowly. I saw tears fall from his eye. I think his tears fell from his eyes moving slower than he had anticipated. I noticed him wiping them discretely and as he was about to walk back towards the building a lady walked towards him and he and this lady exchanged words then she began to walk towards the car and Ma began to really weep. The lady was an older woman. She held Ma's hand, pulled out a handkerchief for Ma and one for herself. Ma was the spitting image of this lady. Ma would wear her hair pulled back in a bun, exactly how this lady had hers. Ma would wear a necklace of a stone that was pink, known as a rose quartz. The lady had one on as well. The lady finally bent down to get a good look at us three. Her eyes lit up and her eyes filled with more tears, she smiled. She never let go of Ma's hand. The man called for the lady and she slowly walked away. Ma rolled the window up but sat there a little while longer. All three of us still sat in silence, but boy were we thinking and asking questions in our minds. We would not even dream of asking questions. Well, we as in Lois and I. Ruby on the other hand....

My Ma was about to turn the car on and the lady came back with a small box and a note. I noticed this time that the lady had on two stones, the rose quartz and moldavite stone which is green. Ma opened the box and there was a green stone just like the lady's stone. Ma put it on the necklace that had the pink stone rose quartz on it, she rolled the window up, wiped her tears and everyone was silent.

On the way home, Ma decided to stop at the park and let us run around. Ma grabbed a beautiful quilt and began walking towards one of the biggest trees in the park. Ruby, Lois and I were chasing each other. Ruby stopped and looked over at Ma and then she ran to go sit under the tree with Ma. Lois and I picked up where we left off and start chasing each other again. Lois and I played for a while. Ruby sat with Ma under the tree. Lois and I were on the swings. The only 2 swings in the park. I watched Ruby and Ma. They laughed, talked and Ma even laid down on Ruby's lap. Ma pulled out the note the lady had given her. Lois and I both jumped off of the swing and started running towards Ma. She did not even look up in our direction. Ma just told us to sit down. Lois and I decided to lay down on the quilt that Ma had pulled out of the car but did not use. Lois grabbed one end of the quilt and I grabbed the other end spreading the quilt out and we laid head to head. I was laying beside Ma and Lois head was right there beside Ma, just the opposite direction. We laid there looking up at the sun, the sky, the trees and just all of nature. We laid in silence for a while. Everyone had questions but we were waiting for Ma. We waited patiently as if we knew she had been carrying something for a while that seemed to be full of emotion and pain. I wanted to know but I was prepared to wait until she was ready and I felt that all three of us knew this instinctively, along with the fact that in those days you didn't really ask questions; but our Ma was different. She talked to us about aspects of life that some adults may frown upon discussing with children. Ma didn't care one bit. She once told us, "I share with you what I know will be beneficial to you three; and sometimes adults try to hide these sorts of things to protect children. They try to make a child feel that they live in a world where you always feel protected. The fact of the matter is that sometimes you don't feel it, but you have to know that you are... Ruby, Lois and James Reginald." We answered, "Yes Ma." "Do you hear what I'm saying?" we respond, "Yes Ma." We continued to lay on the quilt in silence, waiting for Ma to share. Ma began humming an original song. Ma had the voice that was what some would say was before her time. She did all kinds of tricks with her voice. Her voice reminded me of magic. It could have you feel like you were in a trance. Her voice was and still is truly an instrument.

She stopped humming and began to sing the words. [One of the most significant things in this world is love and its beauty is in its strength, it has the power to touch effortlessly....and she began humming again and slowly the humming grew faint. I was watching Ma because when she sang it was as if she was singing directly to you. She'd touch you without lifting a hand. The way she moved her notes it was as if she was massaging your heart.

We laid there, all four of us silently. We knew Ma wanted to tell us but she just wasn't ready. Ruby asked Ma about the stones. I remember thinking Ruby doesn't really care about those stones she was just hoping that would push Ma to spill those beans.

Ruby said, "Ma those sure are pretty stones." Ma looks down at her stones and holds them in one hand holding onto the necklace with the other hand and then Ma sits up and looks at us three and says with a smile, "thank you." She then grabs the pink one and says, "My Ma gave it to me, your big Mama Ruby." Big Mama was quite the rebel. She spoke about things that most of us colored people would consider blasphemous. Ma began to tell us about the stone. "Big Mama Ruby told me that this stone will open my heart if I closed my eyes and take deep breaths, feeling the love that I already am, while having loving thoughts and this stone would somehow amplify the love or hold that love too. The funny thing is I feel it when I hold it and when a sad thought comes, I remember what big Mama said."

My sister's and I quietly sat there looking at this stone as if it were magical and Ma must have figured that out because she grabbed my face and said, "it's" in you, the stone is just a beautiful reminder of all that you are, it's just something else you can hold." My sisters and I still sitting quietly because now we were, well; I was wondering why the lady had the same pink stone and why she gave Ma a green stone.

We sat quietly by this time we were all sitting up; still under the tree. Ruby, Lois and I were waiting and hoping with our fingers literally crossed that Ma would say something about those two people we saw earlier today. Ma began humming again. Her voice sounded as if it were dancing. She stopped and said well, we should be going so I can prepare dinner. The three of us felt a sadness. We knew that those two people were significant. Ma just wasn't ready to tell us who they were. We grabbed our blankets, folded them and headed back to the car. We saw Pop's car parked there. I wondered how long he had been waiting there. He finally looked up. Ruby said, "Pop?" He got out of the car. He walked over to Ma, hugged her tight and fell down to his knees and began crying. At this point, we were all crying and the four of us did not even know why but Pop was obviously crying for a reason. We had never seen him cry before.

Ma was weeping quietly I almost think she really did not want to know what was wrong with Pop. I really felt we were all nervous. Ma knelt down with him she still did not part her lips to ask him anything. Ma just held Pop as he rested in Ma's bosoms. My sisters and I were leaning on Ma's car not really knowing what to do, all we had were tears. Pop finally stood up, helping Ma up. Pop said, "It's my Ma." He let out a loud cry. My Ma must have known what he meant exactly because she started to cry again which made Ruby and Lois cry all the more. I stood there waiting to hear what happened to Grandma Tee. Finally, Ma ask Pop, "When?" Pop answered, "This rising." Grandma Tee was Big Mama Ruby's (Ma's Ma) closest friend and they introduced Ma and Pop to one another. When Ma and Pop were school age, they were inseparable but they bickered all day, every day until around the age of twelve or thirteen. They truly had a bond.

The bond became more intense as the years went on. They would tell each other everything. Everyone thought for the longest that they were courting but they were honestly just friends. Besides, during those days you didn't really date (court) at the ages they were when they met. The only thing you could do then was exchange smiles, hold her books and walk her home; other than that, that was pretty much it.

Grandma Tee practically helped raised Belle (My Ma) just as well as Big Mama Ruby helping to raise James (Pop's). Pop's dad, my Grandaddy was a good man. Grandma Tee loved him very much. I felt so proud to be Grandpa James grandson. Grandpa James returned to the stars, as Grandma Tee would say it. He passed on before I was born. Grandma Tee would always say, "James you're an old soul with a new body, you're too much like My James." At the time I did not know what she meant but I remembered that and when I grew a little older I brought it back up and asked her what exactly did she mean, although by this time I had an idea of exactly what she meant but during those days you didn't hear much about people talking about reincarnation. Mostly everyone in our neighborhood went to Sunday morning worship service and that did not include Grandma Tee or the rest of my family for that matter. Not Ma, Pop, Big Mama or Big Daddy, no one. Well, no one that I knew of at the time. They had a spiritual way of doing things, but I can't say I knew it to have a name though.

Grandma Tee would get up every "New" day (as she would refer to a morning) taking a few deep breaths and then go into the kitchen for a special tea that smelled so good. You could smell it throughout the house. After she'd prepared her tea she would grab her bundle of what look like sticks and burn them. This would also leave a cleanly fragrance. She would walk around humming. No words, only humming. After she'd finish walking through the house she would go in the backyard and sit by the tree planted by her grandma, she would be smiling having such a pleasant look on her face from the time she rose until it was time to go back to bed again that night. I know all of this because my sisters and I always slept in her bed and she would sleep on the sofa that she had in her bedroom. I do not know why we slept with her because she had 4 other empty big bedrooms. I think she just wanted us close to her while we slept. I loved Grandma Tee. She just always seems to know what you needed to feel. She always made everyone around her laugh. Grandma Tee was so beautiful. She had very keen features with a full head of hair, like cotton and she also had dark skin. Grandma Tee's friends would go to the beauty parlor and try to get her to come along and get a press and curl; but Grandma Tee would always put up a fight and she would win. She would say "Ain't a thing wrong with my hair growing on my temple! I'm not putting them cracker chemicals in and on my temple, to try and disconnect me from the all infinite power and have me confused in my temple. I love all that I am. And no one can take that away from me; because it is who I am. Gotta keep my blood pure." What grandma put in her body and her scalp was very important to her. She made oils, soaps, and ointments for the body and especially for the hair. She would insist that Ma would only use those things on us and Ma always did. The funny thing is last week Grandma Tee gave Ma the recipe for all of those products and asked her to promise that she would always use them on us.

Well, we were on our way back home but only to stop and pick something up that Ma wanted to have before going to grandma Tee's house. Pop had to go back to grandma Tee's and finish making arrangements. I asked Ma, "Why does Pop have to go right now?" She said, "because your Pop is preparing for grandma Tee's memorial." Ma asked me to help prepare a little sacred ceremony for Grandma Tee. I had to go and get Grandma Tee's copper pitcher that she had given to Ma. Ma called Ruby and Lois downstairs, and she had some seeds for each of us to plant in honor of grandma Tee. Ma also had a bundle of sticks and grandma Tee's favorite handkerchief. The handkerchief was the color of lilac with grandpa James initials stitched in a deep dark color purple. Grandma Tee had lilacs planted not too far from her tree in her backyard.

As Ma was gathering the rest of her items for the sacred ceremony, I just stood there in the living room staring out of the window. I just could not stop thinking about Grandma Tee, how close I felt to her and how much closer I felt to her in that moment. "James, (pause) James, do you hear me calling you?" "Coming Ma." Grandma Tee lived about eight blocks down and three streets behind us.

When we arrived at grandma's house a preacher man was there. I had never seen this man before but as soon as we got out of the car we noticed this tall slender man who looked a lot like Grandma Tee; the resemblance was eerie.

"Ma." "Ruby, hush!" "but Ma, who is that man?" Ma smiling at the preacher man who was wearing glasses and he smiled with tears falling from his eyes. Ma reached out to hug him and he received the embrace. "How have you been Uncle Pete?" asked Ma. The man replied, "I have been pretty good considering." We never knew Grandma Tee had any family other than a sister and a few cousins, some who lived right here in Wilmington and then there were some who lived in New York somewhere. They were grandma Tee's Dad's family. The only family of grandma Tee's we have been around is Aunt Dot, her six children, and Uncle Willie which is Aunt Dot's husband.

I had to go find Pop. I had to ask him who this Uncle Pete was. Maybe he will tell me. After Ma and Uncle Pete hugged and me and my sisters were introduced and everyone greeted one another, we followed Ma into the house. I told Ma I would be right back, as Ma placed and prepared the items in the bag needed to pay our respects.

Pop was upstairs digging in what use to be his toy trunk. It was a wooden trunk that had different colored paint over it along with a knitted throw at the foot of grandma Tee's bed. She had a lot of things in there. A few of Pop's old toys, photo albums, even a jewelry box that made music when you either opened it or turned the knob on the back of it. I stood in the doorway watching Pop kneeling while searching through this trunk as if he were really searching for something. I moved my left foot forward and the floor squeaked, Pop turned around, stared at me for a moment and turned around to keep searching. I wanted to ask him about the preacher man that Ma referred to as Uncle Pete but I just wasn't sure if it was a good time. I decided to turn around and go back downstairs until Pop said, "James," I, of course, answered, "Yes, Pop?" I mean it was as if he heard my thought and before I could turn around or make any movement for that matter. He asked me to come in; so I did. He told me to sit down and I did. I did not know what he was going to tell me but I knew that it was something, something important. I was going to sit on grandma Tee's bed but I decided to sit in her rocking chair; the one in the corner by her window. By this time my Pop was sitting on the trunk looking down at the floor. He looked to be pondering. I started to become a little nervous. "I never told you this or anyone other than your Ma but for a while when I was a youngster I was ashamed of Grandma Tee. Immediately I responded with, "ashamed? of Grandma Tee? How? Why?" "You see, Grandma Tee was considered to be a rebel, she did things her way. She didn't care who liked her or who didn't like her. Your grandma Tee was a lot like my Granny, Sarah Mae Johnson. One of the special things about Sarah is that although she was a slave she was very proud of her lineage and most people didn't like that about her nor did they understand it. Most of her friends and a few family members thought she had it made because Johnson treated her well. Many believed he loved her because he did not separate Grandma Tee from granny. Many men wanted your grandma Tee. She was physically strong and physically beautiful. She was very clever. She taught herself to read, write and she innately knew spiritual magic. Johnson would not sell her. I would always remember when Ma (your grandma Tee) would get that fire in her eyes when someone would try to tell her that Johnson loved her Mother. She would say, "That is not true. There is no truth in that there statement. There is no way that an orangutan monkey could ever love my mother." She would also say, you do not reward mankind for pretending his behavior is honoring nature. It is nature or natural for a mother and father to be with their children and this behavior Johnson presented is not in his nature. He gets no special recognition from me" "James?", "Yes Pop?" "Your grandma Tee's Father was killed after he killed Johnson's brother for attempting to violently hurt and touch people in places they had no business being touched. Namely, your Great Grandma Sarah and your Grandma Tee." I remember sitting there listening to Pop and I could hear Grandma Tee's sweet voice, humming in the background as Pop was talking. I could smell her sweet smelling tea. When Pop had gotten silent, I noticed tears falling from his eyes. Then Pop says, (while wiping his tears) "Now what did you want to ask me?" My eyes were as bright as the moon. Pop's was smiling. I asked, "Who is Uncle Pete?" His reply; "Uncle Pete is grandma Tee's brother." I had so many questions to ask but I didn't. I noticed Pop wiping tears from his eyes, which made me know that there was more; but in due time, I knew he would share whatever it was. As Pop was still wiping the tears from his eyes, he lifted his head while sitting on the trunk in a daze staring out of the window. I continued sitting in her rocking chair, when suddenly I stood up. I found myself remembering a picture that Grandma Tee kept in her oasis study room. There was a table with a white cloth over it with 9 candles and four pictures and small items surrounding specific pictures. Grandma Tee kept the oasis locked up when people would come over. People stopped paying much attention to the room. The room was off to the side next to a small bathroom near the kitchen area. I asked Pop if I could show him something. I knew where Grandma Tee kept the key to the oasis study room but as we came down the steps and made a right, turning the corner, getting closer to the kitchen I could see that the door was cracked open. Pop stopped for a moment and began weeping. He said, "this is where I found her." I thought this made so much sense because she probably was about to leave out of there to go outside to sit by her tree. Every new day she would spend time in that room. It was so early it was still dark outside. On Saturdays and Sundays, she would be up fixing breakfast and I would be right in there with her. I could not stop reminiscing while standing in that room. Pop shut the door behind him and we stood there looking at all of the history on the table where all of the candles and pictures were. There was a picture on the wall that had been moved to the table. It was a picture of Grandma Tee. Immediately I walked over to a beige colored bookcase that was built into the wall and grabbed the lighter stick that Grandma Tee used to light the 9 candles. I went to the right side of the room and saw the wooden box. This is where the candles were kept. I grabbed a purple candle. I remember participating once when she would do her offerings of thanks and honor. I studied her. I admired her. I felt her in that moment. My Pop and I bowed in front of the table. I began to take deep breaths and heard a song. I began to sing this chant. Pop remembered this chant. Pop grabbed the drum that was hanging up on the nail stuck in the wall and it seemed like we were in the room for hours. The rest of the family were in the front room off to the left, a sitting room (living room). Pop and I had continued singing the chant as we grew louder and louder, becoming more passionate and aware of exactly what we were saying, the outside noise grew still. We heard nothing aside from us two, the drum and bells ringing. Neither one of us had bells in our hands. We continued singing and began to hear what sounded like people from the Continent of Africa singing in harmony with us; sounding just like angels. Tears began falling from my face. I began to feel a warmth, my mouth began to quiver. When we no longer heard the bells ringing my Pop stopped beating the drum. We continued to repeat the chant and gradually began to fade out and then silence in unison. We were still for about 10 - 15 minutes. I opened my eyes and looked over to my right and Pop looked up at me and asked, "What did you hear?" "Did you receive anything?" My eyes were as bright as the moon. I answered, "Yes, Pop." Pop asked me if I could share it with him. He said, " I want to know if it is affirming." I said, "Yes, I saw and heard we must keep this home in honor of our ancestors. This is sacred ground." Pop and I wept because this had never happened to me before. We finally stood up and Pop put his arm around me. We connected that day in a way that we had never connected before.

When we came out of the room I noticed that my Ma was in the kitchen sitting in the chair grandma Tee would sit in. Ma was wiping her eyes. Ma asked, "Are you ready? We are going to the tree to prepare for the ceremony." I replied, "Yes." So Ma, Pop, Ruby, Lois, Big Mama Ruby, Big Daddy Joe and Uncle Pete along with a few of Grandma Tee's friends all arrived when Pop and I were in the oasis study. We were all now headed to the tree. It began to pour down raining. We all laughed and began singing and dancing in unison. We then followed the lead of Ma. She began to hand out several copper pitchers and cups filled with water. Ma began to speak heartfelt words. There wasn't a dry eye. After she gave thanks to the great mother spirit for sending Grandma Tee, she poured out living water and we continued; allowing everyone to speak or not but everyone had to pour. When it was my turn I remember feeling so much peace. Pop was the last one to share and when he did, he spoke the same words that Grandma Tee spoke faithfully every new day.

Oh ancestors, we honor you and the great mother spirit.
We rise as the sun. We breathe as the trees.
Our eyes are as bright as the moon; because
the soul light shines through, so we are born
with natural foresight we move as the waters
flowing freely. As the water returns to its source,
one day so will we; so while we are here in
these capsules. We honor each other in every
thought, every word and in every deed.

Grandma Tee would say these words for herself and her family. Pop spoke them just the same. It had stopped raining for a moment. Ma pulled out her bundle of sticks and took a lighter to it and filled the air with a cleanly fragrance burning it in honor of grandma Tee and Grandaddy James. This would be a day and a week I would never forget for many reasons.

About a year had passed. Grandma Tee passed in August 1954. I am 15 now, Ruby is 14, Lois 13. We were now living in grandma Tee's house. We still had our old home. Ma and Pop owned that property too. They had not decided what they were going to do with the other home until about a month ago when they decided to let a family stay there for a small fee. Ma and Pop had a real big fight about it because Ma had a real connection to the home all five of us had lived in for so long. They wanted to keep the home in the family. Ma knew that we were to come to grandma Tee's but she was being stubborn about it. It was our home that we had lived in for 14 years. Our old home was brick and had 4 bedrooms and 2 baths. Grandma Tee's house was a little grander, but Grandma Tee did not keep much furniture in her home. She was very frugal and found the beauty in simplicity. We all missed her but I really missed her.

It was a Saturday. We were all sitting around grandma Tee's kitchen table finishing up with a late breakfast when we hear a knock at the door. It was a new family that had moved right next door and wanted to introduce themselves. We could hear Ma, but could not make out the words; so Pop got up from the table and went to see who Ma was speaking with. Ma asked the family to please come in and have a seat. They were a very nice looking family. Mrs. Wright was a beautiful woman resembling Ma. It was rather strange. The only difference between Mrs. Wright and Ma was that Mrs. Wright dressed a lot sassier. She was not hiding her figure at all. She was very round in places that mattered most to men. Although I was only 15 at the time, I remember quite well Mrs. Wright's figure. She was the color of honey with dark brown hair; so dark it looked like the color black until the sun rested on her hair. Her eyes were the most peculiar but beautiful eyes anyone had ever seen. Her left eye was hazel green, while her right was a light brown. It did not look scary. It was angelic and her eyes were shaped like almonds with a slight slant. It was quite alluring and magnetic. She had one of the most beautiful smiles. She just seemed to be very warm and inviting. Mr. Wright had more of a stern demeanor; yet he was still a handsome man, at least Ruby thought so. Ruby was smitten with him and one of their sons. They had 3 children, two boys and a girl. Mr. Wright was very tall and really solid. He was very humorous. He was the color of chocolate. He had a very thin mustache. The two boys' names were Otis and Johnny. They were twins, age 15 and then there was Sadie Mae who was 14. I was in love instantly. I did not know how to express this love just yet. We all became very close friends. I felt instantly drawn to Sadie. She didn't know it, well if she did know, it wasn't because of me showing it that's for sure. Of course, later I realized she did know it.

On one hot summer day in July I happened to be standing outside in front of the house. I had a T-shirt on covered in oil. I had just finished helping Pop with one of the cars. A car passed the house three times before it stopped. It was an older white man. I wondered if it was the man who we saw that day with Ma. The man pulled over and parked right in front of our house, almost blocking the driveway. As soon as he turned the car off Ruby and Lois came outside and stood on the porch. The man looked a little apprehensive. He finally opened the door and as soon as he stood up he put his hat on. My eyes were as bright as the moon. Ruby whispered, "That looks like the same man that we saw that day with Ma." The man walked towards us taking his hat off with a grin. I was not smiling. I looked at him with intensity because we really did not have too many white folks coming around here for visits. The last time we saw this man Ma was crying and that's all I could think of and the fact that I had to protect grandma Tee's sacred space. The man looked at me eye to eye and said, "Hello son, is your Mother home?" My answer, "No sir." The man asked, "You know when she will be back?" My answer, "No sir." Then here comes Lois, "Hello Mister." He says," Hi there." and then we noticed his eyes filling up with tears as if he were going to cry. He said while walking away and slightly looking back at us, putting his hat back on, "Would you please tell her that her Father came by." I nodded my head, yes. Lois' eyes filled with tears while Ruby stood there with her arms folded with a blank stare to keep from crying. Although Ma had not told us that's who he was that day we sat in front of the tall building, we all knew deep down. All three of us watched him pull off. We went inside and as soon as we were headed towards the back door, Pop was coming in. "Pop!!!" Ruby cried, "Ma's father was here." Pop knew exactly who we were talking about. Pop could not even hide his feelings although he tried to. He told us to never speak of him again and especially to your Mother. This made Lois very sad from that day on because she and Ma were very close. Lois looked a lot like Ma's father. From that point on Lois became very quiet.

Two years had passed. I was 17. I had just gotten home from school. I was heading towards the kitchen and noticed Ma sitting at the table with my journal. I had two journals and had them since the age of eleven. Big Mama Ruby gave us each a journal and told us to write our thoughts and feelings about our journey as well as our vision for our lives. Then she looked at me and said, "Write what you listen to." At the time I did not know what she meant but by the time I was seventeen I would have written many songs, short stories and had started working on a book. Ma found the journal with songs in it. The other journal with the stories and book in it I always either carried with me or hid it in a place no one would ever find.

Ruby, Lois and I usually walked home together from school but they obviously caught the bus and were sitting with Ma and my journal. Ruby and Lois knew about both journals, more so the journal with the songs in it because they would sing them with me but for some reason we would never sing them in front of Ma or Pop. Pop was a musician, composer and talented genius. He published a book that did quite well, but Pop wanted to focus on playing the piano. He taught himself everything, from reading music to composing to playing those keys. He could also play the drums. He was a paid musician and traveled a lot when we were younger. He was now teaching music at a community center in Philadelphia and he taught piano at a school in Philadelphia as well. He ended up going to college after he taught himself how to read sheet music before he and Ma married.

Ma asked me to let her hear some of what I wrote. I did not understand why when she had already opened and gone into my journal. Big Mama Ruby always told us that our journals were our very own and that no one had the right to go in it. I guess she forgot to mention except for your Ma. She asked me again if I would share something. I began reading the very words I knew that she read already. She said, "No son, I want to hear the song." I hesitated, looked down at my journal and then back up at Ma and began singing a song I had written about Grandma Tee. Of course, Ma began to cry. After I finished singing I looked over at my sisters and we began to sing another song. It was a song about the pain that we knew Ma must have endured not being around her Father and although at the time we did not know the whole story, we felt her pain and so we sang:

I've been searching and missing a piece of me
until I realized that love was here in me.
I was angry, hurt and scared because
I knew you were somewhere
until I realized that love was already here.
Even though I still feel the pain and at times feel empty
I know that its ok and things will get better because
love is always here.....

Ma wept uncontrollably while we were singing in harmony. She cried such a piercing cry that the three of us began to shed tears. Once we sang the last note we realized that Pop was in the kitchen doorway shedding tears as well. He did not say anything. Ma got up walked over and hugged each of us. Pretty surprising that I was 17 and neither Ma nor Pop had ever heard me sing; they had never heard all three of us sing.

Pop had already gone up the stairs. Ma followed behind him. The three of us decided to go out in the backyard. I headed towards the tree that Grandma Tee use to sit under. Ruby and Lois sat under the tree with me. It was around spring, maybe April. As soon as we sat down a cool breeze touched us. I closed my eyes and began singing with my sisters; a song we would sing whenever Ma would drift away. I mean she would be there for us but there were times when she was just not present as if she would drift away to a place that made her forget or perhaps remember. She would go to her room and shut the door. The three of us would sing in private.

Ma and Pop loved us but sometimes they had to go to their own worlds for a moment. They both carried a sadness that neither ever discussed with us but I knew there would be a time that it would be revealed or at least that is what I hoped for. Ruby, Lois and I continued our mini-concert outside. In that moment we felt free to sing after we sang for Ma. After singing for a while we just sat, not really saying too much until Ruby asked Lois a question, "Lois, can I ask you something?" Lois, said, "Yes." Ruby proceeds, "Why don't you have much to say anymore?" Lois looked up at the sky and said, "Because I like listening more." If you're quiet you can really listen to the things that people want to hide and to the words that others are afraid to say. I have listened and learned so much in this quietness about myself, life and those I love." Needless to say Ruby and I sat there for a moment speechless. She sounded a lot like Grandma Tee and big Mama Ruby.

We continued to sit outside for another hour or so and we all brought up random things that we either wanted to know about the other or simply wanted to share with each other. It was one of the best days we'd had in a long time.

Ruby and I decided to go back in the house while Lois decided to stay outside a little while longer. As soon as we walked in through the kitchen Ma was coming to the kitchen and asked where Lois was. I told her and then Ma went outside. Ruby headed upstairs to her bedroom. I decided to go on the porch and sit on the steps to wait for Sadie. Sadie and I had remained very close over the years. She and I shared many secrets. We were the best of friends. The day her family moved next store was the day I met the love of my soul. I did not know with the first visit to what extent our love was but there was an instant bond for certain.

Sadie was dating someone. I knew him. He was very popular. All of the girls liked him and Sadie was dating him. He would walk her home from school. His name was Johnny. He was known around town as "Bird" because of how he flew through women and also for his athletic ability while playing basketball as well as his vocal ability. Needless to say, he was pretty arrogant and was dishonest towards Sadie. I refused to call another man "Bird."

Johnny did not like the friendship Sadie and I had. Of course, I did not care, not one bit what he liked or didn't like. Sadie would confide in me about their relationship and she would make me swear that I would stay out of it. I knew Johnny knew that I knew some of the things he had done to her. I fought the urge so many times to say something to Johnny or Mr. Wright for so long; until one day, I saw Johnny yelling at Sadie I couldn't take it. I boxed the fool up (punched him) and he became very angry and pulled out a knife. I kicked it out of his hand and then he came charging towards me. He didn't know that my fist would be waiting for him again. After hitting the ground with a bloody nose and now blood on his clothes, he angrily walked off. Sadie was yelling for me to stop. I heard her in the distance but was not listening. The whole entire time I was silent. I did not break a sweat. I didn't even know what they were discussing all I saw was something that I did not like and that was the fact that he was trying to intimidate Sadie. I was so tired of listening to the bullshit. The hurt that she would share with me and then not doing anything about it and want me to turn a blind eye to it as well. What kind of friend would that have made me? What kind of man would I be to look myself in the mirror with my head held high as a man and not do anything, not only as a man but as a friend who cared. I rarely heard anything good about their relationship. If she did tell me anything good it would really be nothing spectacular, nothing more than what a stranger would do for another stranger. So I would ask her, "Why are you with him?" Her response, "Because he's not that bad, I know you hear a lot of harsh things but he's really not that bad." I sighed. I finally told her that I could no longer listen to the painful things about her and Johnny. It made me sick. I don't like to take in shit. I release shit. She told me she understood. I went on to explain what it was doing to me physically. She looked downward and then looked back up at me and gave me hug.

The next day Ruby, Lois and I waited outside for Sadie to all walk to school together. We waited and waited and finally, we decided to ring the doorbell. All 3 of us heard a screaming match, arguing and what sounded like things being thrown. I did not know what to do but all I could do was imagine something happening to Sadie and doing nothing to stop it. So I knocked so hard on that door that it sounded like I was about to knock the door down. The door opens and it's Mr. Wright; before I could say anything he says, "Sadie is not attending school today." and slams the door. I stood there deciding whether or not to knock on the door again and next thing I know Ruby and Lois knocked on the door. I was shocked. Mr. Wright opened the door and in a stern voice said, "I told you the first time, Sadie is not attending school, now leave. This time before he could slam the door Lois put her foot there. Mr. Wright was just as shocked as I was as well as speechless. Lois began telling Mr. Wright, "Mr. Wright I DO mean to pry. We heard a lot of commotion and something is not sitting well with me. Now if you'd like, we could go get our Pop to help you." We all knew he did not want our

Pop to come over. Mr. Wright exclaims, "While I appreciate your concern children, everything is just fine. Nothing but a love quarrel, now you need to be minding your own business and stay out of grown folks business."

"Well if love sounds like that, that's only a copy cat of love and I don't want it." says Ruby. Mr. Wright asks, "How do you know what love is Ruby?" "Mr. Wright, I may not be able to tell you all that it is with a fancy definition. I don't believe it can truly be defined; but I can tell you that if I don't love myself and my family are an extension of myself then maybe I have never experienced love. But, I know I have. And I can be certain of what it is not. I may not have experienced romantic love but I know love, Mr. Wright." I began to tell Mr.Wright, "With all due respect Mr. Wright, I know what we heard and it sounded pretty serious. I am sure you can understand our concern so if you don't mind if we could just speak to Sadie for a moment." At this point, Mr. Wright was speechless, angry and embarrassed. He went in the house and before he shut the door we heard him calling for Sadie. The three of us waited outside, standing in front of the door. Sadie opened the door, she said (in a whisper) "Guys I am fine, I heard you from my window. Thank you. (with tears in her eyes) Thank you, I will be outside when you guys get out of school." We were satisfied. We walked off the porch and as I turned around I saw Mr. Wright watching us from the big window right next to the front door. He watched us walk away.

When we came home from school that day Sadie was outside. She was watching us. Lois started running towards Sadie. Sadie smiled. In fact, we were all smiling. We stood in their front yard inside of the gate smiling until Sadie said, "Thanks guys again." We all told her there was no need in thanking us. Sadie began explaining what happened earlier that day. She said that she heard her Mother and Father fussing and that although they argued quite often this sounded different. She said her Mother told her Father that he was about to become a Father again. Her Father began yelling at Mrs. Wright. He was blaming her. Sadie told us that her Ma was standing up for herself as she had always done which is why they argued as much as they did. Mrs. Wright was not a doormat for a wife. Anyway, Sadie went on to say how she heard her Mother screaming get off of me. Sadie busted in on them and Mr. Wright had his elbow pressuring against Mrs. Wright chest and neck area. Sadie pushed her Father and he fell off of the bed and he was heading towards his belt to take it off when he heard a knock at the door. When he went down the stairs Sadie looked out of the window and realized she could not see who it was and raised the window and heard everything along with her mother. Before Sadie could finish telling us our Ma called for us to come in.

More than a few years had passed. I was about 21 years old not too much had gone on. When I graduated from high school I did not know what to do so I took a year off but I knew I had to do something. I was absolutely not going to join the military, although I had often entertained the idea; I knew Grandma Tee would come and give me a few choice words if I had done that besides I was really a writer in my heart. I had already written a few short stories and during this time was still working on a book that I was excited about. The book was about myself and my family and Sadie but after Grandma Tee taught us three the art of meditation. During my meditation time some of the most interesting things would be revealed to me. One of those things that were revealed to me, was college. I had decided to go to college and had about two years left. I took a few writing courses and majored in English. I didn't really understand the concept of teaching me to say what was already in me to say as a writer but I felt like I had to do something, so I did. I attended Howard University. Ruby was attending Temple University. Ruby was going to become a nurse or doctor. Lois was attending Howard University studying Chemistry.

Ma and Pop were still living in Grandma Tee's house. Everything seemed to be fine with both of them. Sadie and her family were doing well. Sadie nor her brothers, Otis and Johnny or Mrs. Wright had heard from Mr.Wright. Mrs. Wright ended up having a baby boy. Sadie was still involved with Johnny Jackass, I mean Jonny Bird. I just did not respect the negro bird ass not one bit; and even though I met someone at Howard University, Sadie was my best friend. She had a piece of my heart. Sadie and I were close when we were teenagers but from 18 up until I left for school in D.C which would be a year later; our bond grew even closer. We would exercise together because Sadie ran track. We would walk and then eventually drive to the grocery store together, run errands for our families together. We would sit on the porch steps and just talk for hours. Of course, Johnny did not like me by this time; but there was a part of him that did not mind me hanging out with her because it kept Sadie preoccupied and distracted from the nonsense that I knew she knew he was doing.

There were many a days Sadie and I would spend time together doing absolutely nothing. There would be an in-depth silence with a constant communication going on. It was as if we were traveling to a space where the only thing that existed was everything that was real like our true spirit form. I knew I loved her. There was one day in particular when She and I decided to go to a park in town and go see a play called Raisin in the Sun.

I had been working as a stock person at the local grocery store and had been saving my money for school but had set aside some to be able to do something different for Sadie that we normally did not do. I went to her house and had a basket of a full lunch prepared in the car, knocked on the door and Otis answered the door; one of her brothers. He was very protective of his sister. Robert, their brother had enlisted in the army.

"Hows it going J.R.?" asked Otis. We shook hands. I responded, "Well, it's going and Im doing just fine." Otis called for his sister and she came down those steps like she had walked off one of those picture shows, magazines or books that Grandma Tee would either read to us from or show us pictures of beautiful women of African decent. Sadie came down the steps in a white dress that she had designed and made herself which was one of her many passions. The dress was slightly form fitting and covering her knees, while a small portion of her upper back was showing. The fabric was cut out in the shape of a heart and her sleeves barely existed. I felt like I was supposed to be getting down on one knee and popping a question.

I smiled at Sadie and said, "Hello, Miss" She smiled and said, "Hello, Mister." She told Otis we would be back around nine o'clock that night, which was fine with me. It was, however, odd because it was so early when I picked her up. I was at her home by noon to pick her up. Sadie yells up the steps to her Ma and so I did the same, just to say hello. We then told Otis bye and were off to what seemed like a real date.

We arrived at the same park my Ma would take us to when we were growing up. I opened up her door and we walked towards a tree. We were sitting under the tree. The weather was fair. There were many other people there enjoying the weather on that day. The park had changed some what having a little more than what was there before. I laid out a quilt and began setting up the space; but Sadie interrupted me and took the basket. She moved it to her side without saying a word and continued setting up the space, which really wasn't too much to do. After we finished, she kicked off her shoes. For the first twenty minutes or so, we said absolutely nothing. For most, that could possibly mean awkwardness. But we Or maybe I should say I on second thought, no... I will say we. We were speaking in our silence. I felt so much comfort as well as connection. After we ate, Sadie laid down. I could see her looking up towards the sky with a question in her eyes. She said "Why do you think we instantly touched each other the way we did?" The touch she was referring to was so subtle without any force, thought or effort. The touch felt like an eternal hug or as if we were surrounded by an ocean submerged in an endless womb of timeless bliss. It was so liberating and so reflective. I could not believe she asked the question because I did not know that she felt the way she did and yet somehow I did know. I just wouldn't allow myself to understand why she would continue to be with bird ass.

Sadie and I laughed and sang songs. I wrote a song about her of course I didn't tell her it was about her. After I sang this song she told me how beautiful it was and reminded me that I never answered her question and I told her that she must not of been listening to the song I just sung for her. The song was entitled "Endless." I noticed Sadie was staring off into the distance as if she were really contemplating. She snapped out of the thought, went in to the cooler and grabbed a few ice cubes and threw it on me and took off running. I chased her towards the swings and we began swinging, not saying anything, initially. We later talked and shared so many things with each other; for hours.

It was becoming dark and we were packing up. I was sad because I knew that for some reason we had to take different paths again. There wasn't much talking on the ride home. That night for the first time we kissed and it was the most electrifying kiss I had ever experienced. I had been with a few young ladies and one older woman; but with Sadie time was no more so much so that I forgot we were suppose to be going to see a play and I completely forgot. The kiss was as if our hearts touched. It was very sensual and passionate and lasted for what seemed like more than twenty minutes. The kiss became a vehicle that afforded us the opportunity to travel into the depths of something so touching, exhilarating, elevating, eternal and heal~thy. It seemed as if we were lost without seeking and comfortable with not returning and so we didn't. We subconsciously and eventually consciously stayed in the comfort of eternity. We were eternally connected. Even if not in the physical. All we did was kiss, no hands wandering. Just a kiss. I would spend the next few years searching for the same "kiss", not even realizing that is what I was doing at the time. That was our last outing before heading to school.

Chapter 2

It was my final year at Howard University. I was pretty serious about my studies. I worked hard to get there. I knew I had to work even harder to finish. I was on the dean's list my entire academic career there. I was in the marching band. I was a part of the concert choir. I was on the debate team and monologue team. I was also a member of the student government.

There was a beautiful woman named Janet that I met on the debate and monologue team. She always brought laughter with her. She had the greatest sense of humor and was very smart. She was studying to become a nurse, just like Ruby. The relationship between Janet and I grew to be very serious. We had been in a committed relationship for a year and nine months. Janet already met Ma and Pop. Pop loved her. Ma didn't dislike her. She just did not feel she was the one for me. I cared for her deeply. I had already met her family and from what Janet says, her family loved me. I was contemplating when I would propose to her but there was such an inner battle going on within. I would keep seeing many reasons as to why I should wait before asking her. You see, Janet wanted to move back to her hometown after graduation. I did not want to move to Virginia. Janet was from Richmond, Virginia. She did not necessarily have to move to Richmond, but she definitely knew she wanted to move back to Virginia. She was actually leaning towards Norfolk, Virginia. I really wanted to move to either New York or Washington D.C.

I was not too fond of the idea of moving back home to Wilmington, Delaware but I knew that the time for a decision to be made would be arriving shortly. The reason I battled asking Janet the infamous question was my heart would always wonder towards Sadie. The answer to an eternal question that I would hear so clearly. The volume was high and yet soothing. It vibrantly spoke boldly. My heart asked repeatedly and I knew this question would never ever eventually fade away in the distance.

Graduation was finally here. I was not as excited as I thought I would be. There was more uncertainty than I had before I began four years ago. I was older than most of our graduating class, not that much older, but older. Even though I was older than most of my cohorts, they were a bit more certain what their next step would be. I became close to a few brothas, B and Malcolm. They were very militant like, assertive and knowledgeable. Both were continuing their education to become lawyers. B was from Philadelphia. Malcolm was from New York. We had the some of the best times. I knew that I would hold those memories close to my heart. We knew how to have a good time. We also knew how to hit our books hard. We felt it was the only way to really be able to compete with the rest of the world. We earned our degrees; both B and Malcolm were very proud of this. I wasn't for some odd reason.

This would be one of the longest and hottest days. We the students were hungry. B, Malcolm and I had to stand in a long line outside to practice for rehearsal. Rehearsal began at 7:00 a.m.; but it was now 11:00 a.m. and no signs of the line even moving. The staff who normally sets up and or prepares for such events got a late start. The line finally began moving a little after 11:00 a.m., our rehearsal lasted another two hours and graduation began at 4:00 p.m. That evening. B, Malcolm and I rushed to go get something to eat and then rushed back to get dressed in time for the ceremony. Those guys were so excited. I was just ready to get it over with. Janet and I had planned to meet up directly after the ceremony at a specific location. For some reason, I did not want to meet up with her and wasn't sure as to why at the time.

It was now 4:15 p.m. We were all lined up to march in the processional to only take our seats. I had so many thoughts going through my mind that I must have rushed things along. As the row that I was in was standing up I remembered the feeling that I felt as I knew they were getting closer and closer to calling my name and then I finally heard it. I walked across the stage. I thought I could hear my family in the distance. The feelings I had were that of sadness and nervousness and then disgust because my last name is Fletcher, Malcolm's was Flennard but B's was Rogers and Janet's was Thompson and we were still on the F's. Definitely not the kind of thing a college graduate should be complaining about but we had been there all day and I was so tired. As the row that I was in was completely finish and seated, I remember no longer being present. I was in deep thought, in a trance wondering where I was going and how would I get there. I was truly missing Grandma Tee. I was wanting to be so close to her. Just one more time. I wanted her to tell me to trust, close my eyes, take deep breathes and know everything will be fine; knowing that in fact it already is. I wanted her to say this to me. I wanted to hear her chanting. I wanted to see her out by her tree. I wanted her to tell me what she could see, to tell me where do I go from here. In that moment I felt a cool breeze all over and I began to shed a few tears of joy. I happened to look down on the piece of paper that I was holding, the program. It said say yes to you and do. I heard Grandma Tee in that moment, "Ask now what do you do? And do you already know because you've been doing it all along?" I smiled.

Another couple of hours and a half had passed and we were just about finish. It really was not that big of a graduating class. There were a lot of speakers as well as all of the formalities that made the ceremony much longer than it needed to be. A group of us were planning to hang out after graduation not considering our families would want to celebrate with us. I had a feeling my family was here because I thought I could hear them when I walked across the stage, especially Ruby. As soon as I heard the announcement congratulations class of 1963 Malcolm and I went searching for B. On our search Malcolm ran into his family. He introduced me to everyone and they invited me to New York for a visit. Malcolm asked me to excuse him. I stood off to the side and when he came back he had B with him. Malcolm began to tell me how his family wanted to take him out to celebrate. We knew that we would not be able to hang out but we just thought we would give it a shot. All three of us had already exchanged our information. As soon as Malcolm walked off, B's family came running towards him screaming and extremely loud with roaring cheers. B introduced me. His mother hugged me with tears. She just kept saying "You young people just don't know how historical this is. Do you know that there are no limits to what you boys can accomplish?" I smiled and she said, 'Now I want you too keep in touch with each other." B and I shook hands. I felt really emotional in that moment. I guess because it was a chapter closing.

I decided to walk back to where I was sitting during the ceremony since there were so many people. As soon as I turned around I could see my Pop's smile from a few feet away. Pop started to cry. I grabbed his hand for a handshake as Ma was hugging me with such a tight embrace. Then I hugged Ruby, Lois, Big Mama, Big Daddy Joe and a surprise, Sadie; needless to say I was smiling from ear to ear. We hugged for the longest time. It was as if our souls, our heart was picking up on silent signals. No words, just connection.

Pop asked if I had made plans or if I was going to hang out with them. I said, "Of course I am hanging with my family". Everyone was so excited. I was at peace now, knowing that Grandma Tee had made her presence known to me today in a subtle way. I received clarity today and I was thankful.

My whole four years here I was uncertain and in that moment I was in peace knowing that I didn't have to know the outcome but I can complete what I started. Pop asked me where I wanted to go. As we were headed towards the parking lot I saw Janet. A part of me did not want to stop. I wanted to keep going. As I was contemplating, Pops spotted her out. Janet locked eyes with Pops. She smiled and then looked at me. I began walking towards her direction. My family followed me with the exception of Ma, Big Mama Ruby, Sadie, and Ruby. They just stood and waved from where they were. Janet and I embraced each other with a hug. The hug was brief for some reason. We then congratulated each other. Her family came and hugged me and then the question I was hoping no one would ask was asked by her Mom, "Would you and your family like to meet us at a restaurant and celebrate together?" Before anyone could respond, my little sister Lois rescued me just in the nick of time. She says, "Well it was supposed to be a surprise but we were driving all the way to Philadelphia to one of his favorite steak and cheese sandwich shops. You guys are more than welcome to join us." I was in complete shock that Lois would know that I did not want to have dinner with Janet and her family. I began to question myself. Was I with Janet because I knew that I could spend the rest of my life with her or was I gaining an experience and learning about who I was. I began reflecting on the ride back home. Sadie rode back with Ruby, Ma, and Pop. Big Mama Ruby and Big Daddy Joe drove and helped carry some of my things in their car. Lois was riding with me in my car. The best co-pilot to ride with when you want to reflect. We had been driving for about an hour when Lois asked me a question, "So have you accepted that you're to get off at this stop?" I glanced at Lois for a moment and immediately realized what stop she was referring to. I responded to her by saying, "Are you referring to our relationship, Janet and I?" Lois responded with a look that said, I know you know exactly what I am talking about. I told her I honestly felt that I should, I just know how much she loves me and how great of a person she is. I guess a part of me felt like I ought to do "right" by her. Lois sat there quietly looking out of the window and then turned to me and said, "big brother, some times what's right is in what we already know. What's right for her maybe you doing what you think will hurt her. I just gave a slight nod and grin. Lois rested her head back on the seat and slept the rest of the way. I began to feel so many emotions. Most having little to do with Janet, more about my next step and how to take it. I spent the rest of the ride just thinking and gaining understanding. There was only an hour remaining on the road trip to Philadelphia. We did go and get that Philly cheese steak before we headed home. It was one of the best dinners I had ever had with those I loved most.

Chapter 3

Well, I was home now and had been home for a month and was working as a teacher in a summer program. Janet and I had officially ended our relationship. It was a difficult thing for me to do but I knew that I would regret it if I stayed in the relationship any longer.

Summer was just about over and I still had no clue as to what I would do. I knew what I wanted to do but had no idea on how to make it happen. During this summer Sadie and I had grown even closer. Sadie would always encourage me to go after my dreams, well not in those words. She did not like that phrase, she would say, "You don't have to chase your dreams, you have to breathe them, live them and do. She was always touching something so deep within not only with her words, but with her laughter, her smile, her eyes, her thoughts.... she just had a way of knowing.

A year had passed and I was overwhelmed with joy for three reasons:

1. I had decided to teach and made it through my first year, while working on my books as well as music.

2. Ruby graduated, became a nurse and decided to go on to medical school.

3. Last but not least Sadie was no longer with Johnny Bird bitch. Sadie and I were stuck together like glue. Summer had come again and I was moving out on my own. I had saved money. I had stopped by on a Saturday to pick up the last of my things. Ma and Pop were both happy and sad at the same time. Ma called me into the kitchen and asked me to sit down at the kitchen table and I did. Pop was already sitting down. He was

staring at the table cloth, holding a cup of tea. Ma was getting herself a cup and asked me if I wanted a cup. I told her yes. The moment was odd. I wondered what they were thinking, what they were about to ask or what they were about to say. Ma walked over to the table carrying two saucers with two cups of tea placing on top of the saucers. Ma sat down herself. It was just us three at home. Ruby was back in school. She was attending Howard University. Lois was finishing up her last year in undergrad. Neither one of my sisters would take breaks from their studies even if it was an actual break. They enjoyed being in their books and away from home or so it seemed. I on the other hand loved breaks when I was in school. I loved them so much because it allowed my mind to be still. I was always thinking and creating during those breaks. I needed that year off after finishing high school and I am thankful Ma and Pop allowed me to do that. As I was contemplating this and slurping up lemongrass, lavender and mint tea, I looked up at both Ma and Pop. I could tell they were both in deep thought. Ma was taking a sip. Pop had pushed his saucer back to the center of the table and looked up at me. He had tears in his eyes. He said, " Son, we need to to talk to you. First we want to say how proud of you we are." I responded with a smile and a thank you Pop. Pop started tapping his fingers on the table. " Son anything you feel you are suppose to be doing with your life, do it. Just because you no longer will be living here does not mean you have to give up on those youthful visions. In my experience those youthful visions are without limitations and fear, they exist in the most purest space. They were placed there for a reason." Pop got up from the table and walked over to the sink and grabbed a box that was on top of the window seal on the kitchen window. Pop walked over to the table and sat back down and held the box in front of him and then slowly slid the box towards me and told me that he wanted me to have it. I did not know just yet what it was. The box was a wooden box. The shape of a rectangle and it was cherry wood, with a lock. He reached inside his shirt and took one of his chains off. One that I never noticed that had a key on it and something called an ankh. I remember Grandma Tee teaching us three about the ankh. He told me to keep the chain and he asked me if I would open up the box. I nodded my head and said, "Yes." I took the key and opened up the box. There were so many pieces of written music, too many to count. There were many pictures and last but not least two journals. When I took the journals out, Pop began to really shed tears and left the kitchen. I opened the first journal and on the first page there was a title, 'memories traveling'. I was not too sure as to what was going on, whose journals these were and why Pop was so emotional until I happened to notice something outside. The chair that I was sitting in was facing the back door which was opened. When the back door was opened, you could see the big tree that Grandma Tee would always sit under.

There was a breeze that must have carried Grandma Tee and PopPop. They looked up at me and smiled. I could literally see them. They were both writing in what looked to be the same journals that were sitting before me. Ma was sitting across from me, but to the left of. She was looking down towards her cup of tea, sipping. She put her cup down. She stood up and walked towards the door. She began staring at the tree and began wiping tears from her eyes. I began to wonder what she had to tell me or if she saw Grandma Tee and PopPop outside by that tree. I finally decided to just ask her. "Ma, did you just see and before I could ask, she turned and looked at me and asked me if I saw them and I told her yes. I sat there quietly for a moment. I decided to ask her all of the questions I've had for some time now. "Ma, I would really like to ask you some questions and I no longer want to assume." Initially she was looking at me, but by the time I finished asking that question she was looking outside. She turned back around, walked back to the table and sat down. She said, "Well, ask me. Ask me anything you'd like." "Ok, Ma." She looked down into her cup, watching her finger circling around in her cup. I took a deep breath. I was pretty nervous even though I was an adult. I asked, "Who was the white woman who gave you those stones long ago and the white man who gave you the envelope?" Of course I already knew who the man was but she did not know that I knew already, well knowing Ma she may have known that I already knew but quite frankly I just wanted to hear it from her. She answered, "the man is my Father, well; I mean he was." I responded, "What do you mean he was, Ma?" She told me he passed. She then began to tell me the story. Your grandma Ruby use to work for Timothy Wright." I ask, "Do you mean the owner of Timothy Wright? Wright Funeral Home? And Wright Grocery and Wright Deli? And Wright everything else... Timothy Wright?" "Yes, son. My grandfather owned all of those things and some and it was passed down to us." I began looking outside at that tree again. I could feel Ma's eyes on me, but I just could not keep my eyes off of the tree; almost as if that tree was going to have answers. "James, let's go sit under grandma Tee's tree, of course I agreed. We sat under the tree and Ma began telling me everything she could think of to tell me. "Son, do you see this?" She was holding her necklace with her stones which had a third piece that I had never seen. I remembered the pink and green; but the third was a locket. She opened it and inside was a picture of a Man and a baby. It was the man we saw that day who handed Ma the envelope and Ma began telling me how her dad was considered "colored" because his dad (Ma's granddad) was a very light skinned black man who was passing for white and really could not stand to look at his son who was the man we saw that day (Ma's biological father), because he reminded him of his heritage and looked just like his mom (Ma's grandmother) who's name was Elizabeth Bella who was obviously a black woman who worked as a housemaid for the Wrights. Elizabeth died at the age of 45 from an infection. She was a hard worker who had relations with my father's father (my granddad), Timothy Wright Sr; who was at one time married to a woman named Martha. Martha was a woman who could not have children. She died also. Timothy Sr. had another child prior to my Father who was about 10 or more years older than him with Elizabeth Bella but Martha practically raised both children as her own after their mom passed. My father's sister's name is Elizabeth as well and she was just as light skinned. They obviously took after Timothy Senior's pale skin but you could definitely tell they had negro in them and to Timothy Sr. they were just a reminder of how he had betrayed his family. My father had broke a promise to Timothy Sr. and it was the same promise that Timothy Sr broke with his father. Timothy Sr. told my dad, your granddad "You owe me your life and a part of what you owe is to never put your loins inside of a negro woman. Even a beautiful one, you will regret it if you do. You will suffer and so would your child. Timothy Sr. told him this while staring right at big mama Ruby. Timothy Sr. knew that there was something going on. Timothy Sr. drilled this in my father. Timothy Sr. tried to erase the fact that his children had "negro" in them and rumor has it he did too. He had many siblings who were about as dark as you son." I then asked Ma, " So that day after the diner, the man was your father and the lady; your aunt?" She replied, "Yes, your Pop told me he came here looking for me one day and that was not too long before he passed." I saw my Ma wiping tears from her face and then she looked up and said, "Now I know you're moving out and have to get settled but tomorrow around 5 p.m. I want you to come over and meet someone. Your sisters will be here as well. I agreed. She said, "Son if you love her as I know you do, tell her because NOW is one of the most loving presents you can accept." My eyes grew big; eyes were as bright as the moon. I never talked to her about Sadie but I am sure it was obvious to those who knew me best. I took a deep breath and said, "Ok." She said, "I don't think your Pop will be able to share why he cried when he gave you that box with the writings in it. It's a reminder for him of this fear, and the lack of fulfillment he has felt."

He has always enjoyed composing music for some of the greats and being a musician but he really wanted to eventually become a literary writer along with Grandma Tee and your Pop Pop James. They told themselves, "these are just sacred writings for our eyes only" but I know as well as Pop it was fear. "Son, I will say it again, now is one of the most loving presents you can accept. Do it all, everything that would allow you to express the loving being that you are."

By this time a tear fell from my eye. I looked up and saw my Pops standing in the door. I could tell he wanted to come out but he just stood there watching us. Ma looked over there and said,

"I'm going to go back in now and I'm going to let your Pop's come out here and sit with ya for a while. As I was helping Ma up, my Pop began walking towards us and told Ma that he wanted to have a heart to heart with me. She held her hand out towards me. Smiled, then hugged me and told me she loves me. I told her that I love her too. I sat back down under the tree with Pop who held a small branch he used to write in the dirt. I did not wait for him to speak. I said, "Pop you don't have to worry about me. I've learned a lot from you. You've taught me some of the most valuable lessons." Although he hadn't yet responded I could listen to his silence. So, I replied to his question. "You've taught me how to love a woman. You've taught me how to feel. You've taught me how to never give up. You've taught me how to treat Ma. You've taught me how to treat my sisters. You've taught me how to be the best son. You may see something great when you look at me but that's because it is the something I see when I look at you Pop. You've taught me respect. You've taught me the greatest lesson as a male child, you've taught me how to be an honorable man and that is what I focus on when I think about what's running through these here veins and that is irreplaceable."

I had listened to Ma, she said, "Now is one of the most loving presents you can accept." So I took the opportunity to share all that I felt was needed to share on that day. Pop looked at me with the biggest smile and humbled heart and said, "James, son (pause) you always were one to tell no lie." We chuckled and then silence. He then said, "Son, any thoughts you have... make sure you spend the most thought on what you can do with what you have access to right now. Don't spend time worrying about what you think you can't accomplish. Just because you think it doesn't make it true. Spending time thinking can be a waste too. Spend time doing what's valuable. If you accept the thoughts that encourage you along with doing, you spend less time second-guessing your decisions. I love you son. Will you be coming tomorrow evening?" "Yes, Pop and I love you too."

The following day I was somewhat in disbelief in regards to all that Ma shared with me. I still had questions but maybe I would get the answers this evening.

I was too excited to spend too much time focusing on that. I was in my own apartment. I had moved to Philadelphia. I was about 25-30 minutes or so away from home. I was still unpacking. I was not only excited because of me moving out of my childhood home. I knew that I wanted to get as much as I could, unpacked today. I had been moving things in for about a week and a half. I just did not want to move in officially until I had my phone turned on and my bed that I recently purchased. As I worked through the day unpacking I began to see that I must have been really focused to have completed as much as I had in my two bedroom apartment. I lived in a development called Meadow Village. A really nice location and not too far from my job. I would be starting as a teacher in the Philadelphia public school district in the fall. As I was finishing up the last five boxes I realized that I had to freshen up because it was now 3:30 and I wanted to be there on time. For some reason I felt like Ma had something else to share, so a little nervousness set in for a moment. I remembered what Pop said about my thoughts, so I decided to change those thoughts and became relaxed. I finished preparing myself and freshening up and got on the road. I was excited to see my sisters. I missed my sisters.

When I arrived I noticed two cars parked in front of our home. It was only 4:45. I wanted to know who was there and if there would be something else revealed. I did not recognize either of the vehicles. I got out of my car with excitement. Ma must have been waiting for me because as soon as I looked up she was standing on the porch with a pleasant smile, a white dress and her hair down which she rarely did. I slowly made my way to the steps and as soon as I touched the porch Ma hugged me so tight. Ma walked towards the door and she walked in and I followed behind her. When we walked in I saw my two sisters and they had grown into beautiful young ladies and although it had not been that long since I last saw them, I could no longer deny that they were adults now, no more little girls. Ruby was standing up in a bright red form fitted dress. She had a headband on, pushing her afro back. She really began looking more and more like Grandma Tee, instead of like big Mama

Ruby. Ruby was in med school and she was determined. Lois was dressed in a bright yellow dress with her hair hanging down just like Ma's. I was hugging my sister's as though I hadn't seen them in twenty years or so. I was so proud of them. Lois would be graduating soon.

At this point, the three of us were standing up in the hallway. I had not made it into the kitchen nor the living room. I could hear Pops and a few other unrecognizable voices coming from the back. Ma had gone up the steps and the three of us decided to wait for her, I guess subconsciously we felt that Ma wanted us to wait. We chose to stand in the hallway until Ma came back downstairs.

When she finally did come back down, she smiled and asked us to follow her into the living room. So we did. Before my sisters and I could enter the room the room grew still; very silent. Ma said, "Ok, I want you all to meet some of our family." My sisters and I smiled and said our hello's and how do you do's, but inside I was confused. Ma said, "This is your Aunt Elizabeth and your Uncle Jimmy, Uncle Jimmy I am just meeting for the first time." In that moment I did not understand how Ma could be so open and warm to the people who had nothing to do with her or her family because of her skin. When they had the same thing running through their veins. My facial expression must have been saying a lot because Elizabeth looked me in my eyes and said, I apologize for not being in you all's lives. I..I..I was a coward who held onto all that my mother shared with me to make sense out of it all. While she was speaking with tears falling from her eyes I noticed she was holding onto the same chain my Ma was holding on to the day before when she was talking to me under the tree. She also still had on the stones. She was wiping tears from her eyes. Aunt Elizabeth looked at us and said, "Any questions you have I am willing to answer." The three of us just stood there looking at her. We were very quiet. I decided to sit down and my sisters sat down as well. I figured Ma must have shared everything with my sisters earlier in the day before our guest arrived. I began asking questions. I asked her why she gave Ma those stones. I asked her about my great grandmother, but I really wanted to know how big Mama Ruby even fell for such a cold hearted creature or as Grandma Tee would say, "an orangutan." So I asked Ma, "How did big Mama become involved with such a cold-hearted character creature?" I could tell that she either really did not want to answer the question or maybe she really didn't know the answer and I noticed Ma looking in Aunt Elizabeth's direction. I had more questions and just as I was about to ask Elizabeth began answering all of them, even the questions I had not asked just yet. Elizabeth began to share, "Well, my brother Timothy, your grandfather, was quite smitten with your Grandmother Ruby. From what Timothy expressed as well as from my own recollection; he fell in love with Ruby when they were really young. I am very much aware that there can be many perspectives and or interpretations regarding the relationship between Tim and Ruby. But I was there and Timmy loved her. Your grandmother was a hard worker. She was highly intelligent. Extremely smart, so smart that the Wrights would call on her to handle a lot of the Wright's business affairs. She was always good with numbers. They trusted her from a very young age. They set aside money for her to do whatever she wanted to do with it once she turned 18 but Timothy really did not want her to leave and go off so far away. I always thought he was afraid that he would loose her to a handsome dark man who was sure and proud of his heritage and his skin unlike himself. Timothy and Ruby did not officially start courting until she was 18; but even then their interest towards each other was very discreet because Timothy Sr. forbid his son to be involved with a negro woman, even Ruby. There was always an innocent flirting going on between the two but at that time no lines were crossed. Timothy and Ruby were the same age. Timothy hoped that our father would eventually change his mind about the 'promise' that Timothy had to make regarding impregnating a negro woman as well as even falling for one. Timothy had hope; he knew that our father thought highly of Ruby. I suppose a part of him knew that our father didn't think highly of Ruby enough to no longer enforce his rule. So they secretly had a love affair that lasted for about two and a half to three years.

One night our father had gotten out of bed to go into the kitchen to fix some hot tea. He decided to go have a smoke on the porch and realized he wanted to open up a bottle of wine. He went back in the house and was headed to the wine cellar which was in the back of the basement. He opened up the door and came down the stairs. There were two bedrooms in the back on opposite ends of the wine cellar. That night he heard his son but was not sure who his son was with until he looked through the key hole. Timothy and I always felt that our father already knew way before that night. Our father went back up stairs without interrupting them. Most of the time it was so obvious between Ruby and Timothy. Ruby tried to be very discreet of course. Ruby was so beautiful and a very shapely woman. Elizabeth turned to Ruby and said, "You remind me of her." Aunt Elizabeth went on with the story and told us how she was there when Timothy told Timothy Sr. about Ruby being pregnant and how he wanted to marry her. Timothy Sr. put his head in his hands, looked up, stood up and walked over to his son and said you already know my answer.

As Aunt Elizabeth was telling us this she was shedding tears. " I remember this day as if it were yesterday because I was there. Timothy cried in front of our father and our father cried. Ruby cried and ran out of the house. Timothy ran after her.

That night I looked into my father's eye's for the first time and saw a hurting young man who wanted to love all of himself, who no longer wanted to deny his own mother or the love of his life. This is how our father became so bitter and passed. It was because of a broken heart that he was trying to mend but without love, it doesn't work." By now there were tears from us all not so much for sorrow but for the valuable lessons that we all were gaining from listening and that we all were embarking upon with our exciting endeavors. Aunt Elizabeth told us that she had some things for us that Ma's dad wanted to make sure we received before he passed. The first thing was a check for each of us in the amount of two hundred seventy-five thousand dollars a piece for my sisters and I. The second was the deed to his house and land along with being the owners of multiple businesses.

Aunt Elizabeth was wealthy herself and she would be well-taken care of. She also married a wealthy man, but she definitely did not need his money. Her husband's name was Benjamin James but most called him Jimmy. He was a real estate businessman.

Aunt Elizabeth handed us the checks and we signed the necessary paperwork. She also gave Ma a pretty box filled with letters addressed to big Mama Ruby and some addressed to Ma. Ma's Pop had been sending her money since she was born. Ma had been well taken care of financially. I knew Ma had always hoped for more than that. We enjoyed dinner and got to know Aunt Elizabeth. She apologized a lot over the course of the night. She apologized for Timothy, her dad as well as herself. She explained how she was simply trying to respect her brother's wishes from staying away from us. That night she told us about her three children and her grandchildren. She couldn't wait for us all to meet each other. What aunt Elizabeth didn't tell us was that she was ill. I felt that she didn't want to dampen the mood of the evening. She smiled and laughed a lot towards the end of the visit. Before she left, she reiterated how she wanted to set up a time for all of us to meet again and so we were invited to her home for dinner. We all agreed and looked forward to it. We planned for the month of September. At the time we did not know why she wanted to wait a few months but nonetheless, we agreed on the time and location.

On September 11, 1964, aunt Elizabeth passed and we met her children and grandchildren for the first time at her returning home service. We became very close to her children. There was an instant connection.

We didn't know anyone there but everyone appeared to treat us well. I was thankful for the opportunity that Ma had to get to have that time with her aunt and the opportunity to be introduced to some family.

Chapter 4

I had been in my place for several months now. I had finally gotten settled. I was finishing up on a novel I was writing about my life when I heard a knock at the door. I asked who it was and heard nothing. I tried looking out of the peep whole and saw nothing but darkness. So I opened up the door and it was Sadie. I was so excited to see her. I didn't even question her to discover how she found out where I lived. I had not seen her in a while. I was pretty certain Ma told her where I lived. I picked her up and hugged her so tight. We spent that Saturday reminiscing about our lives and catching each other up on our present day lives. Sadie was finally finishing up with school and was in the process of owning her own boutique in Philadelphia. I was thrilled. We were sitting in the living room in front of the television. I heard her stomach growling. I turned to her and asked, "Is someone hungry?" She smiled and nodded her head. I got up and went into the kitchen and washed my hands and began preparing a meal for us. She decided to come into the kitchen with me. She stood in the entrance and I looked towards her and she said, "It smells so good. What are you fixing?" I told her, "I am fixing salmon, baked potatoes and a salad- Oh! And lavender tea." I was just about finished and began setting the table. She asked if she could help while she was already helping. She asked where the serving utensils were to put in the serving bowls. I told her where they were. She grabbed them and placed them in the serving bowls. She walked over to the chair to sit down. I sat down. I asked her if she would mind if I gave thanks and she said, "No, of course I don't mind." "We give thanks for this food. May it nurture us and love us by giving to every organ and cleansing our blood. For this meal was prepared with loving hands and a pure heart. Ase'."

I told her to help herself. I waited until she finished preparing her plate but she offered the plate to me. We both smiled and before I could say anything she had already taken the empty plate that initially was in front of me. So I just told her thank you and that she did not have to do that. She looked at me with sass and then said, "I know." We had the best time. After dinner, she and I cleared off the table and washed the dishes. I turned the radio on and we caught the ending of the song titled, 'Try Me, I Need You' by James Brown and I could feel the energy between us charging and then Betty Everett sang to us, 'It's In His Kiss'. Sadie began singing and I had never heard her sing the way she was singing in that moment. She has a beautiful voice. A soul stirring voice, so stirring that after I washed and dried my hands, poured two glasses of wine, I embraced her with a kiss. We kissed for so long I began caressing her back so passionately I picked her up and carried her into the bedroom while kissing her. I laid her on the bed and began undressing her. I continued kissing her while I was fully dressed. After kissing her lips for what seemed like for hours I began kissing her neck, shoulders, and breasts. She was trying to undress me but needed my assistance, so I helped her. After my clothes were completely off I proceeded to lay on top of her and I had both of my hands underneath her head as if her head was resting on my hands as a pillow, We were looking into each others eyes, just laying still. I finally said Sadie, "Before we exchange energy I want you to know what is about to happen with each entrance I give and you receive and vice versa." Sadie says, "Tell me while you're entering." So that is what I did. As I entered her I said, "Sadie, as I enter I want you to know and feel our trust. As I enter in, know that there is healing being realized with each movement. As I enter in, we are giving each other permission to see into the other, see the real me, see my heart, my soul, as we enter and we receive. As I enter in, we look into our souls via our eyes know that love is only connecting with itself in us as us. Know that as I enter in and you receive, I receive and you receive and each time we are experiencing the limitlessness in our bond and all of its loving sacredness. As I enter in, each time healing is being realized in both of us and as I exit hurt is dissipating. As we enter, we receive, knowing we've never left from the omnipresence of this connection being expressed right now. As I enter — trust. As I enter —healing. As I enter —love. As we enter — we receive."

As I repeated the last line I could feel that she was about to climax with each entrance, each phrase she was releasing. I had not yet and that was Ok. I knew we were not finished. She had released and we started again, only she was laying on her side. Her back was facing me and I put my hands on her breasts, rubbing her nipples, flicking them back and forth, stimulating them between my fingers, kissing her back and then I entered her. I was getting ready to repeat but Sadie began to speak, "James, As you enter my physical body know that we were already connected at the heart. As you enter know that I've always loved you and always will. As you enter James, know that I feel so protected especially in this position. As you enter I feel even more connected. As you enter you are experiencing energy of endless healing power directly connected to all of the divine being that I am. As you enter in side of my universe, with each moment healing is being realized and so whenever you're ready it is okay to release. I released and twenty minutes later Sadie began to lay on top of me and began moving on top of me in a circular motion while sitting up. She said, "James, I move on you in a circle because this love, this bond will never end. It will always meet, always know this." Sadie began to lay down on me and kept saying, this love will never end, this love will never end... I released only for us to continue one more time. This time we were very quiet, focused and meant business. The intent behind our words had been set and actually the connection had always been but we were expressing and acknowledging it. The tone had been set, we were tuned in so no words were necessary at this point. We were sitting in the bed. Sadie was sitting on top of me with her legs wrapped around me. This was a night we would always remember.

She stayed the night and I asked for her to come back later the next evening. She did. We were both happy and enjoying each others company. We watched television and played cards. We began cooking, ate dinner and fell asleep. We continued this routine for about a year and a half to two years and during this time she was busy with finishing up with school as well as her boutique. We never established a title for our connection. At the time we both just knew what it was without ever saying it. Our bond just continued to expand.

One evening she came in and I picked up on something, she seemed distant. She said, "James, I am thinking that we may need some time a part so I can sort some things out. I immediately felt a pain in my heart. I grabbed my chest and plopped down on the couch. I could not look at her. Just two thoughts running through my head, 1. There must be someone else and 2. We got along so well. We had few disagreements. I mean we weren't perfect but we were the best of friends. I did not understand. She was not even sitting, she was standing up. I knew that she was serious and that there was nothing that I could say to convince her other wise but I still tried. "Sadie, you know I love you. I do not want you to leave but I trust you and yet it does not mean it doesn't hurt. If you feel you need to go then go." Sadie began crying. I began shedding a few tears as well. I stood up and hugged her for a while and we kissed. It was one of the most revealing kisses. It told me that the connection would always be there no matter where we'd end up or who we'd end up with.

Chapter 5

One year and three months had passed and I had neither heard or seen Sadie; and I was Ok, I guess. I had just finished my book loosely based on my life. I had just gotten an agent who was interested in helping me shop my book to publishing companies. In the 60's it was still a very challenging time if you were a black man, but I was excited. I just had a feeling that everything was going to work out. I wanted to share the news with Sadie but couldn't bring myself to do it. It just did not feel right, at least not yet. I was working as a teacher in one of the toughest schools in Philly and I loved it.

My agent was a close friend of grandma Tee's. He knew big Mama Ruby too. His name was Eddie. Eddie supported my book wholeheartedly. He believed in it one hundred percent so much so that after I told him my manuscript had already been copyrighted. Two weeks later, he surprised me by telling me that I needed to pack my bags because he sent the manuscript to New York and a major publishing company wants to meet with me. I fell to my knees and wept. I immediately went to those journals that Grandma Tee and granddad James had in that box. I was living it for them as their DNA is running through my veins they are living in this moment with me. I thought "I ain't afraid. I ain't afraid."

That night I packed which was a Tuesday. Our meeting was on Thursday at 9:00 a.m. I was ready but I also did not want to give up complete rights of my story. I knew Eddie wouldn't fail me but more importantly, I knew I would not fail me. I prayed that Tuesday night to my higher being and my ancestors. I was in complete trust. Wednesday we were on our way to the Hotel in New York. When we arrived Eddie told me to check in my room and then we were going to dinner and to a night club he would frequently hang out at when he was in town. So I tidied up and we met downstairs in the lobby. The restaurant we were going to eat at was an upscale restaurant and Eddie was not only an agent but he also owned several businesses. He was pretty well known in the entertainment business. He was respected and yet quite the ladies' man. The ladies loved him and threw themselves at him. He was tall, dark and athletic. He was always very well dressed.

After we ate, we headed to the "spotlight" club. I followed Eddie to the VIP section and there were so many women in this area. I knew it was going to be a long night and I didn't want to stay out too late. I wanted to be prepared for our meeting tomorrow. So I left the club early. I woke up extremely early considering that I had gotten in around 1 in the a.m.

I could not believe how well I rested the night before. I was extremely excited. I woke up remembering something that Grandma Tee had once told me. I could hear her voice so clear, she would say, "when you live what's in you most of the time everything needed will already be lined up, waiting on you."

I was up by six a.m. and washed and dressed by a quarter til' seven. I left out of my room and knocked on Eddie's door next store and he was not answering. For a minute I thought, well maybe he went to go and get some breakfast or a cup of coffee. So just as I was headed to my room the door opened and a beautiful woman stepped out and she kissed Eddie, waved at me with a smile and walked off.

I said, "Eddie you're a slick sly cat." Eddie smirked. I chuckled. I said, "Hurry up man." He responded, "Alright man, give me twenty-five minutes. The publishing company is about 13-17 blocks away; we'll make it." So I went back to my room and waited for twenty minutes to come and go and then twenty-two minutes later there was a knock at my door and it was Eddie ready with business attire on. Eddie had on a gray suit. I had on a navy blue suit. We looked like we meant business. We were on our way. We had already walked up six blocks. I just happened to glance at someone in a clothing store that looked familiar. My heart felt as though it was going to come out of my skin. My eyes were as bright as the moon, my heart was shining through. It was Sadie! Why was I happy and not angry? Should I stop or keep going? I must have slowed up with my walking because Eddie asked, "What's wrong, you ok man?" "Yeah; Eddie." I kept walking but what I didn't know was that she saw me and came running out and belting out my name. I stopped and slowly turned around and it was her and we hugged. It wasn't quite 8:00 a.m. and Eddie and I wanted to stop and grab a bite to eat. I told Sadie briefly that I was on my way to a business meeting about my book and hopefully we would see each other soon. A tear fell from her eye with a brilliant smile and she grabbed my hand and said Ok. We parted ways. A few blocks later we stopped in a small coffee shop on a side street and grabbed a doughnut, no coffee for me. I just didn't need it at this point. Eddie did. He had a long night. Eddie and I paid and grabbed our food. We ate on the way. We only had about three or four more blocks to go. When we arrived I stood in front of the building for about ten minutes before I went in. Eddie stood outside with me asking if I was ready. I held my finger up gesturing to hold on for a minute and Eddie did just that. He stood beside me. I opened the door. Eddie followed and he said, "they are on the fifth floor." I could not believe that we were in Harlem and this could possibly be the day my vision becomes a manifestation. We got on the elevator and as soon as we got off I decided I needed to make a pit stop just to make sure I was clean and fresh still. Eddie pointed me into the direction of the bathroom. He waited and when I came out we walked towards the front desk which was to my right when I came out of the bathroom. We were thirty minutes early. Eddie informed the secretary, Mrs. Peters, that we were here for our appointment. She called Mr. Wilson and informed us that he would be with us momentarily before asking us to have a seat. She asked if she could get us anything. I replied with a "No thank you." Eddie, said a cup of coffee, please. I laughed. I whispered to Eddie, "Man she must of have tired you all the way out. That is cup number two." Mrs. Peters brought Eddie his coffee. Mrs. Peters heard my remark and chuckled also. As soon as Mrs. Peter walked back to the front desk, Mr. Wilson buzzed for us to come in. "Mr. Wilson says, he's ready for you now. Please follow me." Eddie and I followed Mrs. Peters into Mr. Wilson's office. After formal introductions, he told us he would be willing to negotiate numbers, copyright and discuss advancement for the follow-up novel. My heart felt like it was going to come out of my chest again. Mr. Wilson told us that Mrs. Peters is his cousin and was filling in for the secretary who was out on leave. Mrs. Peters was one of the editors. Mrs. Peters and the other three editors were surprised that they had very little to edit in the manuscript. So Mr.Wilson wanted me to sign some documents that day. I did not. I asked if I could bring the documents with me and read them over before signing. He agreed. The following day Eddie and I read over the documents that I had to sign, it was official. I was an author within a few months after signing, my book was out there in major bookstores to be read, my voice to be heard and I was so thankful to share.

About six months had passed. I remember going to the bookstore just to purchase a copy. I wanted Sadie to know and wondered what she was doing in New York. Sadie leaving when she did is what motivated me to complete my first novel expeditiously. I at the very least wanted to thank her. I was already working on the follow-up and was thrilled. I was halfway finished. I wanted to get as much writing done as I could that night because on Sunday evening I was invited to a local bookstore for a signing. Eddie and the family would be there. I tried contacting my friends from Howard. Even though I was unsuccessful in contacting them, I was beyond grateful that it was all happening.

And on that day about a year later, May 7, 1968, I woke up with the biggest smile. I was still participating in book signings. The book signing wasn't until 3:00 p.m. on Broad Street. I began my morning rituals which consisted of kneeling before my altar with a heart of gratitude, lighting my candles, singing and sitting quietly in remembrance of those who came before me. I would then breathe deeply and stretch. I would prepare grandma Tee's favorite breakfast which was a black tea with mint, an orange, french toast, and hash browns. I enjoyed it for the both of us. I cleaned up the kitchen and decided to hop in the shower, brush my teeth and get dressed. It was only 10:00 a.m. but I was ready.

I decided to sit down at the kitchen table and write. I was having what was known as a writer's block of some sort but I later realized it was something that I was holding onto that was altering the flow of my creativity where the creator resides. As I began realizing this I heard a knock at my door. I knew someone was coming, but did not want to be interrupted. I asked who it was and it was Eddie. We greeted and he then told me I had another book signing to attend next Saturday in Harlem. I was speechless. "Are you okay man?" asked Eddie.

"Speechless man, just speechless." Eddie then says, "James, I told you this book would touch the people's hearts and that is why I had to support you. I am going to meet you at the signing today at 2:30 I just wanted to stop by and tell you in person." I shook Eddie's hand and told him, "I'll see you then."

A couple of hours had passed. I was now writing. I was excited about this piece as well. I put the pen down and looked over at the typewriter and thought, maybe I should start using that now. So I started to type and I must admit this brought a level of peace to me. From that day forward I used the typewriter that belonged to Grandma Tee that was given to me later that same day that Pops gave me the box full of writings. I love using a pencil and paper then transferring it to the typewriter. There was something about the energy from my hands and touching the paper that for a long time I just preferred over the typewriter in my initial process of creating. I felt closer to Grandma Tee using the typewriter. I knew tonight at the book signing she and Pop-pop would be with me.

When I arrived at the bookstore it was 2:22 p.m. and there was a line already outside. Eddie was standing outside waiting on me and as I was speaking to the people he rushed me in to introduce me to the owner of the store. A beautiful woman and her brother. I was captivated by her beauty. The doors opened at three o'clock on the dot. There were roughly about 200 people there. Most of the guests were sitting, while some were standing. I was standing to not only read an excerpt from the book but I wanted to share a portion of my new book with the people and I asked the owner if it was ok. Afterwards I answered questions and lastly, I signed books. I met many beautiful people who inspired me. I saw my family who had been very supportive.

I only had eight more people left in the line. The last one was Sadie. We embraced each other in the warmest hug. I signed her book and wrote a message in the back of the book. She had just purchased the book.

"James, you look good. How have you've been?"

My response, "I've been exceptionally well. How about you?"

I've been ok. I was hoping soon we could get together and talk. I have to head back to New York. The next few months will be extremely busy for me. I own a boutique and I am also involved in a major expose and I am creating pieces for that event. I will be back for a few days in July. I agreed to meet her then. I was very curious as to her reason for leaving the way she did. Sadie and I hugged and we parted ways.

As I was packing up, the owners of the bookstore came over and said that they really appreciated me coming. They expressed how they both already read my book and how much they both thoroughly enjoyed the book. Hakim and Fatima Mosley are the owners of the guiding light bookstore in Philadelphia. Fatima was a very beautiful woman. She was very humorous and very flirtatious in a respectable manner. So I asked her if she and I could go out for a cup of coffee sometime soon. She agreed and we exchanged information. That evening was one of the best nights I had experienced in quite some time.

Fatima and I had been seeing each other for about two months. As much as I liked her I just felt my heart speaking and thought I should have closure with Sadie before moving on with Fatima with only a piece of me available. Fatima and I continued to see each other just not as often. One day in July Fatima and I decided to go for a walk. We ended up at her bookstore. Fatima and I always had fun but I think we both knew it was nothing more than a genuine friendship at this time and it was pretty cool. We had lunch at the bookstore in the cafe' inside. Fatima and I would do a lot of laughing. We were always joking around. In one of our few moments of silence, Fatima asked, "James, who is she? Who has your heart? Who has your mental?" Of course, I was completely shocked. I stared at her for a few seconds. I shared the story with her and she could actually relate to my situation. She had a very similar story to share. We really learned a lot from each other that day.

Later that day in the evening around 7 p.m. after hanging out with Fatima we parted ways. I was home working on my new book. There was a knock on my door. I opened it and it was Sadie. We greeted one another with a hug, the hug was very intimate and sincere. The door to my place was still open. I closed the door and we walked over to the couch and sat down. Sadie was looking straight down towards her shoes. I was looking directly at her and I knew she was about to tell me something that I was not going to be happy about. I began to feel nervous. I was picking up on how she felt and how she could not look directly at me. Sadie was staring at the floor and I staring directly at her.

Sadie finally looked up with tears in her eyes and said, "I am pregnant." So immediately, I thought why is she sad about it? And yet my heart hurt so bad. It felt like it shattered into a billion pieces. I mean physically I began to feel pain in my heart and I grabbed my chest and stood up to grab a glass of water. I drank the whole glass and just stood in the kitchen leaning my back up against the refrigerator. I still felt a pain physically. I walked back to the couch and looked at Sadie who at this time was crying aloud. I hugged her with so much pain I felt in my heart and yet there was this part on the inside that completely understood why this happened. Sadie did not tell me who the father was but I knew that it was someone who would eventually abandon her, as her father had once done to her and her family. This was a lesson she had to learn that I would never be able to teach her, even if I stopped breathing tomorrow I still would not be able to abandon her. You see we were so connected that even after one's heart stops beating the soul lives on, always remembering. Love is still felt in that remaining heart beat. Sadie cried in my arms. I did not say a word. She sat up and said, "I'm not keeping this baby." I looked into her eyes and told her, "I feel strongly that you should keep the baby but I support your decision either way." She said, "Thank you." She cried some more. She asked me if she could rest a while. She had to be only about 4 wks if that. I told her she could rest as long as she needed. She laid down on the couch. I brought her a blanket and she dozed off. I went to sit down at the table and write. I wrote and was so focused that three hours had passed and I had almost completed this book. I just felt a sense of urgency to complete as much as possible.

When Sadie woke up from her nap. I asked her if she was ready to eat and she said yes, so I made her a sub sandwich. She went to use the bathroom. I began to set the table and she asked if I mind if we ate on the floor. So we did just that. We interacted as if we had never lost contact and that is because we hadn't on a heart ~ soul level.

We played cards and listened to the radio just like old times. I had a television but I rarely turned it on. I just preferred being engaged with people I knew, not engaged with strangers on or in a box.

Sadie and I had talked about many things but one thing that we had yet to ever discuss was religion in depth. We began to share ideas and spiritual practices with the other, for some reason. I asked Sadie "What do you believe? Do you believe in heaven and or hell? Do you believe in a God?" Sadie told him, "No. I feel that we come from a source or something that is eternal but there is no big man sitting in the sky while he waits to send his son to pick us up. I am not sure if there is some big man sitting in heaven who claims to love all of his children, giving them free will but yet if they don't do things the way he wants he sentences them to eternal hell to burn forever. This is a very conditional God, with human flaws. I do feel that there is a greater power as a whole and I am a part of that whole. I am the representation of that source. This is one of the reasons my dad left us because he was a religious man. He could not understand how myself or my mom did not believe in going to church and being a traditional Christian. My brothers were on the fence and questioning things but had not yet made a decision one way or the other." I then asked her if she thought there was an afterlife of some sort and or reincarnation. Sadie then told him, "Yes, absolutely!!! I just feel strongly that there is." James told her that he definitely felt that he had been here before and in fact that he and Sadie had traveled together on their journeys before in previous lives. Sometimes coming back playing in different roles. He said, "I feel this is why we have loved each other unconditionally and why I loved you instantly. Sadie you were placed in my life on this journey to remind me of a friend that I once knew years ago. I did not like speaking of her. Her name was Genie. She was about five years old when we became friends and we remained friends up until twelve years of age but she moved and we lost contact. I always wondered where she was and how her life turned out. We were inseparable. Genie was one of the ones that most people thought we would eventually marry. There was just something special about us two. She protected me as if she were my sister but I was a year younger than she was. She was in some ways over-protective. One day she and her family up and moved and I never saw her again." Sadie's eyes were as bright as the moon. She looked at me with a smile and told me something similar. She begins telling me about her beloved friend Teddy, "Teddy died after he tried saving his sister and mom from a fire. His dad was at work he had just gotten in from school when he noticed smoke coming out of the house. He ran in the house to go get his sister and mom. It just so happened that his sister and mom happen to be out running errands with the neighbor. I was home sick that day from school. Our friend Ben told him not to go inside the house. Ben told him to wait until he got his dad and uncle but Teddy wouldn't wait. He wouldn't listen. He said, "I'm going to get my mom and Tammy out of the damn house." As soon as he did go inside, the house became engulfed in flames. Everyone ran, people were screaming. Ben's dad called 911 emergency but of course, it was too late. Somehow Teddy managed to make it upstairs. He was determined to save his family. His dad was devastated. His mom and Tammy never forgave themselves. I was miserable and blamed myself. I felt if I had just gone to school that day just maybe he would have listened and not gone inside of that house. Teddy was thirteen. At the time I was eleven. Teddy was quite the rebel. He was our little neighborhood militant leader. He was my best friend and there was a not a day that went by that I did not think about him." "What happened to the rest of his family?" I asked. Sadie replied, "His mom and dad are fine or as fine as someone can be after losing a child. Tammy, on the other hand, was ten years old at the time. She became hooked on drugs, running the street and pregnant by age fourteen. She was very angry. She has since turned her life around and is now a community activist. She went to college to study law to become a lawyer." Sadie then told me, "You remind me a lot of Teddy, you know?" I turned towards her and said, "I do?" she said "Yes, you do." "You came into my life not too long after that loss of a great friend. There has always been something magical and therapeutic about the connection between you and I. The connection you and I share is rather similar to what Teddy and I had."

I thought and felt the exact same way about me and Genie's connection in relation to Sadie. Genie was a strong young girl and I knew she would be a strong young woman. She reminded me a lot of my Grandma Tee but in a lot of ways you remind me of both Grandma Tee and Genie. You see, Sadie was not afraid to speak up just like Grandma Tee and Genie. We spent many hours that evening talking. We touched some subjects we had never discussed before and I am thankful we did.

It was getting late and I was ready to turn in. Sadie must have known because she asked if I'd mind her staying the night. "Of course I don't mind" was my response. The thoughts and questions that I had I knew I had to speak and or ask. We went into the bedroom. I gave her something to change into. She went into the bathroom and changed. I changed while she was in the bathroom. We got in the bed and her back was facing me, I held her and wept. She did not know I was, but I was holding one hand over my heart because it hurt like hell. I felt a tear fall onto the other hand I had around Sadie that fell from her eye and then she asked me, "Don't you want to know who the father is? Don't you want to know how or why?" I told her I did and then I said, "Sadie I do want to know who, when and why. Just not now." I felt like I already knew deep down inside. I then told her "Just know love is unconditional, it never abandons you. I feel a sadness but I will feel better when I rise tomorrow." She said, "Ok. Thank you for loving me. I love you James, I held her tight and told her, "I know." When her back rested on me as she laid on her side, her body pressing against me, I felt that she knew I would always protect her and support her. I would always love her. Sadie told me that she would be heading out early because one of my relatives who were close to my parents had just gotten married a fairly young couple and my Ma had invited Sadie and I'm sure intentionally because I had not been around as often. My ma thought that her inviting Sadie would encourage me to come as well. It worked.

The young couple was a very odd couple. They did not seem to fit but everyone seemed to think they did. The wife is a cousin. Rayanna is her name and she is related to my Ma on Grandma Ruby's side. Grandma Ruby and Rayanna's Ma who were cousin's and really close when they were coming up. Anyway, I was drawn to this couple and really did not know why because I don't really remember Rayanna that well. Sadie and I enjoyed the gathering with my Ma and Pops and Rayanna and Ron (Rayanna's husband).

It was getting late so I was getting ready to leave. Sadie said she was coming with me and going back to my place but that she needed to go home to her Mother's and pick up a few things. I really did not know where she was living or who she was living with. I did not even bother to ask. When we pulled up to the house I helped her up the steps. I told her I would wait in the car. I only waited for a few minutes before she was coming back down the steps. I helped her put a few things in the trunk and helped her in the car and then we were headed back to my place. On the ride back home I kept thinking about Rayanna and Ron. I saw them staring at me as if they felt some odd synergy. In the middle of my thoughts, Sadie asks, "Did you notice some kind of connection between you, Rayanna and Ron?" I turned to glance over at her and smiled. I said, "Oh, man, yes!!" That made me feel a little better knowing that it wasn't just me feeling that way. Neither one of us knew why just yet.

Some weeks had passed and Sadie was beginning to show. She was coming over pretty often which made me wonder all the more who the father was. I began to feel my heart physically aching. Every opportunity I would try to write as much as I could because school would be starting soon. I would have to start preparing for the up coming school year. A part of me wanted that school year to begin so that my mind would not be on Sadie and her child.

About two or three months had passed since Sadie had come over to tell me the news. I could barely look at her whenever she came around. My heart would be in pain. She was beginning to show. Her face was full already. We did the usual, card game, ate, talked, laughed and danced. I was tired this night and she was as well. She decided to stay over. We laid on the bed in our favorite position. Her back was facing me. My arms were wrapped around her. I felt that I was protecting her and as though she felt protected. I began shedding a few tears as my hands would wander and stop as I felt the hardness of her stomach, remembering there was a life growing inside of her, a life that I knew nothing about. A life that I did not help to create. I didn't know who the father was and if things would change once the baby came. My heart felt it. I got up to get some water. "Are you Ok?" Sadie asked. "Yes, Sadie; just getting some water." I always picked up on how others felt usually instantly but so did Sadie. As I began drinking the water the pain grew sharp and sharper, feeling like a knife cutting me. I walked back towards my room with tears in my eyes. The next thing I remembered was dropping to the floor, holding my heart as I heard in the far distance Sadie scream....

Chapter 6

The year was 1978. I had become very close to James's Ma and Pop but what was even more interesting was I became extremely close to Rayanna and Ron. Rayanna had a child who was now a year old. A beautiful girl named Love' who spent a lot of time with Sadie, Ma and Pops.

Rayanna began going through some rough times with Ron. Rayanna began confiding in Ma, Pops and myself. "I just don't understand why he seems to be completely changing. It started right after I had Love', my dad tried to warn me," Rayanna said. Apparently, Ron was very disconnected and only thought of himself. Many nights Rayanna felt alone and not just because Ron worked so much, she felt that way because both were very immature. I would often times pick Rayanna, and Love' up and hang out. Rayanna depended very much on Ron and he felt very overwhelmed at times. Deep down I felt they loved each other. Two years later, Love' had a beautiful baby brother, Ron Jr. and three years after Ron Jr. another beautiful baby boy named Malik James.

Rayanna and Ron initially were pretty heavy into the church which was so different for me as well as ma Bella and Pop Fletch. I was asked to become Love's Godma so I honored their request and went to the Christening, even though she was already Love's and honestly her brother's Godma at heart. When Love' was a baby and ever since then, well even before then Love' and I had a connection. I also had a meaningful connection with Malik James and Ron Jr. I became very close to Rayanna, Ron, and their three children adored me. I admired

Rayanna for her spirituality in spite of the fact that I was not a Christian. I still knew that Rayanna was in touch with the part of herself that she referred to as the Holy Spirit. There were many times that Rayanna and the three children over the years had experienced some unexplainable events that involved angels or beings from other realms. I remember one of those events (that took place years later) when Rayanna and the three children were coming from Wilmington, DE to go home to Newark, DE. They were riding on Interstate 95 in a 1988 Ford Tempo at night. All of a sudden, sparks began to fly from the tire. The tire made a loud sound and then there was no more tire on the back left rear tire. There was no pay phone on the busy interstate. Rayanna began to pray and told the children to pray. Malik and Ron Jr. were crying. Love' was annoyed with her brothers at the fact that they were crying until Rayanna told Love' it's ok to feel how they feel and it is ok for them to express it in that way. Then Rayanna tells the boys that everything is okay. Let's pray. Within five minutes a car pulls up behind the car but what was odd was that the car pulled up from nowhere. It just appeared. An older couple got out of the car. Rayanna had gotten out of the car but Love' jumped out of the car as well because she always felt that she was the protector of the family. Love' just wanted to make sure that these people were not crazy. Rayanna told her to get back in the car. The older couple proceeded to assist Rayanna with putting the doughnut on the car. The couple was conversing with Rayanna. She asked the couple what church they were   attending, the elder black man looked at her with a very eery yet pleasant smile and said we belong to the Church of God. During the man's response, Rayanna felt that they were not from this dimension. Rayanna thanked the couple and as soon as she got back in the car she and the children waited for the couple to pull off and they did. She and the children were waiting to see what would happen and the couple drove off and it looked as though the sky opened up and they went into another realm. It was as if the sky literally opened up. Anyway; they had many more experiences like that. I would try to explain that it wasn't your character savior Jesus it was your ancestors and your children's intention and knowing that someone would come but Rayanna would not budge. She believed what she believed.

By the time Malik James was five, Rayanna and Ron were having so many issues within their marriage. She was married to her church and Ron was married to his sexual appetite. Ron was having an issue with infidelity. He slept with Rayanna's sister-in-law and countless others. Rayanna felt as though she needed to hang in there for the family but she would refuse Ron sex for obvious reasons and then for some not so obvious reasons. You see, Rayanna was taught that it was a sin to have sex on a Sunday even if married. She was a virgin when she married Ron and so this was devastating for her to continually be cheated on. She felt shame because of the church. She believed it was a sin to divorce, period. Of course, Bella (James's Ma) and I were outraged and spoke our mind about it. They knew that in 1987 was not the time to risk being in a marriage where infidelity was an issue. Ma Bella knew even more than that, the very thing, "church" Rayanna was running to was the very thing that was subtlety enslaving her to false ideology. I asked Rayanna, "What type of love would force you to stay in a relationship that is not mutual in respect, honor, or love or concern for your whole self?" She began to respond with as I often referred to or called psycho religious regurgitated babble. Rayanna responded saying," I trust the Lord with all my heart. It is obviously in his will for me." Rayanna, " Who's will? Ron's will or your will? These beliefs of enslavement were passed down to us by slave owners to keep us in submission; to keep the matriarchal aspect bound to a white image and view them as the superior group and to take the responsibility off of you, off of us." Rayanna said, "Ok, that's enough now Sadie." I left it alone.

Another few years had passed Rayanna and Ron had divorced. They had been divorced for about three years. She had decided that she could no longer take the pain, the unhealthy lifestyle that she was subjecting herself to. I felt what really did it was when Ron had an ongoing affair with a younger woman and the affair became very serious. One night (a few years prior to the divorce) Rayanna began praying. Ron was out that night. Ron worked a lot of swing shifts that consisted of a lot of overnight hours. Rayanna and Ron were also involved in a popular gospel choir that required a significant amount of travel which is why Rayanna resigned from participating in the choir but Ron continued and this is where he met the young lady who would later become pregnant. Rayanna left the choir when she began attending a church that was a lot more advanced in comparison to other churches that she had attended in the past. The popular gospel choir had a lot of what the church called "perversions" taking place within the organization. Adultery, promiscuous behavior from heterosexual as well as homosexuality was very prevalent in the choir. Not everyone was involved in these behaviors but many were. Ron was indeed one of the ones who was sleeping with a young, small, petite framed twenty-something year old woman who was in the choir. Her name is Katelin. Most called her Kay. She was a hurting young woman. Ron was in his mid-to-late thirties at this time. Before they began their escapade one night the choir practice was in Chester, PA where they had a rehearsal and Ron asked if Rayanna would come and bring the children. She told him yes. She met Ron at the rehearsal. Rayanna had been feeling her intuition (Holy Spirit) was speaking to her for some time, again about Ron. When She arrived with the children everyone was excited to see her and the children. Everyone greeted them and told the children how big they had gotten. She tried staying for the entire rehearsal but it was getting so late and the children had to go to school the next morning. Rayanna told Ron she was leaving and so Ron walked her and the children outside. As he was walking with them, Kay comes outside and calls for Ron. Ron turns around and says, "Oh, wait; Rayanna, I want you to meet someone, a friend. In that moment Rayanna felt it in the pit of her stomach as they were being formally introduced. Then as they parted ways, Rayanna heard a still small voice say, she is going to try and take your husband and sever the family unit. A year and some change later Katelin ended up pregnant and had a son. Rayanna was devastated. Ron told Rayanna but he told her that he wanted to tell the children. Rayanna agreed but out of spite took it upon herself to tell the children. So when he began telling the children they sat there not saying a word. They let him finish. Ron was crying uncontrollably and then Rayanna says with a smirk, "I already told them." The children were crying. Ron was embarrassed, filled with shame. Ron became so angry with Rayanna, He screamed from the pit of his stomach, "HOW COULD YOU DO THAT, HOW THE HELL COULD YOU DO THAT?" Rayanna looked at him with a sly smirk and apologized but deep down she was pleased. Ron asked if they could all pray together. The five of them stood in the middle of the floor in a huddle. The four of them were crying while Rayanna was trying not to laugh at Ron due to his hysterical crying that sounded like he was hyperventilating. Ron asked them for forgiveness but the family as they had known it would never be the same, even though it was pretty dysfunctional. Ron was hardly ever home yet it was all they knew. Ron would often times blame his lack of presence on work but then he would go on trips with the choir or spend hours away at the "gym". Love' remembers her Ma having to make up something to do just to get Ron to spend time with his three children. When Ron would agree to it the children would come over but he would go in his room and watch the game, order the children pizza and a cream soda with salt and vinegar chips and that would be the extent of the rare Friday night occasion. They may have spent the night at their dad's place once or twice which was fair at the time considering he had a roommate.

Rayanna and Ron had been a part for some time now. The fact of the matter was as a family it was all they had all known for the past thirteen years and now from this point on It would never be the same. Of course, a woman can not take a man from any place unless he allows it but the straw on the camel's back was broken after Joe was born. A year or so after Joe was born Rayanna thought to give it one more try but it would not be. They would finalize their divorce, prior to Lil Joe's sister was born, Bionca. Joe and Bionca were loved by Ron's eldest three children. His three eldest were raised by Rayanna to never hold it against their siblings and so they never did.

Rayanna was looking into relocating and starting fresh. She and Ron had been divorced but was just making sure that it was officially over. Ron admitted that he could no longer be married and wanted to enjoy the single life. Rayanna began making plans to try and relocate to California. Love' was not having it. She was getting ready to start high school and loved her city. She loved her church and her friends. Ron jr. and Malik were a little younger so they were pretty content with relocating and going somewhere new and exciting.

Now, before Rayanna and Ron had married Rayanna was attending Norfolk State University. She and Ron were already planning to get married. Ron was in the army at the time. They kept in contact via letters. Ron wanted Rayanna to come home so that they could marry. She wanted to come home as well. She was saving herself for marriage and so they had not been intimate (sexually) the entire time they dated. During Rayanna's academic experience at Norfolk State University, she had become popular amongst her peers in the music department. She had become friends with someone named Craig. He was a music major. A very religious man. Rayanna and Craig remained friends throughout the years. They kept in touch.

During the separation between Rayanna and Ron, Rayanna had a successful daycare business but she decided to close up and start pursuing other options for a career. After the divorce was finalized Rayanna had begun living with her Father with the three children. During this time period, She and Craig were communicating quite frequently. They were becoming closer as friends. Craig had invited Rayanna and her children to come for a gospel choir workshop his church was having and Craig wanted Rayanna to be a part of it. She was willing to attend but she had no idea that Craig was preparing to show her a good time in this small city called, Lynchburg. She had no interest whatsoever of even considering moving to a place called Lynchburg. She still had her hopes set on moving to California. Her dream was to become and actress, model and singer. She loved theater and was always involved in musicals and or plays in her hometown and was phenomenal. At one point and time in her life, Rayanna was asked to go on the road for a season to sing backup for Stevie Wonder; but because she felt like that experience would be compromising her relationship with Christ, she did not agree to do it. Rayanna is extremely gifted and creative but often times did not realize just how gifted or creative she truly was or is. A few months later she would agree to move to Lynchburg to start fresh. Her daughter Love' did not agree with this move and everyone agreed that Love' would move in with Ron. Love' was very angry and hurt that Rayanna was making such a drastic move but as long as Love' didn't have to move she was ok for the most part. She just knew she would miss her brothers tremendously. Her brothers were going with their Mom to Lynchburg, Virginia which is five hours away from

Wilmington, Delaware. The reason Ron Jr. and Malik James were more willing to relocate is they were promised fun, a dog and the opportunity to be involved in sports. As soon as they relocated they realized it was all a ploy tactic to get them there. Malik was and still is to this day a very kind hearted, gentle soul. He is very gifted in a multitude of areas. He was kind on one hand but if he became angry, he was unstoppable. As time went on that rage would develop as result of the neglect and abandonment he felt from Ron his dad. Eventually, the rejection he felt from their mom and the manipulative mind games he felt from Craig. From the time Malik was born Ron just was not in his life. He never really took the time to get to know Malik as a child. When they relocated Malik was eight years old. Ron Jr. was also kind-hearted but he had a very ornery nature about him. Some called it the middle child syndrome. He was and still is also very gifted as well. Both of Love's brothers were very gifted in the areas of music, athletics, humor (comedic geniuses) and academics. Although, academically they did not know they were gifted until later on in life. They were pretty bored with school. They eventually became angry when they realized the promises and lies they were told were just a ploy to make the transition of relocating go a lot smoother. Love' would eventually watch her brothers blossom into beautiful, loving, young men despite the lack of role models they had access to demonstrating what a man really was and is. Love' was fourteen at the time. Ron jr. was 12 and Malik James was 8 going on 9. While Love' decided to live in Delaware she was torn in her decision. Ron and Love' were able to spend some time getting to know each other. Even though Love' was only 14 she had a very old soul. She was very observant and intuitive. Her dad was still pretty busy for the most part and she knew he still felt overwhelmed. He would be responsible for a teenage daughter by his self. As months passed, Love' began to see Ron in a different light. Love' saw her dad as a hurting little boy. She would later learn why she selected the type of men she selected in her adult life.

Ron would confide in Love' about his relationships and ask Love's opinion. Love' loved how Ron seemed to think highly of Love's opinions. Love' was and still is very intuitive and would pick up on vibes from people instantly. In most cases, she was able to mirror how others were feeling, so she could easily tell how others were feeling most of the time. She knew Ron was still searching for a mother's love. Love' remembered the time she asked Ron a question when she was around the age of 8; she and her dad were laying in the bed waiting for her mom to come in the house with her brothers after an outing, "What happened to your dad, dad?" Love' wanted to know because she thought it was strange to never ever hear anything about him or see any pictures of him. Love's grandfather on her mother's side was still around and although her grandmother

(mother's mother) passed, she always heard stories about her and saw pictures and everyone knew how Rayanna and Ron both loved Laurie (Love's grandmother). But she never heard of her dad's dad. Ron answers, "My mama shot and killed him." "Why?" Love' asks. Ron answers, "because my dad was a womanizer who use to beat on my mama. My mama and dad use to drink and argue. I was five years old when it happened but she shot and killed him dead. He fell down on the bed in our house. When the sheriff came he told mama to leave town and take us kids and to never look back. So we did and we ended up in Smithfield, North Carolina." Ron's mother ended up having a total of 13 children and Ron and his Mama had some heated arguments and disagreements. There was a time when he wanted affection from his Mama but she told him to get away and go on somewhere. That hurt him and left a wound. He, later on, had forgiven her but it hurt like hell. Love' didn't really remember spending much time with Ron's Mama. Love' knew Ron was still searching to fill the void of not getting what he didn't get growing up from his obviously hurting parents. I always felt strongly that we all have this innate nurturing ability in us if we are sensitive to it. Love' just wanted to fix her dad, she wanted to heal whatever hurt he felt and just take it away from him.

As time went on Ron began to feel so overwhelmed with raising a teenage daughter. Love' was home alone most nights. She would stay up late an get up early to catch the bus for school. She was not doing well in school. Love' was hurting and missing her Mom and her brothers, the family unit she was used to. So Ron spoke to Rayanna and told her that he thought that it would be better if Love' moved to Virginia with Rayanna and her brothers. He said, he just wanted to be single and that he felt that Love' needed her mom. Rayanna agreed to it and decided to talk to Love' about it. When Rayanna did speak with Love' on the phone about moving there, Love' told her no, that she was not moving. Rayanna also told her that she was getting married to her long-time friend, Mr. Williams. Love' was pissed. She did not feel her mom was ready for marriage again just yet. Rayanna then proceeded to say, "Your dad is the one who thinks that it's best. He is feeling overwhelmed." Love' was heart broken. She asked her dad about what Rayanna told her. Even though he said the same thing Rayanna told her, Love' still felt the pain all the same.

Time was winding down and she would be leaving shortly to relocate. She asked her dad if she could have a going away gathering. It was the most uncool going away party ever, but Love' appreciated the people who actually showed up. Even though Love' was slightly embarrassed by her dad trying to liven up the party. She appreciated it. There were about 15 to 20 people there in a mid-size two bedroom apartment. Out of that number, there were only about five to seven that were really close to Love' that she was going to really miss. Specifically a couple of best friends. One of those friends names is Unique who had been friends with Love' since they were in second and third grade and who have remained friends until this day. The other close friend was someone named Tionna who instantly became close to Love' in a very short period of time. Love' had a few other close girlfriends. Love' also had a few male friends and out of those few, there was one who she had a major crush on for a very long time. He was a very special guy in Love's life. Love' would keep in touch with a few of these people years later. When the party was over. Love' cried so much, some of her friends did too. One of her friends told their mutual friend, Tam, "I don't know what I'm going to do without her." The party was on a Friday night and Love' would be headed to Lynchburg the next night, riding in a van with her soon to be stepfather's brother and a woman who was a close friend of the family who Love' would later refer to her as an aunt. When Saturday night came, she felt so grievous. There was so much pain she felt. She became very bitter. It was the longest five hours of her life. Everyone was trying to cheer her up and Love' was looking at everyone like she could stab them with her eyes. In fact, Love' would have this same look in her eyes for the first few years she lived there. In February of 91' Rayanna and Craig were married. Love' started attending one of the two high schools located in the city in 1991-92 she remembered feeling like she was in a different time period. Not because everything was outdated but because of the educational system. Many of the Caucasians were in all of the college prep course classes and if you were a black student in those classes everyone would say, "Oh, he or she must be really smart." Love' felt as though she was trapped in the fifties or sixties. Love' would, however, meet some of the kindest people and the dearest of friends. She gradually began to stop hating the school, well; either that or just making herself content with everything. Love's stepfather was very popular and or well known within the community. Love' did not like that. Most people only knew her as Mr. Craig William's stepdaughter.

Mr. Williams cared a lot about his image and how he would be portrayed so that meant Love' and her brothers were not allowed to do most things. Love' was able to do a little more than of course what her brothers were able to do because of the slight age difference. Most of Love's friends were able to do a little more than she could so she would always stay the night at one of her friends' homes and mostly it was to get away from the insanity that was taking place at home. Williams was controlling, psychologically abusive, manipulative, and physically abusive to Love's brothers. Love' began to hate Williams and Williams didn't seem to care too much for Love' not being easily intimidated by him. Love' would question everything, especially if and when (which was often) it didn't make sense.

More often than not, Love' would spend time in her bedroom with her brothers. They began to really have hatred in their heart for their step-dad during this time. During Love's freshman and sophomore year she would often say she felt old in her soul and tired like she had been here before. She spent so much time alone at this time to listen to her thoughts and imagine how differently she would live her life once she became an adult. She would later realize she didn't have to wait to live the life she imagined. Love' was so sad in her heart. She was depressed most of the time. She and her brothers felt rejected not by one parent but both parents. Love' didn't understand how both of her parents could allow someone to come into their lives and try to sever the relationship that parents are supposed to have with their children. Love' felt that she and her brothers were put on the back burner. She knew that their parents loved them. She began to see that her parents were hurting children, themselves. There were many times that Rayanna would not agree with what she allowed Mr. Williams to do as far as discipline, punishment and just his overall ideas about raising children. Love' would be that voice because she knew that Mr. Williams was trying to take Rayanna's voice and mold her into what he wanted. Love' began to question men. She began to feel as though perhaps they could never be trusted. Her experience with her dad caused her to believe that men could never be in a relationship and control themselves sexually. Then her step-dad was just a very deceitful, manipulative, vindictive, controlling person. Love' wondered sometimes how he slept at night peacefully. There were times when everyone in their home thought, hmmm... ok, maybe he's not such a bad person and right after he would do something that said otherwise. Love's three in a half years in the new high school were supposed to be exciting and inspiring but they weren't all that great.

Ron Jr. attended the same school that Mr. Williams was teaching at. He was a chorus teacher. Eventually, Malik James would end up attending the same school. Their experiences were a lot different than Love's as far as school was concerned considering that Mr. Williams (Their step-dad) worked at the same school Ron Jr. and Malik attended. Love' was in high school. Some times it wasn't so bad. Guys were interested in her because she was the "new" girl. She was different. She dressed in bright colored sneakers. She spoke differently. It did not take long for the guys to realize Love' was not going to be giving it up at that age, anyway. She was determined to remain a virgin until married. Love' would tell the guys, "I don't have sex at all, so if you think you're getting some, I'm telling you now you need to move on." Love' began to eventually feel left out because everyone had a boyfriend and everyone was dating and some of her friends were sexually active or planning on becoming sexually active very soon. This still did not influence her. She was still determined.

One of the first people she met when she first started attending the high school was a girl named Naseeya. Naseeya was very chipper, personable and friendly. She walked up to Love' and said, "Hi, my name is Naseeya aren't you Mr. William's stepdaughter?" Love' responded, "Hi, I'm Love' and yes I am." Naseeya says, "Tell, Mr. Williams I asked about him, he'll know who I am." Love' said okay and from that point on those two were inseparable, well at least for a few years they were. They were more like sisters. Love' would end up spending most weekends over Naseeya's house. However, Mr. Williams wanted Love' home before or on Sunday morning to be home in time for church.

From ninth grade to a portion of tenth grade Love' and Naseeya would remain friends but Love' was becoming close to two other girls. Tina who just happened to be Naseeya's cousin and Nicole. As Love' became close friends with those Tina and Nicole, Love' and Naseeya began to go through a natural separation. They hadn't had a falling out. They were just experiencing things at a different pace on their journey.

By the time Love' had become a senior, things had become more tolerable at home for the moment. She was excited about graduating from high school and the funny part is that the whole entire first two years of high school she would say, "I can't wait to graduate so I can move back home." Now that the time had come Love' had no real plans to move back home or go to college or do anything. Love' had basically graduated by the skin of her teeth. She did not apply herself because of her anger and her guidance counselor worked hard to assure her that she was not college material and would not be successful academically. Love' believed her. Even though Love' was very unsure about her next step to take after graduating, she was very sure about how much she had grown to love little Lynchburg, well maybe not so much the city but definitely her friends as well as her experiences. One of those friends would turn out to be her first love who's name is Amir. He has a sister name Lovey the same as Love's. One day when Love' had just gotten out of one of her classes, his sister approached Love' and asked her if she knew her brother. Love' did not know her brother by name. His sister asked Love' if they could meet around the same time the next day so that she could point out her brother to her. Love' agreed to meet. The next day came and his sister pointed him out and Love' smiled so brilliantly and her eyes shined as bright as the moon. His sister asked Love' what she thought and Love' told his sister she thought he was cute so his sister gave Love' his number and Love' gave his sister her number. Love' really thought Amir was really a cutie, she loved how shy he was but she had to play it cool in front of his sister. That night they talked on the phone for hours and hours. They instantly connected. Amir was tall, he was six foot and three inches, basketball build, had light skin with hazel color eyes unless moody or aroused then they were an olive color. He was on the basketball team. He was number 00. He had a beautiful smile, round face, sandy blonde, brownish, red hair. It wasn't too long after they officially met that Love' and Amir were a couple. Love' was four foot and eight inches, shapely, with deep dimples, brown skin, almond shaped eyes with a short bob, pixie cut hairstyle. There was an obvious foot difference in height but the connection was obvious they shared. Her family loved Amir which said a lot to Love'. Whenever he would come over to pick Love' up, Rayanna would notice the way he looked at Love'. One day Rayanna was watching out of the window after Amir had picked Love' up and Rayanna said she knew then that Amir was in love with her daughter. She said she could see how proud he was that he was picking up his baby as he opened up the passenger car door for Love' and shut it for her. Love' and Amir were so in love that hey had planned out their future together. They were moving to Maryland and Amir would become an engineer while Love' would become a teacher in her own school and an author.

Amir and Love' began to become even more serious, so much so that sex became an issue. Amir was ready, he was sixteen. Love' was seventeen going on eighteen but she was not ready, and was afraid. She did not know if all of the things she had heard about boys and or men leaving you were true. Love' was mature about a lot of things but naive about many things as

115

well. Love' and Amir began having oral sex. She did not feel as though at the time she could talk to her mom and definitely not her stepdad, so she talked to Ron; her dad. Ron would constantly express how Love' and her brothers should always feel comfortable to tell him anything. Ron really voiced this specifically to Love' simply because she was the oldest. Even though he had not been there as the best father in the past he got that point across because Love' had no problem telling her dad what she and Amir had done. She called her dad and told him. He tried to keep calm but inside he was clueless on how to handle it. Ron listened and then hung up the phone. He told Love' that he would call her back in a little while. She assumed that he had to call someone to ask for advice on how to handle it or he really needed to process this information he had just learned.

While Love' had not been penetrated vaginally she had crossed a boundary that would forever change her life and their relationship.

There were times when Amir and Love' would be in the car holding hands as they would be driving to their destination. They had a song that was their song, 'Your My Baby' by D'angelo. Amir would play this song every time just about that they would get in the car. Initially, it was just Amir and Love' but then later it turned into Tina, one of Love's best friends, and Jay, Amir's close friend. The two couples would have a lot of fun together over the summer.

I remember how Tina and Love' would be in the mall every Saturday night knowing that they would run into Amir and Jay and then they would head on over to the dollar movie but this weekend was different because Amir had to go to his family reunion in Maryland and Love' was really missing him. Amir must have been missing her as well because he left early Friday morning and then on Saturday night as Tina and Love' were walking towards the food court in the mall, Love' says, with a sigh, "I really miss him." As soon as Love' said that, Tina looked towards the entrance of the mall and saw Amir walking towards them. Tina says to Love', Awwww, look Love', "It's Amir!" Love's mouth dropped in shock and then she could not stop the big ass smile she had on her face. Amir told her he couldn't wait until Monday before he saw her. He told her that he missed her and wanted to surprise her. He told his family that he was headed back to the "Burg". The two of them hung out that night and had a wonderful time.

Amir began really wanting to have sex with Love'. Love' felt as though she could not oblige. Love' felt bad because she loved him. She told Amir that if he really wanted to have sex that she would understand if he wanted to go sleep with someone else. She let Amir know that she would always love him. Amir thought about it and decided that he would in fact call it off. They both wept. The next day in school they saw each other in passing. Love' did not know how to react. She was sad, angry and hurt, but loved him. Amir had a pitiful expression on his face. They said Hello to each other and kept walking in opposite directions. Later that day Amir called Love' and told her, "I can't do this to you." He said he thought about it the whole day and said to himself, "I can't do this to this girl." Amir apologized and they were back together again, but not for long. About two months later Love' began sensing the same change she sensed prior and Love' started to become jealous, scared and territorial because Amir began pulling away. Love' ended it this time. She believed that there was a part of Amir that wanted Love' to end it for him. Love' told me she was in prayer and heard the Spirit tell her to let him go and that they would be reunited again, that it wasn't over but over for right now. Love' cried when she told Amir this. She explained how the voice of God instructed her to do this and how painful it was but that she knew one day that they would be reunited again. Amir thought she had lost her mind. He asked, "Why?" she said, "Because I know you really want to have sex and I know that Spirit is telling me this. And even though it's hurting me, I have to listen." Amir was hurt and angry as well as confused but that night it became official and the song by Brandy, 'Broken Hearted' became Love's depressing anthem.

After Amir and Love' had been broken up for quite some time, she had become very close with a guy named Neek. Neek and Love' were just friends. They talked on the phone every night faithfully, long hours; sometimes from 11:00 p.m. at night until 5 or 6 in the morning. It didn't matter how late the other one called. They were there for each other in a way that Love' hadn't experienced with anyone up until that point. He just genuinely cared for her without expecting anything in return. Love' cared for him. He was handsome, hilarious and listened to her every word. She listened to him. She didn't understand their relationship because she knew that they would never pursue anything because of their mutual friends.

If Love' was hanging out she couldn't wait to get back home to talk on the phone. He was her best male friend at the time and it was amazing. He was her distraction (for lack of a better term) during the time she and Amir were no longer an item. She always wondered what would have happened if they had pursued a relationship out of it. They loved each other without any strings attached, no expectations, just pure, genuine friendship. They never kissed, they never did anything physical, never. He told her he respected her. She would cherish the friendship for the rest of her life. Neek came into her life when she began to feel that all men wanted was something in exchange for their company or conversation even though she had not compromised her beliefs completely at that time she felt great knowing that there was someone other than herself who saw her value, honored and respected it without question and via action in the way he treated her.

A few years had passed and things were just as dysfunctional in Mr. Williams home as they had been. Sometimes people can become complacent in their dysfunction even when they know it is not a healthy environment. I would come to visit from Delaware quite frequently. Although no one told me how dysfunctional things were I could definitely sense it. Love' had attended the local community college for a semester right after graduation but realized that she was not ready for college. She was so unsure about a lot of things in her life. She knew she wanted to work so she did. She ended up working with one of her best friends from high school. Tina and Love' worked at a place called Tri-Tech. It was an assembly line job. Love' did not stay there long. The money was ok for someone who recently graduated other than that she was not going to get very far working there. She knew she had to find something else to do, but what?

When Love' was around the age of twenty Mr. Williams received a phone call from a very close friend that was a music teacher at one time but during this time recently became head of the music department for one specific school district in the Hampton Roads area. Mr. Williams was asked to become the chorus music teacher for a very popular high school in the area. Mr.

Williams did not want to take the position and at the time no one understood why. It would pay more. He would be doing what he loved in a predominately, historically African American school. Mr. Williams prayed and began seeking for the answer. He heard the answer that he had hoped he would not hear. Mr. Williams used to tell Love' and her brothers, "The very thing that you may not want to do is usually the very thing God would have you to do." So it became official and the family would be relocating to Portsmouth, Virginia. Love' did not want to go and no one could believe it. As much as she initially hated the "Burg", she did not want to leave it. She had developed close friendships with people and family members of Mr.Williams that Love' and her brothers had become close to. Lynchburg had become her home. So just like when Ron jr., Malik James, and Rayanna relocated to Lynchburg from Wilmington, Delaware without Love' initially, it happened again. Love' stayed while everyone else relocated. She stayed with Naseeya only for a month or so and then Love' was ready to start over again. She absolutely grew to love what was initially known as the 'Tidewater area' now referred to as 'Hampton Roads'. Love's love for the area did not take as long. She still did not know what her plans were. She started working at a local drug store. Love' and her family were living in a really nice area. The house had five bedrooms, a very spacious living room, dining area, eat-in kitchen, a master suite bedroom with jacuzzi and loft. This home also had a huge back yard. The community was a well-known African American community where most of the homeowners were doctors, lawyers, etc. Her brothers still had a few more years before graduating high school. I remember Love' feeling slightly envious of the fact that her brothers had the opportunity Love' wanted and that was to attend a predominately African-American school. She just felt it was completely different. The choir had a richer, fuller sound. When the school would sing their school alma mater, it sounded like a heavenly choir. The whole entire student body could sing. Listening and watching the high school band was like attending the Southern Classics where all of the HBCU bands would perform. The cheerleaders were awesome. The staff was like family and the students were a part of that family. Love' thought her brothers were so fortunate to be able to experience something so beautiful.

They had a beautiful home and four months later they would become evicted. Williams was a teacher. He had been teaching for over twenty years by this time. He was able to afford the rent. The homeowners wanted them to purchase the home but they would have to come up with twenty thousand dollars. Twenty thousand that they did not have. Rayanna became very angry with herself and towards Williams. When Rayanna's dad transitioned years prior he left thirty thousand for her and her children. Williams took the money and bought furniture that he was making payments on and a conversion van that eventually was repoed. No one knew where the rest of that money went. Love' was working as a pharmacy tech but that was not enough money to help with the rent which happened to be eighteen hundred dollars, and often times he was late paying the rent. Rayanna was frustrated because he was making more than enough to pay the rent and she was also frustrated because this habit had been going on since they first married. Initially when they moved in with Williams in Lynchburg the rent was five hundred dollars for a nice three bedroom home, with one full bath, family room, a living room, eat-in kitchen, dining area and finished basement. He would still be late paying the rent. As a matter of fact, to this day he still owes money for that house. For the entire time that she was married to him, she and her three children would always live in worry that something would be cut off, from the cable to the electric even the hot water. There were times that they didn't even have toilet paper to wipe their asses. There were also times when they did not know where, when or how their next meal was coming. What was interesting was that they never saw the child support. Williams would take it. It was a miracle that they were even able to move into the five bedroom home in spite of poor credit.

One evening after finding out that they would have to move if unable to pay the twenty thousand, Williams called for family prayer time. Rayanna, Love' and her brothers along with their aunt and two cousins, who had moved in with Williams and Rayanna while living in Lynchburg, Virginia. They lived with Williams and Rayanna in Hampton Roads as well for a short period of time. Aunt Miria and her two children are one of Rayanna's brother's ex wife and her two children. They all sat and listened to William's plea to God for a miracle. He told them that God had instructed them to march around the house seven times like God had instructed in the Bible regarding Jericho. Love' looked at him like he was crazy. He also told them to repeat these words: "Money cometh to me now." Love' and her brothers along with her cousins were laughing so hard inside as they watched through the window at night, Williams, Rayanna and Love's aunt march around the house until they all laughed aloud. They were mocking them. Love' said, "I am not participating in this. This is ridiculous. He doesn't have the money and if he did receive a miracle he would spend it anyway. All five of them (Love', her brothers and her two cousins) found the whole family prayer meeting ridiculous." Love', Ron and Malik had watched this sort of behavior for years now and rarely believed anything he said because of the many times he said, God said this or that and then when it didn't happen he would tell them they didn't have enough faith or they didn't pray enough or praise God enough. I can not imagine what this was doing to their psyche.

Two weeks later they had to move and did not know where they were going until one of Williams brother offered for the family to come live in his two bedroom town-home. Williams, Rayanna, Love', Ron and Malik were sleeping in the living room. This only lasted for about two weeks when they moved into a home across the street from a cemetery. Love's aunt and her two cousins had moved into an apartment.

While living in Portsmouth Love' and her family had moved at least three to four times in the first two years until they finally found a house that they would stay in for a year. The home was right across from Mr. Williams home church. Williams and Rayanna ended up becoming the ministers of music there. As time went on Love' had become serious about her relationship with God and was very in tune with her relationship so much so that she preached her initial sermon. Love' knew that a lot of people showed up not for support but to be a spectator. Their pastor at the time did not feel that Love' was ready just yet to become a minister and boy was he right. She got the people up and praising God but Love' needed to experience some things and learn some things, at least that is what some of the elders thought. A year and a half later Love' would become a licensed minister at her step-dad's, (that she was now referring to as Daddy) and Mom's church. The church was one of the best Churches that they had ever attended. The members were all under sixty initially. They all truly loved each other so much so that every Sunday the members would end up staying afterward just to fellowship. Eventually, the fellowship turned into dinners after church. The youth were so serious about God. They would have lock-ins where they would pray, fast and intercede on behalf of their pastors. I remember when Rayanna and Love' told me about one time in particular when Ron Jr. was asked to get on the drums and began to prophesy through the drum. I remember them telling me how his facial expression was, it looked as if someone or something had taken over him, like he was in a trance. The members were instructed by the spirit to dance. It sounded like they were in a country in Africa and that experience sparked a memory from years ago when Love' told me about a time where she remembered her mom in her bedroom praying, when she and her brothers were a lot younger. Rayanna began singing a chant that sounded like an African chant and all of a sudden her children became frightened because they heard other people harmonizing, and singing the chant with Rayanna and she and her children knew no one was in her bedroom but her. There were several other events like that, that really made the members love the church. The church was just so different up until the issues that Love' and her family had at home showed up in the church. Several events took place where Williams began to reveal his insecurities in a way that made others feel uncomfortable. He and Love' had one of several arguments and he kicked her out for the third time. Love' moved in with a friend named Cali and member of the church. Also during this time some of the members of the church had moved in a nephew his name was Big Boi. He was definitely "street" and Love' loved that about him during that time in her life. He was trying to get his life on track. Eventually, she and Big Boi ended up sleeping together in the member's home. This would later haunt Love'. It was only the second guy she had ever been with. She believed she was pregnant by him and she would later find out that she wasn't. This was humiliating, to say the least, especially being though that she was the pastor's daughter. You see a prophet/pastor had laid hands on her womb after she had slept with Big Boi and said that she was carrying. Love' took that in the literal sense. She was wrong. During this time after feeling rejected, humiliated all over again, Love' began partying, going to the club, drinking and smoking weed. She still had only been with two guys by the time she was 23, but she still felt ashamed even though her first was a close friend whom she had known for 8 years. She felt like he was safe and they would always be in contact with each other. Things did not always go as she planned. She had planned to remain a virgin until married. She and the young man eventually lost contact. It would be two years later that she would have sex again and that would be with Big boi. She felt rejected once again and hurt and yearned for a man to love her. Big Boi was the complete opposite of Phil, her first. Subconsciously Love' went for the one she knew her parents would not approve of. She also loved the idea of being a 'savior' to a man. Not much longer after Love' began to reflect and get serious with her relationship with God again. She loved her church and was slightly still embarrassed about what she had done by sleeping with Big Boi. Not just sleeping with him, but sleeping with him in the church member's home and going plum crazy for Big Boi afterward. Love' had to forgive herself for her disrespectful behavior to both herself as well as towards others.

Chapter 7

Rayanna had been praying and said she heard from the Holy Spirit that her children were to be in the ministry full time and that they were to be full-time intercessors. This was confirmation to not only Love' but Malik James as well. Ron Jr. was enjoying life. He was dating someone and ended up getting her pregnant. He was working and he joined the army reserves and was really not spending much time at home. When Williams found out that Love' and Malik James had heard they were to be in the ministry full time he said that he was not in agreement with that, and that they needed to either get a job or go to school. Love' looked at her Mom and said, "Tell him mom what you told us." She said, "I didn't say anything." Love' and Malik James were speechless and heart broken again. They once again felt rejected. They truly believed that they were doing what God or the Holy Spirit had instructed them to do by having, 'crazy faith' and yeah, it was crazy alright. They were only believing and living what they were taught to do. Which was at all cost even in persecution, even when faith doesn't make sense because after all faith is the substance of things hoped for and the evidence of things not seen according to the Bible in the book of Hebrews. I recall having a conversation with Love' and Rayanna about faith. Faith began to not make sense to Love'. She was trying to hold on to her faith as she and her younger brother had both been kicked out of the house but Love' was already living with a friend and member of the church but when October 24th came which was a day after Malik turned eighteen he was put out and all he had was his bike. Malik came over to Love's friend's place and told Love' that it was official, that he had nowhere to go so Love' was certainly not going to leave Malik out there by his self so she left her friend's place to be out there with Malik. Williams began spreading lies about Love' and Malik James. He told the members of the church that they were suicidal, homicidal and demon possessed, and a lot of other things. He was spreading these lies right before he kicked them out and while they were both homeless for a few months living on the streets they believed that they were doing it for righteousness sake, at all cost. Love' and her brother Malik had also been kicked out of the church because they would not be controlled by their daddy (step-dad) and they felt they were listening to the voice of the Holy Spirit. The police were even called on them at church so that Love' and Malik were no longer welcomed there. As Malik and Love' walked out of their parents church, Malik says, "All we're saying is to have a relationship with God for your self." While living on the streets they had been robbed at gun point by some drug addicts. Once Rayanna heard about this she discussed it with Williams and his plan was to invite Love' and Malik James into the warm house, prepare a meal and hope that they would change their minds. The plan seemed to work for a while. Love' and Malik James looked physically sick and were exhausted. Everything was not ok in the home but everyone tried to pretend as though nothing had ever happened.

Williams had an "adopted" son that was in and out of their lives because he was in and out of prison. Every time he would get out of prison Williams would offer his home to 'D'. Love' found their relationship strange and there was something so plastic about it. He was now living back at home now after getting out of prison. I remember when Love was fifteen she had the thought and or the question had come to her, "Was D ever molested by Williams? Was Williams ever molested?" Those questions and the feeling she had when those questions came to her she would always keep in the back of her mind. D may have been in their lives for a total of three to four years and not consecutively. He and one of William's brother were on and off drugs and at one point it was said that he with one of William's brother stole Rayanna's wedding band (she had from her previous marriage) for drug money on the day that Rayanna and Williams were getting married. Anyway, I remember the time Love' was having a discussion with her mom about church and Williams interrupted with anger in his heart. Love' merely made the point that the church would not succeed if the family within the home was not on one accord and operating from love. This statement must have struck a chord because Williams got up with fire in his eyes and told Love' to stop talking to his wife aka her mom, Love's response was, "She's my mom and I can communicate with her as I please." Williams did not like her statement and began 'bucking' and shoving Love' with his chest and then Rayanna began to scream for D. D came running down the steps and just in time because Williams had balled his fist up and pulled his arm back and was about to punch Love' in her face. D grabbed Love' and began weeping and hugging

Love' as she was in shock, stating, "You were about to punch me in my face." Her eyes were as bright as the moon. Love' was thankful that Ron Jr. and Malik James were not there or it would have gone in a completely different direction. D took Love' outside and they talked until Williams went to bed and they came back in the house. Her brothers Ron and Malik were told what happened and were very angry and hurt for many reasons mainly because of their Mom, Rayanna did nothing to stand up for them most of the time while married to Williams.

As time went on Love' had another argument with Williams. At this time he and the family had moved to Suffolk, Virginia. Ron Jr. was married with a little girl and a newborn baby girl. Ron Jr. and his wife were definitely going through their trials. Ron Jr. married a female version of Williams. She was controlling, manipulative but deep down Love' knew there was a good heart in there somewhere underneath whatever pain that she had endured. Malik James was living at home along with Love'. Love' was about 24 at this time with no direction, no healthy self-image nor self-worth.

It was Bible study night at the church and Love' had started re-twisting her locs and she needed to sit under the dryer so that her hair could dry. Williams came to knock on her bedroom door and told her to be ready for church in thirty minutes. Love' told Williams that she was not going to church. He told her that she was. They argued back and forth until Williams told her to get out. Love' laughed and told him, "No!" He called the police on her and the police officer told him that he could not put her out without a thirty-day notice if she had been contributing to the household or receiving mail there. So Williams was angry and he told Love, "You need to make sure you have somewhere to go before the thirty days is up, so be making plans now." The same day and a few hours later her cousin called her. The same cousin who at one time, along with his sister and mom, lived with them told her that his mom, Love's aunt, had told him that Love' needed a place to stay. So Love' would be moving in within a few weeks, she would be relocating to Portsmouth, Virginia. This move would change her life.

Love' began to start smoking weed, black and milds, and drinking again. She did not drink or smoke weed everyday but she was doing it more often then she had in the past. She had smoked and drank before but she stopped when she began getting serious about God. Love' began to question a lot of things; mainly her faith. Love' remembered one of the many conversations she would have with me' and one was when I told her that the Bible says that faith is the substance of things hoped for and the evidence of things not seen. " Our ancestors before slavery lived with sight, foresight, insight, etc. They could see beyond, they saw with their mind's eye. They carried very strong, loving and powerful energy. Of course, there weren't as many distractions back then, but none the less I have not seen a reason to believe in anything that your religion promotes other than love and I don't need anything outside of me to validate me. I don't need to participate in a cannibalistic ritual on certain Sundays to honor my higher self or a supreme force." As far as I am concerned, faith is ok but it should not be habilitating. In my experience with those who professed to have a religion seem to have limits on the divine power that resides within and those who could see knew that everything just was and or is. Love' listened to every word I spoke to her but it was not the time for her to really grasp it just yet. I felt like I would just water it over time.

Love' was so frustrated and began doubting herself with all of her heart because she could not find work. Her car broke down, on her but she would manage to get to the club every weekend with her friends. Her cousin/roomie had the weed all of the time. She was trying to have a great time even though deep down she was miserable. She had many talents, gifts and or abilities but did not know how to utilize them in a way that would create opportunities or support her financially. Abilities or talents within a child typically have to be cultivated and nurtured or it can possibly slow the process and or realization within child of their greatness. The fact was that Love' and her brothers grew up in a very toxic environment.

Love' thought she would give the church thing another try and so she visited Williams and Rayanna's church and it was so dead. The fact that they were pretending that it still flowed with the same flow of 'anointing' was ridiculous. Love' may have been in what some referred to as a "backslidden" state but she knew the feeling, the presence or energy of love, Holy Spirit, and or anointing that had once flowed there effortlessly. That would be the last time Love' would step foot in that church. The church had become so plastic just like how they grew up, how Rayanna and William's marriage was. Everything was about image and covering up the truth. Love' was hurting and could see the pain on everyone else within the family as well as the members of the church. She was not willing to pretend that everything was okay when she knew that everything was not okay in her personal life as well as within the church.

Love' had really gone through a dry spell of not being able to find work. During this time she and Amir had been in contact off and on for the past few years and he would come to visit. He would help out as best as he could. There were a few visits where he would come in town just to spend the day with her. He'd buy her groceries, he would take her out and he would take her to one of his favorite spots, which was a record vinyl store. They finally engaged in sexual intercourse after only about 7 years of knowing each other. During this time she and Amir were both going through things internally. They had a very interesting connection that would seem to last for many years to come. After all those years of not having sex with Amir it was finally happening. The thing was is that Love' was not really present to really experience it. She loved him but there was a part of her that was hurting so much and that part of her was becoming numb. They lost contact for years, yet again.

Some time had passed and love' finally found work as a waitress in a hotel restaurant. The hotel was close enough to where she could walk. She did not stay there long but it was a job bringing something in. She knew she had to make plans to do something with her life but she still just did not know what; well, she knew but she just did not have enough confidence at the time to realize that she was more than capable of doing all that was in her to do and some. This would eventually be realized within Love'.

It was 2002 one of Love's friends was graduating from the same community college that Love' had years ago dropped out of, her friend Naseeya. Love' and Naseeya throughout the years had definitely kept in touch but they definitely did have a few off periods where nothing would necessarily happen but just little to no communication. During this time they were definitely hanging tight and Love' was excited for Naseeya and they were going to celebrate. Naseeya would be traveling three in a half hours from Lynchburg to Portsmouth, Virginia so that they could attend one of the popular clubs at that time which was known as Piccaso's. Love' and her friends loved that place. It was a Friday night when Naseeya and Love' went out to celebrate. Love' never seemed to have any money during this time but she had just done someone's hair and so she had made a little extra cash just in time to celebrate.

When Naseeya and Love' arrived they went to the bar and got a drink. After sipping on their drinks they went on to the dance floor. Naseeya did not like men dancing all up on her. Love' at the time did not care she just loved to dance. A young man approached Naseeya. Love' could not hear what was being said but she definitely noticed that they were interacting. After they finished conversing the young man and Naseeya approached Love'. Love' initially believed that he was interested in Naseeya. Love' thought she heard what sounded like, Naseeya saying, "I'm not from here, this is my girl" So she pulls him up to Love' and he says "Hey, what's your name? Do you think I could call you sometime?" Love' responded, "My name is "L" and gave him her phone number. Sometimes it's hard to tell in a club what someone looks like and what type of energy they have because there is just so much going on in a night club atmosphere but Love' really thought he may have been very handsome. Later on that night after Love' and Naseeya left the club Love' began talking about how attractive the guy was. Naseeya began to tell Love' how he had asked about her but she thought she would let Love' have him but instead of Love' being upset with Naseeya's response she told Naseeya, "thank you" with a smirk.

Love' knew that everything happens for a reason. They went back to Love's and her cousin's place and crashed.

The next day which was Saturday, Naseeya was headed to one of her girlfriend's place in Norfolk, Virginia to spend some time with her and then headed back to Lynchburg. Love' spent the day and night by herself. Her cousin was rarely home. Love' spent the night, writing and thinking and smoking a black and mild while on the phone. Every once in a while she would watch T.V. but not too often. So if she wasn't thinking or writing she would be on the phone. For the most part, most of the people she hung out with were not in the house on a Saturday night, well; everyone except for one of her closest friends, Cali. Love' spent a lot of time talking on the phone to Cali but for some reason, they did not talk on the phone that Saturday night. Cali was and still is married. So it is very possible that Cali was enjoying a night out with her hubby or a night-in. Love' spent the night talking to her cousin, Tae. Love' told her about one of the guys she met that night. Love' remembered he was wearing a fitted hat representing Philly. Tae told her, "Girl sometimes you can think they look good in that club but when you meet them, you see how tore up you were in the club and how many drinks you had that f'd with your vision and the guy comes over looking like a lit cigarette." Love' chuckled and told her, she had only had two drinks that night but deep down she was a little nervous. Then she thought, "Why am I nervous when he hasn't even called yet? I mean he may not ever call." Love' stopped giving it much thought and on Sunday he called.

Phone rings...

Love: Hello

Young man: "Hello, Hey what's up. This is Mozique. Do you remember me? I was wearing a Philly's fitted?"

Love': Yes I remember you. Hey!

Love' and Mozique conversed for a little while and he asked her if she'd mind him stopping by. Love' agreed to it. From that day he would forever touch her heart in a way that no one had with the exception of one high school 'sweetheart' and even still there was something different with the connection she felt with Mozique.

A couple of hours later Love' heard a knock at the door and nervously headed towards the door because usually Love' did not meet people in the night clubs and especially being tipsy. Anyway, Love' asked who it was knocking on the door and the voice replied, "Mozique." Love' opened up the door and was no longer nervous. He was extremely handsome, having what some refer to as that it factor for lack of a better term. He had on a matching fitted baseball cap with his gear. He sat down as Love' did and they just conversed and chilled and Love' truly enjoyed his company. They laughed, of course. The visit was a very innocent visit. During the visit Love' found out that they were both from the same hometown. They jokingly said you rarely meet anyone from Delaware outside of Delaware, maybe in Philly, or the tri-state area but other than that it is very rare.

Love' instantly was fond of him. He ended up leaving at a decent hour. Love' remembers that she did not want him to leave and she thought how odd that was. As soon as he left Love' wanted to tell someone, so she did. She called Cali and told her how she enjoyed his company and how handsome he was and last but not least that they were from the same state. Cali was that friend who always asked questions; the kind of questions that made you think. So thanks to the many questions that Cali was asking Love', she began to remember that she still did not know much of anything about him and not to mention that Love' seemed to be the second choice based on what Naseeya said. Love' simply did not know enough about him. Mozique would call more than Love' did because, well; she didn't call due to fear. They talked on the phone that week. Love' and Mozique shared some parts of their personal journeys. She remembered each time they talked on the phone she was hoping that it would be the day that he would ask, do you mind if I come over to hang out even though it had only been a week.

Well, after a few weeks he came over during the middle of the week on a Wednesday. The both of them had been conversing over the phone for the past few weeks. This would be the night that Love' realized he saw her value before she did. He left an imprint on her heart. They hung out for a little while and had a real chill time. They would talk on the phone in between his visits. He came back over two weeks later after his last visit on a Saturday night after he had gotten out of the club. He called of course and asked if it was okay to crash at Love's spot. Love' told him it was fine. It was close to two in the morning and he had been drinking. Deep down Love' began to feel sad because she initially thought he was different. She began to think he was coming over for one thing and one thing only but because Love' did not know her worth or have a healthy self-image she was already making the decision to go against how she was really feeling and share herself with him. Love' heard a knock at the door. She was nervous and excited. She asked who it was and when she heard Mozique, she opened up the door. He came in and they went into her bedroom. They laid on the bed and Love' said sharply and yet nonchalantly "Well, (pause and sigh) come on." She was just assuming that that was what he wanted. They gave each other a peck and Mozique laid on top of her. He put a condom on and all of sudden Mozique became soft. Love' immediately became embarrassed. She thought he was not attracted to her. He said, "L, lets just lay here and go to sleep." Inside, Love' was so thankful because she really did not want to do anything with him. They quickly fell asleep that night. He had his arm around her. It was one of the most peaceful sleeps Love' had ever had on her blow up mattress. She still had not gotten a bed yet and Mozique never judged her for where she lived and what she didn't have. Love' was so broken during this time. She had been through so much and had not been taught how to deal with the feelings of rejection or any of her emotions. She was just so tired of going through the whole routine of getting to know someone and getting hurt.

When they got up in the morning, Mozique told her that he would be coming back over either that night or the next day. Love' said "ok" even though she was very puzzled regarding last night. Love' had gotten up to go jogging. She came back in to go grab some money so she could go to the corner store for a black and mild. As Love' sat there smoking her cigar. She realized she was feeling those feelings of rejection. Monday came and that evening Mozique would keep his word and came over. When he came over, the two of them sat in their usual seats. The seats that they would sit in in the living room were really a love sofa but you could pull the couch apart so one of the sections was across from the other. Mozique and Love' were laughing and Mozique was cracking jokes on Love' by calling her a hippy because of how eclectic she was and still is. All of sudden, Mozique gets up from the part of the couch he is sitting in and lays on his back on the floor. Love' just kept on talking until he reached his hand out for her and she held his hand for her to lay on top of him. While Love' was puzzled that he would want Love' to lay on top of him in the living room, Love' hid her perplexed thought and laid on top of him. He touched her face, held her chin and kissed her. They kissed for what seemed like twenty minutes or more, without the wandering of hands. Without anything except for a kiss. Love' had never experienced anything like it and to this day she hasn't. It was as if they were exploring. The kiss and the movements were not messy, aggressive, fast or rushed. It was sensual, passionate, soothing, explosive and within each movement during this kiss each moment was electric. There was something so eternal about it. It was pure bliss and more than anything an innocence that touched Love's heart. She could have kissed the rest of the night and not done anything else. She doesn't even remember how, who or why they stopped kissing. She said she thinks it was just that they both stopped after minutes and minutes, simultaneously. After they finished they got back up and sat in their seats and continued to converse. They never spoke about the kiss.

Mozique left two or three hours after that. He called when he got back to Va beach where he was living. He began to share with Love' the reason he moved to Va Beach to stay with some family was because he was leaving for boot camp to join the Navy. Love' and Mozique met in May and he would be leaving sometime in July. Needless to say Love' was crushed and or disappointed. He was going to Louisiana for three months. He told her that he would keep the same number and that he would not be able to talk on his phone for a while. He told her that his phone would be off during this time. They continued chatting. Love' told him that he needed to make sure she saw him before he left, he said, "Of course." That night when Love' got off the phone with him she wrote him a letter that she never gave him. She needed to express how she felt because it was just so unusual how she instantly trusted him. She felt crazy for feeling how she felt. Mozique really touched her heart, Love' was really a bit emotional because of everything she had gone through up to this point. She was ready for a change. She knew that there was something very special about him, something so powerful that manifested in the kiss.

The following week they did not see each other. She felt that they were both pulling away but more so him. A few more weeks had passed and they were still chatting on the phone but not any visits until closer to July and she remembers because both of their birthdays were close to the other. His is June 30th and hers, July 8. His is actually the same as Love's baby sister Bionca. They were both Cancers. He came over in July and they hung out. All they did was talk and laugh. When he was about to leave, she asked him if he could drop her off at her cousin Tae's place. He agreed. When they arrived at Tae's place, Tae was standing outside and so Love' rolled the window down and introduced the two of them. Afterward, Love' rolled the window back up and told Mozique thank you. He said, "No problem and you're welcome." And then right before Love' opened the door, he said, "I can't be in a relationship with anyone." Love, said, "OOOOkay." They both said goodbye, Love' went inside and Mozique pulled off.

The next time Love' would see him would be right before he left for boot camp. He did not stay long. She just wanted to see him before he left. They chatted a bit. He left and he called when he got in the house. It was a sad moment for Love' for many reasons. Some of those reasons she was very aware of but some she would eventually become aware of. They hung up the phone and he was off to boot camp but soon Love' would have the opportunity to move to Atlanta, Georgia.

Chapter 8

A month later Love' had relocated to Atlanta. Many people viewed Love's decision to relocate as a way of her running away from the pain and fear that she carried within her. The pain she felt from the rejection she experienced most of her life. So because she carried that fear and pain of rejection she was constantly inviting in the same experiences externally. The fact is that rejection is always a growing opportunity for one to realize their internal strength, their connection to their internal source, for one to realize who one is through self awareness and for healing to be realized through self love and acceptance. Love' just had not realized that just yet. Atlanta would be one of her teachers.

Love' moved to Lithonia, Georgia in September of 2002. She moved in with her aunt and cousin for a little while. This would be one of many of her life changing experiences that would really reveal who she was as well as how she saw herself. Was she living her life based on what was within her or based on what everyone else said. She would soon learn how at this time a part of her was laying dormant.

About a month and half later she was working in a popular store that would soon be relocating and remodeling to turn into a super store. She did not like the job not because of the actual duties or responsibilities but because of the people who worked there. Love' was so different in regards to the way she dressed. She was an introvert for the most part during this time. In time she later connected with some great people. She just didn't force a connection with people. If she didn't trust you she would definitely be very reserved. A few of the managers did not like her. Love' was and still is short. At the time she was a size five-seven. She was very curvaceous, with a flat stomach. She had locs and had been growing them at that time for about four years. Her eyes are almond shape. She has dimples and a beautiful smile. She can be a very kind-hearted person but she could also be a very bold person and by the time she and this particular store parted ways she had become a little tough and even more angry. This superstore was so "street" and unprofessional so much so that many of the managers were stealing. It was about survival even in this store, Ha! There was so much drama. People including managers would lie on others to get employees fired or arrested. She had already picked up the habit of smoking black and milds, weed, cigs etc... Smoking is one of the most expensive and poisonous habits to have. There were times where she didn't even care if she ate as long as she had her vice of choice she was ok. Not too much longer after she moved to Atlanta, her friend Naseeya moved out to Atlanta. She had planned to do so a while ago. So Love' thought it was great to have a friend from home.

While Love' was living with her aunt which is her dad's (Ron's) sister she began to feel as though they were getting tired of her being there. She had been there for three months and she wasn't making enough money to really be able to afford to move into her own apartment. She did not have a car and the public transportation was horrible. She asked Ron if he could help her get a car. He told her 'no' flat out. Love' became very angry. Her dad saying No took her back to the time when he told her 'no' that he would not help her with attending college after her high school graduation and by this time Ron had remarried. He married Katelin aka Kay. One of the many women he had an affair with while married to Rayanna. After Ron told Love' that he would not help her purchase a car Love' told Ron, "That's not right. If Kay wanted you to buy a car for Bionca, you would." Ron began yelling on the phone, crying and hung up on Love'. Love' was too angry to cry. She did curse him out when talking to her aunt and in her mind. She was hurt. A few days later her dad called and asked if she had cursed while having a conversation with her aunt? Love' lied. She told him that she did say hell but she never admitted to the f-word. She was upset but she got over it all rather quickly because he agreed to help her get a car. A few weeks after she got her car; her aunt told her she needed to find somewhere else to stay because her aunt and cousin were looking for something else and would soon be moving. Love's cousin had been laid off from his good paying job and her aunt was the only one working a real job at the time. Within in that month, a whole lot happened.

Love' was reminded periodically by her close friend Cali to call Mozique. Love' figured she would try again because she had tried to call a month prior but the phone went straight to voicemail. Love' did not want to leave a message. So she tried again and this time he answered. Love' was so excited on the inside when she heard his voice.

Mozique: Hello?

Love': Hello, It's L-

Mozique: Yoooo what's up? (with excitement in his voice)

Love': Nothing much, I am not going to lie I would call from time to time just to see if you would answer.

Mozique: Oh, yeah? I just cut my phone back on not too long ago.

Love': Oh, ok. So how is it or was it? Are you still there?

Mozique: It's alright. I am still here in Louisiana.

His friends are in the background yelling, "Yooo who are you talking to, some bitch?"

Mozique: NO, NAH MAN!!!! she is not like that man, No! she ain't no bitch, don't call her that either!!!!

Love' : smiling.

Mozique: So you don't have the same number?

Love': Oh! No, I have moved to Atlanta. I am in Lithonia, Georgia.

Mozique: Oh how long have you been there?

Love': Two months or so.

Mozique: What made you move there?

Love': Needed to get away and start over. Staying with my aunt and cousin but not for too much longer.

Mozique began singing 'Why Don't We Fall In Love', by Amerie in the background.

Mozique: Listen to those words, are you listening?

Love': Yea, I don't care for her voice but I like her songs.

Love' was thinking to herself "Wait, is he? Naaaa."

Love': So where are you going to be stationed?

Mozique: California

Love': You are going to fall in love with some Amerie look alike.

Mozique: Why do you say that?

Love': Because you are.

Love': (Boldy) I know if we had stayed in VA, I would have fallen in love with you.

Mozique: What makes you say that?

Love': (Watching the movie Brown Sugar) Because I just know I would have. Every time I see Brown Sugar it reminds me of us.

Mozique: (Silence) What makes you say that?

Mozique began singing Amerie's song again.

Mozique: Is this your number you called from?

Love': Oh, yes it is.

Mozique: Ok. Well, I have to go now but I'm going to call you back.

Love': Ok.

And he did just that before he headed out to Cali. Love' and Mozique didn't talk long because Love' had company this time. Love' had met someone who had come through her line while she was working the cash register about a month prior to calling Mozique. His name was J. He was about five foot, ten inches. He was dark skin with cat-like piercing eyes, a mustache, well; a full beard and locs that he had been growing for a little under a year. He asked Love' what her name was and asked her where she was from, then asked if he could have her number. She told him that she was from Delaware by way of Virginia. For some reason, most people thought she was from further north. She told him her name which at this time she was going by L. She gave him her phone number. He called that night and for six months they were in a committed relationship or so she thought. Anyway even though Love' was extremely happy to hear from Mozique, Love' was drawn to J and all of his dysfunction. The relationship was very intense and peculiar. It became very abusive. She realized later on that she was truly broken and was going nowhere fast.

Love' and J had very few good moments and so when they did, she tried to hold onto them so tight. In the beginning of their relationship was when she began seeing the signs of a controlling person and during this realization, Mozique called her when he moved to California. He called just to make sure she would have his new number. He said, "write this number down." She said, "I will write it down later but I do have it, it is on the caller ID" They conversed for a few but Love' was so distracted by dysfunction and relied on the caller ID that she never wrote the number down. Two weeks later she remembered that she never wrote the number down and she had already moved out of her aunt and cousin's place and was staying at a co-worker/friends one bedroom apartment that offered for Love' to stay until she found something else.

Love' called her aunt to ask if by some chance the same number was still on there but it wasn't. Love' was so upset with herself but I think her friend Cali was more upset than she was. Cali could not believe that Love' did not write his number down as much as she would talk about Mozique and the connection that Love' thought was mutual. Love' would tell Cali, "I mean even if nothing were to ever come out of that connection but a friendship I would be just as thankful for that. You don't connect with people instantly like that everyday. Well, at least I haven't."

Love' continued trying to figure out a way to find his number. She was still in the relationship with J but she really wanted to communicate with Mozique. She wanted to feel that connection again from someone who didn't want anything from her, who didn't mind her "weirdness", who seemed to enjoy talking to her as well.

Love' continued to entertain the toxic relationship but deep down she already knew it would not last. Love's friend, Naseeya wanted to meet J, Love's current guy so Love' decided to bring him over to meet her. Naseeya cooked a birthday dinner for Love'. She asked Love' to taste it. She tasted it and found it to be delicious, but Naseeya offered it to J by feeding it to him. One of the other times Love' brought J over Naseeya answered the door in a towel, now mind you; Love' told J to stay in the car but where Love' parked, J could see her and she could see him and Naseeya made it obvious that she wanted J to see her in her towel, she was not discreet, Love' thought to herself most people would hide behind the door if they just had to answer a door in a towel especially with being aware that someone else's man was going to be present. Love' felt uncomfortable both times but she developed a horrible habit of suppressing how she really felt and calling it forgiveness. You see in order to forgive you have to be real. It would be about four years later when she would finally bring it up to Naseeya, and the only reason she did was because she was about to introduce her to her new man and began to feel uncomfortable. However, this didn't happen for four to five years later.

The thing about toxic relationships is that usually in the beginning things start out exactly the way you think you want them to and both parties involved have mastered the art of masking the pain with being "kind". One is usually the passive one, the other is usually aggressive; having the same deep rooted issues which are ultimately fear and uncertainty. The relationship may start out exactly how you think you want it but the new relationship becomes old quickly. The fact is fear and uncertainty are fertile ground for illusions, delusional thinking, or flat out denial. Oftentimes, many see the signs but bow down to fear. The fear would explain one of the many incidents that took place between J and Love'. I remember when Love' wanted to cook a meal for J but he lived with his Mom. His parents were divorced. He had two older sisters as well that of course did not live at home. J's mom considered him as her roommate. Love' noticed that his mom did not like her' the first time she was introduced to her and Love' picked up on it immediately because Love's eyes were as bright as the moon. It was as if his mom secretly envied Love' like a jealous girlfriend. She saw a look in his mom's eyes that just wasn't normal. Love' bought the ingredients needed to cook Chicken, baked mac and cheese and greens. The thing is, Love' had no idea how to prepare mac and cheese. Love' was in her twenties. You see, she vowed at an early age to not learn how to cook intentionally so that she'd never have to serve or cook for her man or husband. She saw how her Mom, Rayanna served Williams and Love' began to hate the role of a submitted woman from a biblical standpoint. Of course, her mom and her daddy (Williams) knew that vow would eventually go out the window.

Love' had to call her mom to ask how to prepare mac and cheese. During Love's and Rayanna's conversation, J began yelling and cursing at Love'. Rayanna was trying to come through the phone. She could not believe what she was hearing and the fact that Love' was tolerating it. Her mom began to pray for her. What her mom had been feeling all along about J was confirmed. Rayanna never had a peace about him. Love' defended him just as she had watched her Mom do in regards to the type of behavior Williams displayed. Williams had never become physical with Rayanna to Love's knowledge and yet somehow Love' attracted this type of behavior from J. She later realized that abuse was abuse, some hit and some hit with their words. J did both. He became physically abusive one time after they had sex. Love' did not want to perform a particular sexual act. He wanted her to watch pornography while having sex and this made her feel uncomfortable, initially. After they finished he became angry again because she was ready to leave and did not want to stay the night. He began fighting her. He would not get off of her. He had his arm pinning her down and pressing down between her chest and neck. Love' was fighting back and cursing him out. There were a few more volatile experiences that really revealed to her not only what she thought about herself but how there were things that she had been programmed directly and indirectly to believe about herself that simply weren't true.

Love' was completely drained after the first three months of their relationship and not to mention she had moved out of her Aunt's place unexpectedly. Even though Love's friend, Krystal was being hospitable Love' knew she needed her own space. Love' had also gained a really special friend, a young lady named Tasha. There weren't too many people who liked Tasha at work, but Love' and Tasha clicked instantly. She was a very sweet and compassionate person towards Love' they became very close friends but she was not in a position to offer assistance at that time.

Love' stayed with Krystal for a couple of weeks until a supervisor asked her if she was still looking for a place. Love' told her yes. Anne, her supervisor, told her that she was looking for a roommate. Love' asked her how much was she charging and when Anne told her, Love' knew that she would not be able to afford it but she knew it was better than sleeping in a one bedroom apartment and imposing on her friend and co-worker. Love' agreed to pay 500 a paycheck, which is nothing; but it was for someone who only brought home no more than 550 and sometimes less than that a pay period.

The first few months of her new living situation was great! She and Anne got along really well. Anne immediately did not like J and Anne had no problem making it obvious as to how she felt. She had a very heavy accent. She was from Jamaica. She was struggling to pay her bills. She lived in Decatur in a gated community. A very nice one. Love' was still involved with J when she moved in her roommate's place but the relationship she was having with J was on its way to ending.

One night Love' had invited J over to stay the night. Her roommate had gone out of town for a week to Florida. Later that night when he asked her "Have you ever noticed how you can't sleep whenever we sleep in the same bed together?" Love' was shocked that he had noticed that. She said, "Yes, I wonder why that is?" He said, "It means our spirits do not agree." J was very knowledgeable and introduced Love' to new ideas about religion. Later on that night she and J decided to sit out on the balcony as they were sitting Love' began to pray while resting her head in J's lap and a man appeared fully naked. Love' became frightened. J appeared calm. J told her that everything was ok and to ignore him. Love' found it difficult to ignore him considering he was talking in some strange foreign coded language and standing there butt naked. His penis was in plain sight. She thought, "how perverse!" When the strange man walked away Love' told J she was going back inside.

J and Love' both decided to hop in the shower and then put their night clothes on, he began fondling Love' and she thought it was odd. He did not want her to take any of her clothes off. She knew something was off with him but she was not sure what. They never actually had sex that evening. This really raised all kinds of flags for Love'. He told her he had to go home. So he asked if Love' could take him back home.

Love' grabbed her keys and her purse. When they got in the car, they were both silent. Love' could tell that J did not want her to ask any questions but being a young woman she just had to; before he could get out of the car. "Is everything Ok? Are you mad at me?" and the infamous question, "Are you cheating on me?" Of course, his responses to all of the questions were very simplistic and to the point, one-word answers. Love' knew something was off and she knew she could always ask for it to be revealed. That night she went home and cried while asking for it to be revealed and had a very detailed dream. In the dream, Love' and J were in his bedroom while his mom prepared herself for a date night with her new beau. In reality, she had just started dating a man after J and Love' became serious. In the dream, J was becoming very jealous and worried. He was telling his mom what to wear and what not to wear. She ended up wearing a black and white blouse and black and white bottoms with this very broad, silver almost literally chain like costume necklace piece. A very odd piece of jewelry around her neck. She left to go out on her date. Everyone in the dream had on black and white. The entire time that J's mom was out on her date J was very anxious. He kept complaining about how long she was taking. Love' remembers distinctly J watching his watch to check the time. He and Love' heard someone at the door so she and J together went down the stairs. J walked ahead of Love' as Love' was walking she turned around to see a black and white cat and a black and white dog engaging in a sexual act. She told J, "Look at what the cat and dog are doing!" His response was as if it were a normal occurrence. Needless to say Love' found that strange. Love' woke up from her dream after she witnessed that act and immediately began to cry. She knew exactly what it meant and she would soon be addressing the matter with J.

Later on that day the revelation of the dream just kept becoming more and more obvious that J and his mom were involved in an inappropriate relationship. Love' remembered seeing a picture of his mom's dad and how scary and soulless he looked and it's exactly how his mom looked and how either J was beginning to look or had already looked but Love' was in a place now to see it. You see the fact that in the dream everything was black and white meant that everything was right there in black and white, right in front of you. Then the obvious the cat and the dog having intercourse which typically does not happen; many would consider this as perverse and or unnatural. Love' began to research animal totems and dream meanings when animals appear in dreams a few of the many things a cat may represent in a dream is trusting your intuition due to the fact that cats see very well at night or in darkness. Everything became so clear. Love' saw how jealous they both were, J and his mom; due to the fact that they were seeing other people. Love' didn't know how she would bring it up to ask him what had been revealed to her via her dream but she was certain that she would.

During this time she and J were really not communicating as much. He kept telling her that everything was ok but yet and still he would continually be rude to her, condescending and very short with her. It was as if he wanted to start an argument with her.

Later on in the day Love' decided to call him and she asked if she could come and pick him up so that they could talk. He asked her, "About what?" She told him, "About a dream I had. It was revealing and I just wanted to let you know that you can tell me anything but I do not want to discuss it over the phone." J agreed and so Love' went to go pick him up and they arrived at Love's place. J did not even sit down. He stood up, prancing back and forth. Love' asked, "Do you mind sitting down?" He told her, "I am good. Now, what is it that you wanted to tell me?" Love' was so nervous she didn't know what he may say or do. She stumbled over her words initially and prolonged it for as long as she could and then finally she just came right out and asked him, "Has your mom ever molested you? And are you two in some sort of sexual relationship?" He began cursing Love' out and took off running out the door. J lived a pretty good distance away from where Love' lived. It would probably take about and hour and a half to two hours walking. Walking is what J was planning to do. Love' grabbed her purse and keys and ran behind him. He was trying to jump the gate because again, Love' lived in a gated community. He could not figure out how to get out other than jump over the gate. People were yelling at him and Love' was calling for him as well. The people began to ask Love' if she was ok and she explained to them that she was. One person said that they were just about to call the police on him. Love' got in her car and pulled over to offer him a ride. He said, "ok." He would not say a word. When they pulled up to his place he took Love's keys because he was angry. He was being the most irrational and all of this type of behavior displayed was revealing to Love' all the more that something was off. When Love' finally got her keys back it would be the last time they would ever see each other. She attempted to contact him one last time. She called him and he answered. He was very short in his response. She told him that she did not mean to offend him but she knows without a shadow of a doubt what was revealed through her dream was accurate. He asked Love' to tell him about the dream. She did. He asked her to share the interpretation of the dream and she did.

J: So what do you think the dream meant?

Love': The dream revealed to me that you and your mother are having an inappropriate relationship. It started when you were young.

J: How did you come up with that from that dream?

Love': The cat and dog do not have sex or mate. Your response in the dream was as if it were normal for that type of behavior. You were extremely jealous of the man that your mother was seeing in the dream just as much as you were in our waking lives when your mother started dating a man right after I came into the picture. Your mother hated me when she first met me. As though I threatened her. Your mother is enslaved to her father, the one who molested her and now you are enslaved to her. The fact that everything and everyone was in black and white, was symbolic as well. It has literally been right in front of me in black and white.

The whole entire time Love' was talking, he was listening. He was listening without saying a word. A man or a boy who feels his mother is being disrespected is not going to entertain that conversation and especially someone who was as volatile as he had been. Sometimes you hear clearly when the response is silence. He never came out and admitted to it. They got off the phone that day without arguing. It was one of the only conversations they had that was actually gentle.

Love' wept for him as well as her. Not too much longer after that, she would be moving back to Virginia. Love' had been in Atlanta struggling for a year. She was tired and ready for the next part of her journey She was moving back to Virginia.

Her brother Malik James rode the bus from Virginia to Atlanta so that he could ride back with her. He spent the night. He helped her load the rest of her things in the car and then they were off and ready to hit the road. It was the longest drive ever. Malik James and Love' definitely had a bond. They went through living on the streets together and being robbed at gunpoint. They talked about what was going on with their parents' church and home life. But not before long Malik James was sleep. Love' was enjoying the drive. It gave her time to think, cry, grieve and feel all of those things without shame.

When they arrived her mom and daddy were excited to see her. By this time Love' and Williams were trying to have a better relationship even though Williams didn't seem to know how to have anything but a surface plastic relationship. It was as if he would only allow people to get but so close to him. He obviously had a wall up. Love's parents asked her what her plans were. Love' didn't know but she knew she needed to hurry and think of something because she knew that her car payment would be due and her car had a contraption in it that when you did not make a payment the car would not start. Her parents talked her into signing up with a temp agency. She signed up where her brothers were working and they sent her right to the same company that her brothers, Malik James and D (the one who was in and out of prison) were sent to which was a warehouse in Suffolk, Virginia. Love' was and still is not the type of young women who can work in a warehouse but she needed the money. That job only lasted three weeks for Love'. She said it must have been a subconscious thing but in her mind she thought she was moving fast enough. Apparently she wasn't and one of the supervisors warned her but she thought she had improved in speed but she did not and they let her go. She later realized that it reminded her too much of a sweat shop or being a slave, working hard and fast for production for little pay. Well, a month later her car was repoed and slowly Love' became depressed. She cut all of her dreadlocks off which she had been growing for about five years. Her hair was cut into a mini afro and she sewed her locs into a purse that said, "God's promise". Her parents thought that it was creative but they wanted to know what the next move was again; specifically Williams. Love' knew that she needed to figure something out before Williams became impatient and kicked her out again.

Love' really wanted to go to school. She as well as her brothers were considered late bloomers. They did everything on their time. At this time Love' was in her twenties and still had no clue of how she would accomplish the things she wanted to accomplish. She remembered years ago writing in her high school senior book and telling Amir that she wanted to be an author and a teacher that owned her own school for inner city youth. Her plans would remain the same in future years to come and yet expand but Love' had no direction on how to go about obtaining some of these things. Love' would wonder why didn't the high school's have a networking system in place where the students could spend time being mentored or following an individual that had already accomplished what the student wanted to accomplish or a closely related career field.

Williams and Rayanna had discussed the possibility of Love' and Malik James moving back to Delaware to stay with Ron for a while. Love' knew he was trying to avoid us being put out again even though Malik James was working it was time for Love' and Malik to permanently leave the nest. So Love' and

Malik James agreed. In 2006 Love' and Malik James had relocated to Wilmington, Delaware. She and Malik James were both working at Target in Brandywine. Love' had applied to Delaware State University and was waiting to hear back from the school. Love' knew because she had done so horribly in high school, it was a possibility that she may not be accepted. If she was accepted she knew that it would most certainly be a probationary admittance.

Ron was married to Katelin. They had two children whom Love' and her brothers loved. Love' felt that Kay sometimes felt as though she and her brothers were a reminder of the fact that he was once married and that she had at one time been involved with a married man and not to mention how much Love' looked a lot like Rayanna.

Love' felt rejected by her biological parents a few times but she knew it was because her parents were dealing with their own feelings of hurt, fear and rejection. They were repeating the cycle in some ways to their children who were now all adults but were all still learning how to release the pain. Both parents had married people who were also dealing with internal, pain and rejection as well which ultimately drew more attention to the disconnect that she often felt from Ron and Rayanna (her parents). Initially, Love' and Rayanna got along pretty well and yet Love' felt that there was a wall building there between them and she did not know why; it would be revealed later on down the years.

Chapter 9

Love' had been accepted into a program at Delaware State University that admitted students for a probationary period. She had to maintain a GPA of 2.5 or higher. Love' was so ready. Love' left in August of '06 and returned to Ron's in November for Thanksgiving break. During this time she had been conversing on Myspace with a young guy that she was drawn to. His name is Marquis. He was a few years younger than Love' but he had one of the best listening ears. They both had a few commonalities; rejection, pain and fear.

When Christmas break came Love' went to her dad's home and over that break she met Marquis in person. He looked a lot different in person. She was not physically attracted to him as much as she thought from the picture on my space, but she was drawn to him nonetheless. They continued their friendship and it evolved into a committed relationship. She was in love and so was he. Some of her family did not approve. They felt she was settling. While Love' was in school it was a truly humbling time for her first year in 06'. She was in her twenties staying in the dorms with a bunch of typical freshmen. She couldn't be embarrassed because she was so tired of her life she had no room for shame. She just wanted to be successful. She was talked about of course for being so old and living on campus in a freshmen dorm. She didn't care. She was focused at this time; for the most part, but she really began missing being around Marquis. She was thankful to have somewhat of a normal experience of college life. She met some really great people while in school, especially when she was involved in a research program for scholars. She also met about two or three buddies. One of them she became very close to during that time. Her name was Kenny and she and Kenny had a ball. Kenny was about twenty-one. Kenny had given Love' the nickname Lulu.

Kenny and Love' would become a pretty cool support system for each other their first year attending Delaware State University.

Anyway; within that year on one of Love's breaks from school during the summer of 06 (after her first year) Love' and Kay had a few disagreements. Kay wanted to take Love' to court for a phone bill. Love' used both house phone lines. The main house line had long distance (unlimited) but Love' was in the attic which is where the second line was. No one told Love' there was no long distance on the second line. Kay knew she made long distance calls but never said anything to Love' until... Kay spent a lot of time up in the attic as well and would often times answer the phone knowing that Love's friends were in Virginia. What Love' didn't realize was that Kay thought that Love' had over heard her on a phone call as she was speaking with someone that she did not want Love' to know about. She would also later attempt to evict Love'. This meant Love' had to go to court not because she owed any money but because she wanted Love' out of the house and all of this while she was trying to get her life together and finish school. Love' knew that she would no longer be welcomed to stay there at her dad's, so she had to make other arrangements. She did not know what to do because she knew of no one in the Dover area. However; her mom, Rayanna, knew of a friend who knew of a pastor who asked members of the church if they would be willing to allow a college student be a boarder. There was a woman at the church who agreed to be introduced to Love' and after meeting each other Love' was able to move in with her for the following year which was 07'. Also in 07' Love' had to go to court for the eviction and phone bill, which would cause her to miss class until Ron told her that he was not going any further with it. He thought it was completely unnecessary. Ron found out that Kay cheated on him. He would soon be separating and they would later divorce but what Ron never told Love' was that he never followed protocol for the case and Love' naively took his word for it without following protocol and so to the courts it just appeared that Love' was a no show and now there was an eviction on her credit that was not even necessary. She began feeling very rejected. She didn't understand how Ron would allow this and so she internalized it. She began feeling unworthy of anything or anyone. Love' knew that she was not perfect but she knew that she had a genuine heart. She was still a hurting little girl.

Although Love' was focused on her education, she really missed Marquis and he truly touched a part of her heart. And she touched him for sure. What they had in common was pain, rejection and fear. How would their love evolve? How would they evolve? She wasn't sure but she was tired of her heart being broken. So she was determined to make it last. They lived an hour apart but soon after she started attending the University. She met an influential woman who not only looked out for her financially with not only an office job but asking Love' to watch her grandchildren which also afforded her the opportunity to drive her extra vehicle. After the 'nanny' position was over she gave Love' the car for free! Now Love' was able to get back and forth to school without using public transportation as well as go to Wilmington to see Marquis and her dad, Ron.

Marquis was attending the church he grew up in and Love' would visit from time to time considering his church was in Wilmington and she was in Dover. Eventually, she would join this church becoming a member for a short period of time, because she was beginning to have a change of heart and begin to see religion in a different light.

Marquis lived in Wilmington, Delaware with a cousin that she felt did not like her so the feeling became mutual. Love' felt that his cousin was entirely too controlling. You see Marquis had been homeless as well. He had dropped out of high school at fifteen because he was so bored even though Love' didn't drop out of high school she was just as bored and they were bored for the same exact reasons. The first reason being that they both were and are extremely gifted in different areas or ways, of course. The second reason was that they were tired of learning the same nothingness that you really never use again. School was just so redundant to the both of them.

While Marquis stayed with his cousin who was about six years older than Love' he was enrolling in job core to get his GED and

Love' was trying to encourage him to get a move on it. She would be his support system as well as him being hers, initially but eventually that would change.

One day, on his way home to his cousin's, the feds tore the house apart. Apparently, she was selling crack cocaine and whatever else. Someone snitched on her. He now had no place to go. Love' really wanted him to move out of the state and start his life somewhere else and she would move where ever he moved to after she graduated but Marquis was not trying to hear anything about leaving his hometown. This became one of many ongoing arguments between them. Love' wanted more out of life but it seemed that he was content and this frustrated Love' and yet this did not bother Love' enough because they continued with their relationship. Marquis ended up moving in with one of his sisters, temporarily. He did not get along with his sister. He lived with his sister until his cousin was ready for him to move back in with her. His cousin Shirley never received time in prison after the feds busted in her home but her boyfriend did. Marquis did not have his own room and he was paying her more than half of his check every pay period. Love' began to question their relationship and a few other things.

Chapter 10

While Love' was attending school, questions began to arise and or resurface after leaving Atlanta and honestly throughout her childhood. She had questions about religion but she always thought it was the devil trying to make her doubt. She was always so fascinated with African history and proud of it. She began to take many classes that would begin to redefine her or allow her to be re-introduced to herself. She would begin to realize that she along with many others had been bamboozled. As she was learning and researching things she was meeting people who were on the same path and discovering and or rediscovering things about their beliefs, ideas and truths regarding faith as well as history. One of her professors Dr. Toure' began talking about how long the ancestors had been on earth and how that means the Bible could not of have been as accurate with the Adam and Eve story and that is where she began to read up on so much information that resonated with her. On her quest to find the truth she and one of her brothers would eventually go to an African priest and priestess. What she didn't realize until later was that the truth was in her. She began to study how facts had been completely distorted and manipulated. The history of Africans had been completely stolen and taken to stamp European images on them. The biblical stories were taken and turned into a circus of patriarchal bondage instead of kept in the sacredness of pure symbolism and honored in oneness with nature. Love' became even more angry and sad, but she definitely wanted to keep learning. She began to share this information that she was learning from books like; 'They Came Before Columbus' by Ivan Van Sertima; 'The Origin of the Word Amen' by Dr. Osei and Dr. Issau along with Dr. Faraji. Love' also began listening to professors, experts and theologians. She realized that he who controls the image remains in power. If they lie and demonize a culture because of some who's mind could not perceive anything beyond the physical then all they had was an illusion and so that is all they could create. They were deceiving themselves and it was a must to convince everyone else.

Love' began to hate Caucasian people during this time in her life. This was not always the case. It really began while living in Atlanta. I remember when she told me about the time she was standing outside of her job smoking and a white man with beautiful golden blonde hair, keen features and a beautiful smile approached her.

Man: You are very beautiful.

Love and Man were now both smiling and blushing.

Love': Thank you, you are too!

Man: Thank you!

Love' remembered the feeling she felt and she did not like it. She thought, "Oh I really must be beautiful if he noticed it." That's that BS. She was beginning to see it because after that thought came she began to evaluate that thought and dig deeper. It took time for her to evolve from that programming of self-hate. She did not like feeling like his opinion was more important than her own because of him being Caucasian. Even though she experienced some very obvious racism towards her growing up she still did not hate Caucasian people until that thought came to her; when that attractive European American man spoke to her.

As she began to learn while attending school she began to see so many connections and gain much insight due to the two melaninated special professors she encountered while attending DSU and later the two other professors at another University (NSU); one African American woman and one Caucasian man who seem to have had much respect for "Black Culture." Love' would go through what is known as the stages of the grieving process. She was in denial for a very short lived moment, then extremely angry, bargaining with the lies that she was used to believing, depression and hurt and lastly acceptance. She later realized she did not hate European/Caucasian people, she loved her melanin and it was as if she could not do that without being made to feel she hated Caucasians. It was the system that she hated. It was the superior complex of Western Society that she did not like. The white supremacy images displayed in education and television or any other form of media. She just had to grow to a place on her journey to realize this. She would then eventually realize that life is beyond the physical in many ways. Love' was one of the kindest, gentlest people you would ever meet. She just had to grow through her process of healing. Love' was so excited and liberated in some aspects. She and her brothers went through this part of their journey together.

Exposing lies and feeling free to not feel obligated to live out of fear of going to hell.

Marquis began to open his eyes as well and began reading. Love' nor Marquis could continue going to church. Love' felt stupid for stepping foot in a church. She said, "I am a temple. I'm already a member and do not need to be a part of the physical building when my true essence is beyond any of that."

This was an exciting time for Love' as well as her brothers. Love' was so thankful to have her brothers travel this part of the journey with her.

Love' and Marquis had been together for about three years now and still most of her family did not think she should be with him. They felt he did not have anything to offer her and they weren't even talking about the physical, more so spiritual and or mental as well as financial. Love' loved him but often times would question whether or not she should be with him or not. She would wonder about this so often because she loved him but they were so different. Questions would run through her mind, "What will happen if we get married?" "How will we raise our children?" They had so many different views, their diets were different, the way they were brought up was different; so they bumped heads often but the relationship continued. During their relationship a dysfunctional pattern started, well; actually it started within the first year and that was Love' telling Marquis often, "I don't know if I can do this" she would be referring to their relationship. Marquis became so tired of the back and forth and he told her that she had one more time to do it, that if she did this again he would honor it and end it for real. I mean this had happened so many times that they both had become accustomed to the dysfunction. This hurt him tremendously and while Love' did not mean to do this because in her heart she loved him, however; there was a serious inner battle going on within her. She knew that she would never truly be happy within their relationship. She would always be trying to change him into something that he's not instead of accepting him for who he was and he would be trying to do the same to her. She nor Marquis were honestly happy within themselves. They were on a journey to becoming or realizing that their happiness had nothing to do with anything external...

Chapter 11

Around this time Naseeya and Love' were talking to each other about the other's love life and Naseeya was very much aware of how close Love' and Marquis were becoming so she wanted to meet him. Love' was excited but deep down she was hesitant because she remembered those issues she never addressed regarding J years ago. Love' began to reflect on her friendship with Naseeya. She began remembering one time back in high school when Naseeya had said and done something to embarrass Love', so Love' began talking about Naseeya to the wrong person. It was a mutual associate of Naseeya and Love's; and that person asked Love', "Do you think Naseeya would appreciate you telling that information?" Love' felt so stupid. Love' knew she was wrong even though the mutual associate had no idea what she had done to Love' and why Love' was saying what she was saying. It did not matter though, Love' would keep that valuable nugget with her for her journey and truly learn how to be a friend and some may say almost to her disadvantage. She had a challenging time letting go of friends even when they continually showed her they could not be fully trusted.

Nasseya brought her man and they met Marquis, they all went out to a restaurant but it was always in the back of Love's mind how she behaved towards J. After they met and Nasseya drove back home, Love' finally decided to talk to her about it. She and Nasseeya prided their friendship and sisterhood on how open and honest they were with each other so Love' thought it's only right to share how she felt but boy did it backfire. Naseeya told her that she thought it was stupid that she was just now bringing it up about an ex that Love' was no longer even involved with and it was a tad bit late but Love' thought it was better late than never. Naseeya told her that she didn't need to get attention from anyone else's man to validate herself. Well, Love' was speechless because she never once said that that was the reason for her actions. She basically told Love' she wanted to have nothing to do with her because she felt as though they were never really friends. Love' was heartbroken but also realized later on in time that everything happens for a reason and that not everyone is meant to stay in your physical life; some you keep in your heart through the memories.

When she and Marquis had reached year three in a half they both had hurt each other out of fear, rejection and pain the same things that pulled them together would be the same things that would repel them from one another and yet this was the same year that Love' was feeling like she needed to be married and began feeling as though Marquis was just stringing her along. Closer towards the end of their three years Love' became so frustrated. She would be graduating soon or so she thought and she was just really wanting to start planning for their future, but Marquis had enough sense to realize that neither one of them were ready.

During the summer of 09' Love' told Marquis that she didn't know if she could continue on with the relationship. Marquis ended it and for six months they were not a couple. He would not do anything intimate with her and she was miserable. She did not believe that he would last for as long as he did but he did. Marquis was also on Love's cell phone plan so she was checking the phone bill to see who he was talking to. A certain girl's name showed up as one of his five favs as well as the number. She asked Marquis about this one girl. Love' knew it would eventually be trouble but there was nothing she could do about it at the time. She became more afraid that she would lose him forever or was it that she just wanted to make sure no one else could have him; either way, she didn't like it. For months he and Love' conversed. He tried to make her suffer and or punish her for all of the going back and forth she had done. He would say, "I know I wasn't perfect in our relationship. I know I've done some fucked up things but it just wasn't as often as you with going back and forth and I told you how what you were doing made me feel and yet you still did it."

Marquis was not the very romantic or thoughtful type. One time Love' had spent money on a hotel room for the weekend and his boys called him because they were having a party and he went and left her in the room. Love' was hurt and there were a few other things that just really had Love' questioning their relationship more often than not.

During their "break" Love' had received an unexpected call from Amir. They had not talked in a while. He wanted to come visit her. Even though she was not in a committed relationship, she still would feel as though she wasn't loyal if she would have agreed to Amir visiting. Amir did not understand Love's logic. In his mind there was no way that Marquis wasn't doing what he wanted or dating who he wanted. Amir didn't like this one bit. Also during Marquis and Love's break, Mozique would be in the back of her mind. She would just wonder where he was, if he was married, or had children. She wondered about him ever since she realized she had never gotten the number off the caller ID at her aunts in Atlanta. She would also wonder about Amir but they always kept in contact even if a year had passed or if they communicated every few months they managed to always remain in contact. There were so many times when Amir would do something to piss Love' off and or vice versa but they had an unconditional love and would always remain friends if nothing else.

As I mentioned earlier; in November of 09' Love' and Malik James went to go see an African priest and priestess. They were referred to her by one of her professors. Love' and Malik James were excited and nervous. The priest lived in Washington D.C. When Love' and Malik James arrived they began to feel so nervous. They knew it was because of the fact that they were taught that your ancestors are evil, your culture is evil. What they experienced was so far away from all the lies told about African culture. The priest and priestess knew that Love' and Malik James had someone in their immediate family who was a minister. They knew so much without her or her brother saying a word. They even did the cutting of the chicken head. One for Love' and one for Malik, the chicken representing or revealing the spirit or energy of that individual that the chicken was sacrificed for. After slitting the head the chicken would continue running around in the designated area. Depending on how long the chicken ran without the head is said that represents the strength of the spirit. The priest and priestess told Love' "Your brother's spirit is strong. Are your parents ministers?" She told them yes. They also did a spiritual cleanse where they were wrapped in white apparel. The priestess told Love' that she would give her man the best loving he had ever had with what Love' was washing herself with. Love' believed her but yet at the same time, she thought, "Oh, you must not know I already do that." Well, Love' ended up saying that to the priestess and she said it's going to be even better. After Love's washing ritual. The priestess let Love' get her clothes back on and waited and prepared an orange for her to eat while Love' was eating her orange with a dark herb on top of it. Malik was preparing for his washing ritual. The priest stood outside of the bathroom door while he told Malik what to do. When Malik was finished he too ate an orange with the same dark herb on it. Afterward, they asked the both of them to come into their alter room. The priest asked if there was anything that they wanted to know, that this was the time to ask. So Love' nor Malik James wasted no time due to the fact that what they were doing cost a total of three hundred dollars. Love' and Malik James later realized how silly that was. While it was their full-time job, Love' was thinking "Well, whoever is telling you about our lives, why didn't it or they tell you I am a struggling college student and that my brother is struggling musician?" Anyway, the first question Love' asked was about Marquis. She asked if he was "The One". He responded saying, Yes, he is just confused and hurt right now. The priest then asked, "Do you have a child?" and before Love' could answer he saw that Love' would soon be having a child and this is exactly what he told her. Love' became weirded out by that. In her mind, she knew that was out of the question. She knew she really wanted to have children but she knew she wanted to be married first and she didn't see that happening anytime soon. The priest then began to just tell them things, things that he could not of known. Then Malik James asked a few questions about his life about the path that he was on. They conversed for a little while longer and then Love' and Malik James were on their way to Virginia for the Thanksgiving holiday. Malik and Love' discussed their experience the whole way there. Love' couldn't wait to tell Marquis, even though they were not back in a relationship officially. They still communicated on a regular basis.

When they arrived in Virginia, their mom and step-daddy were very happy to see them. Love' had been gone for a little over three years and Malik James was now living in New Jersey and had been there for about two in a half years. Ron Jr. was living in Chesapeake with his wife and two daughters. They were all excited to be together again. Rayanna definitely had raised her three children to be close and to protect one another because she always knew that there would be times where they would be all each other had and she was definitely accurate. There were many times where they would defend each other regarding Williams. Love's brothers would always blame her for the fact that she started calling Williams, daddy. Ha! Love' knew that he needed to be nurtured and so she tried her best just as she had done as a young child for her dad. She saw the pain in both of these men and she wanted to take it away or try and fix it for them and when she began to realize that she wanted to do that she took a look at some of the men she had become involved with and realized that she was trying to save her dad and her daddy by saving the men she chose to be involve with especially Marquis and J's crazy ass but then again, she was just as crazy during that time for running behind J.

As soon as Love' had some alone time she called Marquis to tell him what the priest said. He found it interesting of course. That week was an exciting time in Love's life and she could not wait to get back home so that she get things rolling in school.

As soon as Love' got home she prepared for school which would be back in session the next day. After she finished preparing she thought she would check her phone bill again just to see if Marquis was still talking to this one girl in particular. Love' just didn't have a good feeling about it and she asked Marquis what was going on between them and he told her it was nothing. Love' knew that he was trying to make her regret what she had done previously with going back and forth and it was really beginning to hurt Love'. So she told him it was best that they didn't talk at all and he did not agree with that. She noticed that this girl and Marquis weren't talking as much as they had been for some reason. Love' and Marquis were conversing more often than what they had ever conversed but they were both still very afraid. They were still not officially a couple. They had not been a couple for almost four in a half months at this time. It was now December of 09' and they would not be an official couple again until February of 10'. There had been many times that they had made passionate love. One time in particular when they were making passionate love and Love' began to cry and he cried along with her. It was a beautiful moment. She felt loved and they shared it between the both of them. In February of '10 they were a couple again and decided to celebrate. They spent the weekend together and it was the weekend that Love' and Marquis's child was conceived. Love' knew it that night. She was terrified. She felt that Marquis had done this on purpose. Love' searched and searched for the semen and could only find a little. She asked, "Where is it Marquis, where is the rest of it?" She just kept asking over and over again, she was searching for it everywhere and realized she should go to the bathroom as if that were going to help. Marquis admitted to her later that it was intentional to prevent her from ever leaving him. A day later Love's cycle came and left and was very light, she was really only spotting. She went to go purchase a pregnancy test. When she got back to the house, (the place she was staying in Dover with the senior woman named Lucy) she took the test and it came back positive. She took the second test and those results were positive as well. She called Marquis immediately and told him. They were both terrified. Love' called her mom next and Rayanna was very disappointed along with Williams. Love' began to feel so many mixed emotions. She wanted a baby but she wanted a child after she finished school and after she was married. She nor Marquis had no idea how they were going to take care of a child with the way their circumstances already were. Marquis did work a part time job working twenty hours a week and Love' was working two jobs both part time but right before she became pregnant she was without either job. One was a student assistant and the other was the nanny position. Love' was basically living off of her school refunds which were usually a pretty decent amount and range from five thousand to eight thousand. More often than not it was usually seven or eight thousand dollars.

The following weekend she decided to go to see Marquis who was still living in Wilmington. She needed to be around him for comfort and support. When she arrived he was very distant and cold. She asked him what was wrong and he told her nothing was wrong but Love' knew different. She asked him to walk her out to the car because there was always so many people in his cousin's place in which he had moved back in with his cousin as soon as she got a new place. Love' never felt comfortable there. They both sat in the car and Love' began to express herself about how she was feeling scared and how it was making her even more scared because of his lack of emotion, affection or anything. Marquis told her, "I am scared too. I can't afford to take care of a child and neither can you." Love' then said, "So what are you trying to say, you want me to abort the baby?" He told her, "no and you know that!"   Deep down Love' was seriously contemplating it. She just began to feel even more strongly that she would be either raising the baby by herself or there would be so much drama that she would end up hating him. On the other hand Love' did not want to abort the baby. There was a part of her that was so excited. She was just wanting assurance that everything would be okay and that she would be able to complete school.

When Love' arrived back in Dover, she knew that she had to call her dad, her brothers and a few others that were close to her. She definitely did not want to tell them. The men in her life were very hurt, disappointed and angry. They felt that the relationship between him and Love' would not last. Her brothers saw Marquis as someone who would not bring anything to the relationship. He was what some would be referred to as 'hood'.

Love' knew that she would not be able to go through with an abortion so she scheduled an appointment with the doctor to confirm what she already knew and of course the results came back positive. They told her about how far along she was. All she could think about was calculating how much time she had before the baby arrived. According to the doc office, the baby would be due in November of 10'. This meant that Love' would be interrupting her education and probably would be transferring to a school in Virginia.

She would try her best to avoid relocating. Love' was barely eating. She was looking for a job constantly and was having a difficult time once again finding work. The only thing she qualified for was WIC. She just could not afford to buy enough food. She could not get any more assistance than that because she was a recipient of financial aid grants. She did not want to ask anyone because she knew what most of her family and close friends would say and that was, "Well what is Marquis doing? Why isn't he helping?" Love' began to become very frustrated with him. She would ask for money for food and he would say, "I can't. I had to help my cousin out." There were two times where he did help and sent twenty dollars so she could go to the dollar store and buy some inexpensive groceries. She would go to all of her doc appointments by herself except for one. Love' asked him if he could catch the express bus to Dover so that she would not have to drive to Wilmington to pick him up and then drive him back in time so that he would not be late for work and then drive back to Dover. He said, "No." She asked, "Why?" His reply was "Because I don't have the money to catch no bus." Love' knew he didn't have the money, but she thought he would try to make a way. She told him it was only five dollars and that she would take him back; but he still would not do it. She began to feel so lonely during the pregnancy. She kept trying to explain to Marquis how she felt but he just wasn't getting it. Marquis told Love' that she was nagging too much about everything. You see during their relationship Love' didn't trust Marquis and not because he had ever done anything for her to not trust him but she was remembering what other men had done to her, cheated on her, lied, never kept their word and Love' was willing to compromise on most things other than cheating. Marquis became so frustrated with being accused when he knew he wasn't do anything. Men and women have to realize that what they start doing in the beginning of a relationship the young woman will more than likely expect it throughout the relationship.

Love' became so very angry and it wasn't just because he told her she was nagging but he also told her that they would not be hanging out for his birthday weekend like they had planned. Love' and Marquis began to argue about everything and on this day Love' told him, "Fuck you! See this is why I start feeling that maybe we should no longer continue the relationship but there is a part of me that wants to continue." She then told him, "It's best that I move back home with my mom and daddy. This is what my dad (Ron) suggested as well. My dad says I need my mother during this time." Marquis, said, "First of all you're not going anywhere and second of all, didn't I tell you that that would be the last time you threaten me with that?" She said, "I am just expressing myself." Love' and Marquis said some harsh things but it was mainly Love'. She could not get him to see how much she needed him there in every way possible. He continued to live his life as though nothing changed. Love' felt as though Marquis did not believe that she would actually move to Virginia without him. The thing was is that her parents offered for him to come stay just until he got on his feet and once he did, they wanted them to marry. Marquis did not want to leave his family and his hometown. Love' really did not like his decision. To her, his family took advantage of him, but nonetheless they were his family and he was not leaving them. His mom was not in his life. She gave her children to Marquis dad's parents for the majority of their lives. His dad was locked up for twenty years and he had just recently gotten out of prison. He and his dad were very close, considering how long he had been locked up. Anyway, the next day Marquis called Love' before he started celebrating his birthday. He had gone out the night before as well. He and Love' were arguing and she was still upset about what they had conversed about the night prior. Later that night Love' decided to check the phone bill again. When she did, she noticed that the same girl he was conversing with over the phone when they were on their break he spoke to last night right after their argument. Love' knew she said some harsh things to him. She began to feel a horrible feeling within. She did not ask him just yet if he was still talking to the girl (she later found out her name was Tiffany). She decided to wait until she went to school the next day. She went to the library to print out some school work and she then checked his Facebook and Myspace profile. Love' became angrier with herself in that moment. She continued searching his page. Deep down she knew that it was absolutely ridiculous to even feel the need to become a private investigator but she knew that he would never confess because that was the one thing Love' made clear to him. She told him she would know if he ever cheated and especially if they were sexually intimate after the fact. She would know that someone else's energy was integrated because it happened to her in a previous relationship. As she was scrolling down his social media page things became to come back to her memory that at the time didn't set well with her but she brushed it off. For example, the time she wanted to be intimate but he told her no, let's just chill. This was not like him. He said it in such a way that exuded some sort of guilt and now she knew it was because he knew she would know. What she saw while scrolling made her heart jump and butterflies flutter in her stomach. Her eyes were as bright as the moon; sol light shines through.

She saw a meme of two cartoon-like characters laying in the bed with a caption that said, " Last night was great. Thanks for an awesome night." With hearts blinking everywhere. So as soon as Love' saw this she chuckled to herself. She really wasn't sure how she felt. She was shocked, angry, hurt, etc...Around this time she was about two or three months pregnant. She was trying to decide on how to handle this. She knew that if she had asked him he would deny it, especially over the phone. She decided to send a message to the young lady's inbox. Love' told her who she was and then Tiffany asked if Love' would mind her calling. Love' of course told her that she didn't mind. She and Tiffany began to exchange information. Tiffany and Love' were very respectful towards each other. Love' made it very clear to Tiffany, "I just want you to know that I am not angry with you. I do not know you or have a relationship with you to be angry with you. I have no animosity towards you. I just ask that you be completely honest with me as I will be with you." Tiffany began to tell Love' everything. How they met. How long they had been conversing over the phone and how he had stopped calling out of the blue and then he would text or call every once in a while. She told Love' that they had slept together once. Love' was in complete shock. Love' told Tiffany that she was pregnant with his child and that when she and Marquis were 'talking' is when they were on their break but then Love' asked when they had sex and she said it was not quite a month ago, a few weeks ago. Love' knew exactly when it happened because they had just had an argument and it seemed as though he was intentionally starting arguments due to his guilt, apparently. On the night that Love' believed he slept with this young lady is the night that Love and Marquis were on the phone and someone beeped in the line and he got off the phone with Love' to take the call. He said that he would call right back and didn't. Love' called him but he never answered or responded and even the next day he didn't respond until late night. She knew in her gut at that time something wasn't right. Love' was in shock. It took her a long time to really accept what he had done and to release the emotions of how she really felt. It was the strangest thing because she somehow knew that he loved her. He had never done anything like that and was a good guy. He worshiped the ground Love' walked on. His family would say he was whipped but he would say to Love', "You're the best thing that could of ever happen to me. If anything were to ever happen and we are not together, know that I will always love you and that will never change." Love' knew he meant that but it didn't change the fact that he had slept with someone else and not only slept with someone but while Love' was pregnant. He slept with Tiffany raw. No protection. Then right after Love' told her that she was pregnant, Tiffany told her that she thought she was also. This pissed Love' off completely. All she could think of is what will I tell our child about a sibling that was born a few months later.

Love' asked Tiffany if she would mind a three-way call. Tiffany agreed. But first Love' wanted to call him first and ask him a simple question. If he would deny it, she would then do the three-way call. Love' asked Marquis if he and Tiffany had ever seen each other. He was telling Love' that he had never seen Tiffany and that they had only spoken on the phone. They met through social media. Anyway, Marquis denied the fact he had ever been to her house but he did admit to the fact that she had stopped by over his cousin's place of residence. He told Love' that everyone was angry with him and no one liked her. Love' asked him, "And that's all that ever happened?" He told her, "Yes." Love' told him that she had a call coming in and needed to take it and that she would call him right back. So she and Tiffany decided that Love' would call and converse with Marquis as if everything was okay while Tiffany was on the phone. Love' did just that and asked him about Tiffany.

Love': Did anything ever happened between you and Tiffany sexually?

Marquis: Huh?

That was a giveaway response right there.

Love': (speaking in a loud tone) Did anything ever happened between you and Tiffany sexually?

Now Love' already knew Tiffany's name from when they were on their break she would see her name on his fav five list so he was not shocked about that but he was shocked by her line of questioning.

Marquis: No, Why? What makes you ask that?

Love': Well, I was just wondering and I saw on one of your social media profile pages a meme that a girl named Tiffany posted on your Facebook profile.

Marquis: What did it say?

Love': A meme of two cartoon like characters laying in the bed with a caption that said, 'Last night was great. Thanks for an awesome night.' With hearts blinking every damn where. So why would she put that up there?

Marquis: I don't know, I'm not her.

Love: Are you sure you don't know why?

After that question Marquis became very quiet.

Marquis: NO, alright, why do you keep asking me about Tiffany? Stop bringing her up!

Love': Wow, alright. Hello?

Marquis: Hello?

Tiffany: Hello.

Marquis: Hello?

Love': Yes, Tiffany is on the phone.

Marquis: WHAT????? Hello? (with a nervous chuckle)

Love' just wished she could have been in person to see the look on his face.

Tiffany: So you never fucked me?

Marquis: Nope.

Love': This is not the fuckin' time to lie, Marquis. I need you to be honest and come clean or you're just going to make it worse for yourself.

Marquis sat in silence for a minute.

Marquis: Well, yeah.

Love': Yeah, what?

Marquis: Yeah, it happened one time.

Love': Now she is saying she is pregnant.

Marquis: She ain't no pregnant. Tiffany you know damn well you ain't pregnant.

Love': Did you take a pregnancy test?

Tiffany: No, I said I might be.

Meanwhile Love' hears his cousin in the background laying him out. They did not like what he had done, especially when a woman is carrying your seed.

Marquis: Babe, I know you're mad. I'm sorry. I am going to make it up to you.

Love': What idiot were you listening to for advice? Because this was the stupidest, most selfish thing you could have ever done to me, to us.

Marquis: I know. I've been carrying the guilt.

Tiffany: WOW! I can not believe I believed every word you told me. Well, Love' you can have him. I don't want anyone who would do what he has done to the both of us.

Love': I totally understand; but I have a child on the way with him so it's not that simple for me.

Tiffany: Love' you can call me back when you get off the phone.

Love': Okay.

Love' really wasn't in the mood to talk to anyone, but she continued to talk to Marquis. All she could think about is how he had shared himself with someone and it wasn't even worth it to him. He engaged in sex unprotected.

Marquis: Hello?

Love': Yeah.

Marquis: So what do you want to do?

Love': I need time.

Marquis: How much time?

Love': Are you serious right now? I don't know. I can't time it.

Love' and Marquis continued conversing over the phone and all Love' could do was think about how he risked his life and hers by engaging in unprotected sex.

Love': Why did you do it? Why?

Marquis: Because I was angry. I was hurt about some of the things you said. You kept accusing me of cheating on you and I hadn't.

Love' tried to be angry but couldn't for some reason. She was hurt and shocked but not angry. She wanted to be mad and curse him out but that is not what she felt in her heart to do which was very unusual for Love' considering the circumstance. Anyway Love' and Marquis continued to discussed the situation for the next week or two.

Love' was trying to work it out to stay in Delaware but Marquis was not helping enough. He offered for her to stay with him in his cousin small two bedroom apartment but Love' was not having that. She did not want to be stressed living in a cramped apartment with more than enough people already living there. She also felt that there were too many people in and out of there. People were still selling drugs around there and she just did not want to be around it. So she told Marquis again that she would be leaving in a few months. He was not trying to hear anything she was saying. He kept telling her how that was not right. He asked her, "How will I get down there to see the baby?" Love' could not believe he was asking her how he was going to get there but then again she should not have been surprised.

When the time came for her last doctor's appointment before she'd be moving to find out the sex of the baby, Love' was excited. She initially wanted a boy. She began to feel differently about having a girl. Deep down, initially she wanted a girl but she thought she would probably end up with a boy just because. It was not that she did not want a girl but she wanted to be the first one of her Mom and Dad's offspring to have a boy. She knew that Marquis really wanted a boy. Love' had a change of heart because she began to accept who Marquis was and felt he was not ready to be an example to a boy. Marquis already felt that things were working out in Love's favor and so when she called to tell him it was a girl she was so excited and thankful. She kept asking the doctor if she was sure that it was a girl. The doctor stated "Well, we can't say 100% 'yes it's a girl' but we're almost certain that it's a girl. There are surprises sometimes." Marquis was sad and became angry. He said "I bet you are happy, you get everything you want, everything you've prayed for or asked the ancestors for." Love' began laughing so hard because she thought he was joking but she quickly realized he wasn't joking. He was seriously upset. Love' began to wonder if he would have tried a little harder to be there for her a little more if she were having a boy. He was just revealing to her all the more that she had to move back to Virginia in order to have the support that she would need during this precious time. The time approached quickly where she would soon be leaving and she needed new tires on her car before driving five hours by herself. She knew that Marquis would not ride home with her. She decided to ask one of her brothers. Malik James lived in

New Jersey. He was getting his hustle on. He is an absolute artist. Love' was so proud of her brothers and sister. She loved all of her siblings.

Malik James agreed to follow her to Virginia. She was still trying to work out how she would pay for her tires and get home but she knew it would all work out. She asked her dad for help. He told her that he did not mind helping to get her there but he felt that Marquis should also contribute. So Love' agreed and asked Marquis if he could purchase two tires for her car in order to get her back home. He asked her to find out how much the tires would cost and then depending on how much it was he would do it. Love' was shocked but a part of her knew that he would do something to help because he knew that what Love' told him was true and the fact of the matter was if she stayed she would have to drive herself to the hospital or deliver the baby herself. He had no way of coming to Dover and she explained a few more reasons to him that he was obviously in agreement with. So when June came, Love' was on her way to Chesapeake, Virginia.

She was very nervous because she knew there was a chance that Marquis would not be able to come in time for the delivery.

Once she moved, she had to keep begging him to do things that the doctor wanted him to do in regards to his family history. They wanted to test him for sickle cell and for one other disease. She and Marquis were on the phone when she asked if he could go to the doctors to see if he had the traits for certain diseases. He told Love' "I ain't going to get tested at no doctor's office; because I have no medical insurance." Love' continued to plead with him and he continued to refuse. Deep down Love' knew it had nothing to do with her wanting to know if he had the trait for the disease for her it was just a matter of seeing if he would make a sacrifice. Was he willing to do something? Because to Love' it seemed as though he wasn't and the baby wasn't even here yet. While Marquis and Love' were going back and forth for a while about him getting tested, his cousin yelled in the background, "DAMN, HE AIN'T GOT THAT SHIT! AIN'T NOBODY IN OUR FAMILY HAVE THAT SHIT. WHY DON'T SHE GET A TEST TO SEE IF THAT BABY IS YOURS!?" Well, Love' was fuming after that statement. Love' was yelling on the phone telling Marquis to put her on the phone. She told Marquis, "First of all you don't just have one side of a family so just because it's not on your pop's side doesn't mean it's not on your mom's side and furthermore; that is exactly why she will never be in this baby's presence without me being there. She is rude, immature, abusive and mean as hell! Marquis wanted his cousin to be the godmother of his baby as well as help name the baby. Love, said, "Hell to the NO!"

Marquis blamed Love' for relocating back to Virginia. The remaining four months of her pregnancy he told her it was all her fault. If she had stayed, then he wouldn't have had to try to find out how he was going to get all the way to Virginia. Love' would tell him, "You act like I am in another country." They argued so much. They both were frustrated that they were in the situation that they were in. They took it out on each other. Love' became very sick while pregnant. She was trying to remain positive. Everyday she would meditate and repeat wonderful affirmations to herself and the baby. Love' sang to the baby a lot. She wanted the baby to know that she loved her even though at one point she thought about aborting the baby. She only thought about it because she knew that she wasn't ready to be a single parent but she had a feeling that it would turn out that way. Marquis was not a bad guy but Love' and Marquis were complete opposites and they would have a difficult time seeing eye to eye.

Love' had a doctor's appointment in Chesapeake, Virginia. When she would leave the doctor's office she would call Marquis but it had gotten to the point where those phone calls had to be few and far between because somehow and argument would start. Rayanna was wanting them to come together for the baby's sake. Rayanna and Williams kept offering for Marquis to come to VA but he kept refusing.

Chapter 12

Love' had begun working at a department store for about 5 months in Virginia. Marquis was not sending anything and they were still together at this time and she needed maternity clothes and a few other items for the baby. She did not want to have to depend on the baby shower completely. She and her parents planned the baby shower. Love' bought the invitations and mailed them out. Her parents catered it and prepared activities. Love' did not want to have to tell her long time friend slash ex-boyfriend but the day finally came when she had to tell Amir and she was scared for some reason. She did not want him to know. Maybe in the back of her mind she wondered if they would ever be together again or maybe she thought he would be disappointed or hurt like her family was. She told him though and he couldn't believe it. He was in shock. He asked her if she was marrying Marquis but she told him, no and yet honestly she didn't know what they were going to do just yet.

Love' set the date for the baby shower for October 2, 2010. She did this because she planned the shower on Marquis' pay period. She specifically asked him when was the best time for him so that he could come. He called her on that Thursday and told her that he would not be able to come because he had to pay his cousin rent. Love' felt very alone, hurt and angry.

The last doctor appointment the doctor told her he had some concerns. That doctor appointment was on the 27th of

September, a few days prior to the baby shower. He wanted Love' to come back on the 30th of September. The doctor wanted her to be seen by the diagnostic ultra sonographer technician. The woman began asking Love' questions. She asked her how far along she was and when Love' told her, her eyes widened and the woman asked Love' if she was sure. Love' said yes. Love' asked her why and the sonographer told her that her amniotic fluid was really low to be so far along and by this time Love' was between 32-33 weeks. The technician told the doctor and the doctor told her to tell Love' to come and see him. Love' became very nervous. She knew something was going on and she didn't know what. Rayanna kept telling Love' that to her she did not look right. Love's skin was very dark and she was swollen to the point that the month prior to working only not quite three weeks she was put on bed-rest. Love' still did not think anything was wrong with her. Anyway, the doctor told her that if nothing changes over the weekend that she would have to have an emergency c-section. He said the amniotic fluid is just too low and your blood pressure is too high.

Love' was in a state of shock. She was trying to be strong but she was terrified. She was trying to be excited for the baby shower that was coming in two days and she discovered Marquis would not be coming to the shower despite the fact that it was planned out of convenience for him to be there. Some of her former church family, her high school best friend Tina, her children, family members and a few love ones, like her godmom Gigi came. She was so thankful and somehow her heart ached. One of the last presentations was a surprise. Her parents Rayanna and Williams wanted her to watch a DVD. Love' began to cry. It was a DVD her step-dad had done of she and her brothers when they were babies. The DVD had images of them as they evolved into adults. Then there was another DVD of images welcoming the baby with powerful song choices on both DVD's selected by Ron Jr. So her baby shower was captured along with childhood memories so that she could always remember that time and be thankful. It was a very touching moment for Love' and she would always remember it.

After the shower was over. She called her child's father and asked if there was any way he could get there because there was a strong possibility that she would be having an emergency c-section. He said "See, this is what I was talking about. If you had a just stayed here I wouldn't have to be trying to figure out how I'm going to get there. You wouldn't have to worry about being by yourself or feeling alone." Love' became angry and got off the phone. It just wasn't the time to discuss anything like that. She then decided to call him back and try to explain the severity of what was going on but all he could do was think about himself. Love' got off of the phone again. The doctor told her that she would definitely be having a c-section on October 4, 2010.

Love' would not talk to him until she was on her way up to be prepped for surgery. As he was talking to her the same cousin that told her maybe she should get a DNA test asked to speak to Love' trying to be encouraging but Love' was not really present. She knew her life was about to completely change.

Love' and Marquis had decided on a name and they argued on the last name because he wanted the baby to have his last name but at the time Love' felt that was one of the most ridiculous things ever. She said to him, "What do I look like giving the baby your last name and you're not doing anything to help me with the baby before the baby is even here? How dumb is that for the baby to have your last name and I have a different last name?" She and Marquis had decided upon one name, but because Rayanna was more involved she allowed her mom to give the baby a middle name. The original name decided upon was Aniyah. Love' decided to name the baby Ziariah (pronounced Zi- r-ree-uh.)

Before going into have the surgery they noticed that Love's blood pressure was at the level of stroke zone. Love' asked the doctor if the baby would be fine. He told her, "Honestly, the ones who we have to worry are the parents of the wimpy white boys. Girls are fighters and specifically the black babies." Love' smiled she knew she needed to hear that to calm her nerves. Anyway, they needed to hurry so that she could have the c-section. Rayanna was in the room with Love'. Rayanna was excited.

Love' was still in another zone. She was not present. She was in a state of shock. When the baby came out, the doctor said, "Oh she is feisty, I think she is mad with me." Rayanna began crying while Love' lay there in shock. They allowed Love' to hold her for a brief second and then they rushed her away so that she could get on a breathing machine. You see they had given Love' steroids to prepare the baby for her early arrival. Ziariah was only three pounds and eleven ounces. Love' blamed herself for her emotions, for her not being able to eat right as well as smoking a Capone which was a small cigar. Love' had to go to the recovery room immediately. Rayanna took Love's cell phone. Love' was trying to argue with her mom but she was so out of it. Rayanna said, "I don't want to hear it, that boy is not going to take you out of here, stressing you out, this is a very critical time, it's recovery. I will bring it back after you've left the recovery room." Love' wanted to argue it down but she knew Rayanna was right and besides she dozed off. As soon as she would doze off the nurses would come in picking and poking and doing all kinds of things. Love' was in the recovery room for about two days. They finally came to get her and take her to the labor and delivery ward and wanted her to begin pumping milk from her but the milk would not come. The doctors told her it was emotional which made Love' feel even horrible. So much was going on with her emotionally as well as physically that she was totally unaware of. The nurses had to come and get Love' to go and see Ziariah because she had to have a feeding tube. She was no longer on a breathing machine. The day she was born which was October 4, 2010; they had her on a breathing machine for a few hours and that was that. She still could not eat on her own. Love' was trying to nurse her because they told her that perhaps having Zairiah on the nipple may help bring the milk down. Ziariah was like 'What the hell is this?' because her little face frowned.

Love's breasts were very full and her nipples were too wide for little Ziariah's mouth, well; this is what Love' was told and that is what it looked like to her so she said she would just pump and give it to her through the bottle.

Love' went back to her hospital room and called her mom . She wanted her to bring her phone back. So Rayanna did just that. When Rayanna came she told her to still not get herself worked up, that her focus should be on Ziariah. There were days when she did not want to go see Ziariah because she had so many emotions but mainly guilt. Love' did not like walking around much because she felt like her guts were going to come out. It's one of the most painful feelings. You just don't want to move. After she went to see Ziariah that evening she would just hold her, kiss her and stare at her. When she went back to the room she finally decided to call Marquis. He argued as soon as she got on the phone which caused her blood pressure to raise. Her head was pounding. She was trying to talk, but she couldn't yell over him until she finally couldn't take it anymore and said, "I could have died or had a stroke. They don't even know when they're going to let me leave. I have been here four days and they already know they are going to keep me tomorrow. They can't get my blood pressure to stabilize. You haven't even asked about your daughter. All you want to know is if I gave her your last name and telling me if I had of just stayed there then you would have been able to participate. Well, how long are you going to keep saying the same damn thing? You haven't even asked if I'm okay?" Marquis began to feel bad for a moment. He asked how Love' was doing and then he asked about Ziariah. Love' told him that Ziariah would have to stay in the hospital for a few weeks at least. This made Love' sad because she didn't know what the hospital would be doing to their child. On day eight, Love' would be leaving the hospital and leaving Ziariah for two weeks which was the longest two weeks ever.

The day that the phone rang for Love' to come pick up her baby was the most exciting day of her life. She had to go get a car seat and a few other things. Love' was excited but what would happen by Ziariah coming home would shift the atmosphere in the home and the dynamics between Love' and Rayanna.

Love' was exhausted with Ziariah waking up every few hours to eat. Rayanna would come up very often to try and take over. She was trying to show Love' how to feed her and show her things that Rayanna already knew that Love' knew how to do.

Rayanna was acting as if Ziariah was her child. Love' thought that Rayanna was going crazy for a moment. Love' and Rayanna would argue a lot about the baby.

Love' did not know what to do because she knew she needed the help but at what cost? Love' would be going back to school in a few months. She was looking for work that would not conflict with her school schedule which was a challenge for her because she just wasn't sure if she would come home and find Ziariah nursing on her grandmother, in fact, that was a joke that even Rayanna's two brothers said to her. Love' could do nothing with her own child without Rayanna trying to take over. If Love' mentioned it, then Rayanna would tell her how this or that didn't matter. Love' would be thinking 'Well, if it doesn't matter you should not have a problem with me doing whatever with my child.'

Love' wanted so much to know what it felt like having a child that she could do things with without feeling like she was being a bad mom for every decision she made. Love' began to realize something else was going on and it had nothing to do with her. There was trouble in lover's paradise. Ziariah was a distraction for Rayanna for what was and what wasn't going on within her marriage with Williams.

Months had passed and Ziariah was about eight months now. When Love' would come in from school. Ziariah would be so happy but Love' would come in the house, stressed, tired and not really present until her mom, Rayanna talked to her about that. Her mom told her, "Your face should light up every time you see her so that it makes her feel wanted and loved." Love' began to feel bad again, she knew her mom was right. Love' remembered times of exhaustion where she didn't feel like being bothered with Ziariah. Not because she didn't love her, but because she was so tired. She was so angry with Marquis and subconsciously she began to feel some sort of resentment. Her mom told her that anytime she needed a break she could always sleep and let Ziariah sleep downstairs with her and Williams but Love' didn't really want that either. Ziariah was already spending so much time with her grandmother (Rayanna). Love' made it clear to her mom that when Ziariah turned a year old that she would be attending daycare. The daycare owner was a friend of the family.

When Love' started working and was in school everything was pretty good between her and her mom and everything seem to be good between she and Williams as well. She was doing well in school. She missed Delaware State University but she liked Norfolk State University just as well. She had transferred and only had a year and a half left before completing. There was a slight difference in that she had grown to know more of the people at DSU and staff included. She would soon be graduating and she could not wait.

Love' and Amir had been back in touch with each other and he asked Love' what her address was. He told her that he was going to send her something for the baby. A week later she received a card with a check in the envelope in the mail. A check for a hundred dollars. Love' cried. She was so thankful because Marquis had not even done that. Marquis and Love' were no longer a couple. Love' became too frustrated with his lack of drive and commitment to his daughter. While Love' knew that Marquis loved Ziariah and her as well she just felt that they needed to work on things individually for a while and maybe that would help. He did come to visit once when she was two months and then again when she was a little over a year old. Love' and Rayanna would travel to Delaware and he would see Ziariah then. Love' rarely went over to his family's place because she just didn't want Ziariah around certain things and certain behavior but she would tell him, he and his family were always welcomed over her dad's, Ron's, home.

I remember when Love' told me that when Ziariah was around eight or nine months they had taken a trip to Delaware and Marquis had come over to see his daughter and while he was supposedly playing with her. She had taken one of her hair bows out of her hair and put it in her mouth and was gagging on it. Her dad was laying on the floor without movement, no reaction he calmly said, "Hey, yo she got something in her mouth." It was apparent to not only Love' but Love's sister that she was about to choke on it. Love' asked him if he was high from weed. He denied that he was, which made it even worst. Love's sister Bionca was about to curse him out. Love' just did not trust his judgment, she had watched him for years and how he allowed people to do things and say things to him and it concerned Love' and that was just one example. Love' knew that Marquis was sad and depressed because he wanted his family, Ziariah and Love'. Love' knew that he wanted his family but not enough to move and be with them when he had several opportunities to do so. She didn't understand why he just wouldn't move. She was so certain that he could find an even better job if he just moved. He was still only working one part time job. Working four hours a day, twenty hours a week for about three to four years at that time. Love' had goals and she was determined to accomplish them with or without Marquis.

Chapter 13

Love' began spending a lot of time at the Chesapeake Library in Chesapeake, Virginia during this time. She was taking care of business to prepare for returning back to school after her first semester at NSU as well as looking for work. While handling her business she happened to notice a friend on a social media website. She had requested this person to be a friend on this popular site because she thought it was someone she knew from years ago that she had been trying to search for, her friend Mozique. For so long when she lost his phone number by never getting it off the caller ID, she carried regret. For some reason, initially she did not think it was him a year prior. After she sent the request she just didn't think much about it until a year later; almost two years later.

She decided to look on his page and through his pictures before reaching out to him. She was nervous as she was looking through the pictures. It appeared that he had just had a baby girl who appeared to be a year old. She was not sure if it was him because a lot of time had passed since she last saw him. When they first met, Mozique had a young baby boy face. While some of the pictures she was scrolling through had the same features as a younger Mozique. Love' was not used to seeing him with facial hair, slightly buff and tattoos. She finally messaged him stating, "Ooook for the longest time I've been wanting to know this, now I requested you as a friend thinking you were someone I knew from years ago. I am still not sure if it is you,

but did you ever live in Virginia for a second? If not oops;).”
Love' continued scrolling through his pictures while she waited
for a response and then saw an older picture and her eyes were
as bright as the moon. She went back to his inbox and said,
“Wait, I think it is you, omgggggggggg, hope to hear from you
soon and what a beautiful daughter.” When he finally replied,
she was so nervous and excited to see what he would say,
“Whatsup....yea it's me lol...haven't seen nor heard from you in
a while, how have you been?” Love' responded and he never
responded back until she told him a dream she had about him
regarding his writing. Years ago when they first met he had told
her that he was a writer and had many ideas. She just wanted to
encourage him to write if he wasn't already. He was shocked
and told her that basically he had not had time to write due to
his job and traveling but that was it. Love' didn't really know
what she was expecting for him to say or do. It most certainly
had been between seven to eight years that had passed since
they had last spoken or seen each other and for some reason
she never told him what happened or how she lost his number.
Love' began to feel bad again even though it was not intentional
that she lost contact with him. She felt slightly embarrassed that
she reached out expecting a little more in return from him. She
then began to question what she had felt all of those years. She
began to doubt whether he had wondered about her and what
she thought was a connection between them. She thought

maybe it was just a figment of her imagination. As hard as she tried to not to think about him he lived in the back of her mind and never left the memories of her heart. She was not expecting for them to settle down together or anything. She just thought that one day she would be able to see him again even if it meant that she had to travel to the other side of the coast where he was now residing or even just to talk to him but at this point, it did not look like that would be happening.

Ziariah had turned a year now. She had adjusted well to the daycare and Love' loved it, because Ziariah loved it. It made Love' feel all the more at peace with her decision. Love' only had a total of three semester's left before she graduated. When Love' was attending DSU her major was Elementary Education. When she transferred her major became Interdisciplinary Studies. She did not want to switch her major but she did not want to be in school for another three years due to a lot of credits not transferring. She had already been in school for four years. Love' was ready to be finished so she could pursue other things. She wanted to move out of her parents' home and start a new life for her and Ziariah. As time went on she and Marquis knew that they still had feelings for one another but Love' just couldn't see how it would work. He called often and they remained friends the first few years of Ziariah's life.

Love' was still facing the reality that she was parenting by herself. Marquis wanted to be in Ziariah's life but he wanted

Love' to move back to Delaware. Love' did not think that it would be wise to do so at that time. She really had no desire to move back. As time went on she often contemplated the idea but that was as far as it went. Love' had known even before they conceived Ziariah that she could no longer be upset with Marquis for being who he was. She had to examine herself. He had not really changed. The characteristics that Love' was recognizing were present for quite some time but they were magnified when she and Marquis conceived Ziariah. In fact, the dysfunctional behavior that she and Marquis often displayed was magnified.

The dysfunction was yelling because it wanted to be released. She finally accepted that what she had dealt with within their relationship had nothing to do with Marquis and everything to do with herself and what she believed about her own self-worth.

Around the Fall of 2011 Williams adopted son returned from prison. He came to stay for a while, and all of their lives completely changed forever. Love' was living in Chesapeake with her mom and Williams. Love's brother Ron Jr, his wife and two daughters were still living right across the street.

Everyone was very happy to see D. Everyone had high hopes for him. He was and still is very intelligent, gifted and posses unlimited potential as most of the inmates in prison do. For a long time Love' would wonder what happened to him; specifically, as a child. She remembered hearing stories of his upbringing and things about his biological parents. Love' would often think about how unusual D and Williams relationship was. She could never understand the anger they had towards each other but yet they always seem to want to reconnect. Love' noticed the same pattern between the both of them every time he came back into their lives. The reunion would be great. Then Williams would become so agitated for no reason and instigate an argument between he and D. D would become angry and say that he needed to get out of here and then end up doing something illegal to end up right back in trouble again.

As I stated previously, I remember Love' telling me how she remembered when Rayanna and Williams were getting married and how D and one of Williams brothers who were supposed to be there in the wedding decided to go smoke crack that day. Rayanna accused D of stealing her wedding band that she had when she was married to Ron. Rayanna knew that he had taken it but he of course denied it. Williams use to speak on D's anger issues often. He use to speak on D's rough upbringing. Things never made sense to Love'. D had been married before and had actually just divorced when Rayanna and her children had moved into Williams home back in Lynchburg, Va in 91'. D had one daughter at the time. She was the flower girl in Rayanna and Williams wedding. He later went on to have another daughter with the love of his life. Things really were not adding up but later on it would all really make a lot of sense.

When D had gotten out he decided this time that he was enrolling in community college. He was on parole so he had to live at the address in Chesapeake during his probationary period because this was his agreement already established with the probation officer and courts. They were all beginning to believe that he was really changing this time. He seemed to be focused and everyone was really hopeful. Love' and her brothers did not like how D always seemed to kiss Williams ass. They did not understand the dynamics in regards to their relationship. D would go above and beyond for Williams approval. He really considered Williams and Rayanna his dad and mom. He knew his mom and was very much in touch with his biological mom but he considered Williams and Rayanna his parents also and Love' and her brothers as his siblings. He loved them as best as he could.

The holidays came around it was November 2011. Williams birthday was on November 28, so Thanksgiving was always two celebrations in one. Williams would make the best yeast rolls ever!!! Everything would be delicious. A few days after the family gathering celebration D and Williams had gotten into a disagreement and again it was over nothing. The disagreement really did not make sense. Williams wanted D to wash a pan out for him that was in the sink. Love' had been home with Ziariah all day but for some reason, he wanted to pick on D.

D had been spending a lot of time over Ron Jr's house. Love' and Ron Jr.'s younger brother' Malik was visiting for a little over a week for the holiday. Love' and her brothers didn't think that Williams wanted D spending so much time with Ron and Malik. Williams of course would never tell them that. Anyway, D told Williams that he would wash it a little later because he had just gotten in. At the time D was in his forties. The way Williams was acting towards D you would have thought D just cussed him out. It was all about not having that control. He wanted to make sure he still had it. This is what Williams tried to have with all four of them, Love', Ron Jr., Malik and D. It didn't work as long on Love' and her siblings. You see growing up, Love' felt as though she had to be the protector for some reason. Her mom began to become too laid back and passive. She allowed Williams to make all of the decisions even when she and her brothers knew that she was not in agreement with his decisions. Love' spoke her mind about everything when it pertained to her brothers and her mom but specifically her brothers. There were so many manipulative mind games that Williams played with them. Williams would use "God" a lot to get what he wanted out of his wife and her children. There were times when Williams would either work late or maybe go out of town. Whenever the family, including Rayanna, heard his vehicle drive up on the gravel in the driveway, everyone would take off running. Scattering away like little mice. They did not like being around his energy. He tried to control everyone. And now years later he was still trying to control them. D ended going upstairs to his room and asked Love' to come in his room so that they could discuss what just happened. That night D decided to go to the store and get something to drink. Malik and Ron Jr. drove him to the store. Little did they know he was stealing the drinks. They were angry with him that he would not only take the chance on them being in trouble or an accessory but that he would most certainly be violating probation but D was a hurting boy on the inside and it was obvious to his siblings.

The next day he and Williams were still not getting along. D began feeling uncomfortable and was ready to go back to Lynchburg but that would also be violating his parole and or probation agreement. Love' nor her brothers thought that was a good idea because every time he would move back to the "Burg" he'd find himself connecting with the same people and end up right back in prison. There was one time that D had come to stay with Williams and Rayanna from 2004 - 2005. Malik and Love' were taking D's youngest daughter back to Lynchburg. He had a second child born in 97'. His eldest was the child who was in Williams and Rayanna's wedding.

At this time Williams and Rayanna were living in Suffolk, Virginia. While in Suffolk D would periodically ask Malik if he could drive his car just to run to the store real quick and D would always bring it back intact. What Love' and her brothers had to realize was that while they had a challenging upbringing there were people who felt they had to constantly scheme to get what they could get out of people. D had obviously been planning this for a while and he had the perfect set up to do it. D's youngest daughter had come to visit Rayanna and Williams in the summer and it was time for her to return to the Burg so Love', Malik and D rode to Lynchburg to take her back to her mom and stepdad's home. When they arrived they dropped off Nyah, D's youngest child. D did not really know his youngest due to the fact he was spending so much time locked up. D then asked if he could take the car to go visit his boy real quick and he would just drop Love' and Malik off at their uncle's house (one of Williams' brothers). They waited over there and waited and waited. They ended up spending the night. They were calling and calling D's cell phone so much so that by this time he had turned his phone off. Malik had no way to get in touch with him. Love' was angry because she didn't understand why Malik was letting him drive it in the first place with no license. Love' and Malik had to go downtown and file a police report. They had to get their cousin to drive three in a half hours back to Suffolk to drop them off. after returning to Suffolk, Malik received a phone call from Lynchburg city police telling him that they have the car at the impound and he would have to pay over three hundred dollars to get it out. Malik was furious. All of this happened so that D could get crack. D was hurting and so he didn't care who he hurt in the process. It all made sense to them now. He had to ask Malik periodically to use the car to gain his trust so that there would be no hesitancy from Malik when D would ask him in the Burg.

Anyway, all of that took place during '04 - '05 regarding D stealing Malik's car. Years later in 2011 after he had stolen the wine from the store D shared something with Love' that she had been knowing all along but it would be affirmed.

D: Sis, what I am about to tell you, you can not repeat this and tell anyone especially mom.

Love': Ok, I'm not.

D: When I was younger, around 9 or 10, Dad tried to get me to masturbate him. He also did a few other things and allowed one of his brothers to suck me off. This was my first orgasm.

Love': I knew it.

D: How?

Love': I just did. I paid attention to the both of you and how your relationship was and it was strange and a dysfunctional pattern. I remember growing up wondering if someone had molested him as well. Of course, I put it out of my mind but deep down I've always known.

D: Wow! Well, yeah. Don't say anything to anyone, not even Mom. I only told you and my little brothers because I felt like you all had the right to know, especially since you all have children. I do not believe he would ever do anything to the girls (Ron Jr.'s girls and Ziariah). Nonetheless, I feel you all have the right to know. I am tired of him playing the role of perfect.

Love': So what if he is still doing it now? He is a teacher, you know. Oh my Ancestors!!!

The police became involved not much longer after D had told his siblings and the siblings had convinced him to tell their mom. Rayanna was hurt needless to say. D and Williams conversed about the subject prior to police involvement but there was no remorse. The police became involved and showed up at Williams job. They took him in for questioning and he admitted to doing sexual acts to several boys.

Everyone was angry, embarrassed and some were confused but most importantly everything began to make sense about how controlling he was, deceitful, and manipulative but yet Love' manage to see a hurting little boy that had been hurting for so long he knew how to mask it.

Williams was arrested and once he admitted to these acts he never came back home again. That night the police had to rush him to the hospital. He was overweight and had health challenges for a while. His blood pressure skyrocketed. He was taking medication for diabetes and he had not taken any while in jail. Love' and Rayanna rushed to the hospital as soon as they heard he was there. As soon as Rayanna got there he and Rayanna hugged and wept. Love' waited a while and gave them a moment and then she went into the room and hugged him and wept. Williams was a shame. He kept apologizing. He also was dealing with prostate cancer but he had been fine for almost twenty years and the doctors couldn't understand it but things would soon change for him and for all of them.

He was the sole provider for the condo Rayanna, Love' and Ziariah were living in. They would soon be moving. Apparently, Williams was behind on the rent so in the midst of all that was going on Rayanna, Love' and Ziariah would have thirty days to vacate the premises. Neither one of them were making enough to cover the rent. Rayanna asked her church for assistance in the moving and not only would no one help, but Rayanna's pastor was rude and showed no compassion and told Rayanna she should not leave her husband. He told Rayanna that she should stand by him especially during this dark time he would be facing. Rayanna and Williams were no longer pastoring their church they started backing '02. The church had changed so much, no anointing, no sincerity, so plastic and many people left. It was what Love' had told Williams years prior that actually manifested, "If your family and house isn't right then how do you expect to lead a church?"

Malik had come down to assist in the move along with Ron Jr., who still lived across the street. Love' and Malik became very angry towards Rayanna and Williams church, the church that Rayanna and Williams were members of. It was during this time that Rayanna and Williams were sitting down as pastors and only bore the title. The pastors of the church they claimed as their own in which Love' despised acted as though Rayanna had done something wrong. Malik began breaking things that belonged to Williams. Malik began cursing and really wanted to go to the church just as well as Love' did just to curse some people out. They could not believe how insensitive a person could be during this time. Never mind the humiliation Rayanna must have felt or the anger she felt towards herself. I was very sure that Rayanna must have had several questions, the main one being, "Did he ever do anything to my boys?" Rayanna could not get that question out of her mind.

Malik stayed and helped Love' and Rayanna with the move. Ron Jr. would come over to help as well. No one else helped them move with the exception of one couple who were former members of Rayanna and Williams church they pastored a few years back. They were there supportive throughout the ordeal. For the most part it was Love' and Rayanna packing up and mainly Rayanna because Love' was still trying to graduate and take care of her daughter.

Once Williams was sentenced to 10 years and would continue being on house arrest, he asked permission if he could go to Love's graduation. Whomever Williams asked granted him permission to attend. He would not be able to get out of his van. He was staying with a former church member who had no children. He was no longer allowed to be around children.

D tried to give him advice on what to say while in court so that he would have a lesser sentence but he chose to listen to his lawyer instead and recanted his admittance which was an unintelligent move on the lawyer's part. He showed no remorse in court and D told him you must show remorse and let them know you haven't done anything since that time which was over thirty years ago according to Williams but did D really know that for sure that he had not done anything since that time? In fact, the reason he told his siblings was that he saw Williams hanging out with a young boy that was a student of William's from the high school that William taught in. This young boy had spent that Sunday in church with Williams, Rayanna and D. The boy had gone out to eat with them after church. This sparked all of the memories that D had regarding what happened to him as a child. He began wondering along with Love', Malik, Ron Jr. and Ron Jr.'s wife if he was still doing it? At this point, no one really knew but no one wanted to take the chance on it still happening. Everyone was thinking that something would happen sooner or later and that everyone would wake up from this dream.

Love' was graduating in another 2-3 weeks and she had been conversing with Amir and so he was planning to come for a visit and attend her graduation. She was so excited even though a part of her did not believe him because he had been saying that he was coming for a visit and would never show up. This was not like him but he started to do this more often than not. When he would do this it would hurt Love' but she would always pretend that it didn't bother her and that it was no big deal. No matter what they always managed to keep in touch with each other.

Love' was excited to be finally graduating. Her long time friend and one of Ziairah's godmoms, Tina was coming and bringing her two girls. By this time Love and Rayanna had moved into an apartment. A two bedroom apartment. They were living in Portsmouth. It was definitely a downsize but it was a decent apartment complex area to live in.

It was finally the week of graduation and she hadn't heard from Amir. She was beginning to feel that she was about to be disappointed again. She nervously contacted him and he told her that his friend's mom died. She felt bad for his friend but selfishly she wanted him to be at her graduation. Love' asked him who's mom and he told her who it was but she thought she remembered this friend's mom had already passed. So when she talked to Tina and told Tina who he was referring to she told Love', "Girl, that boy's mom passed years ago." Love' was hurt even more she could not understand why he felt the need to lie. If he didn't want to come all he had to do was say that or just tell her he couldn't make it. She knew there had to be a reason why he told her that and she knew she would eventually find out. She decided to tell him, "That is not the reason you aren't coming." He told her the reason was that he had a baby on the way. Love' could not believe it. Not much longer he had another baby on the way by someone else.

Anyway, Love' was still excited to be graduating and starting a new life for her and Ziariah.

Graduation day had arrived and a few of her family members had come from out of town. While she was sitting there waiting for her name to be called, so many things were going through her mind. She really doesn't remember what the speaker was even talking about. She was hot, hungry and tired. She began thinking how stupid college actually was. Thoughts flowing through her mind, such as:

1. So, now I owe all of this money for a job that will never be able to pay me in a year, what I have accumulated in loans.

2. What I really want to do does not even require that I have a degree.

3. Why does school cost so much when it's supposed to help the economy?

4. Who's idea was it to charge people for education?

5. What was their motive in overcharging?

6. I should be guaranteed a job once I graduate.

7. So, I have to have experience in my field but I just graduated so I don't have experience in my field.

8. I must give back to my community in some way with this degree I earned and work with youth.

Love' had several more thoughts but the one that she slightly entertained was that she may not even be able to find a job with the salary she would like to have. She would soon experience just that and some.

When they called Love's name, it was surreal for her because she knew that she had done something that she was told by a high school counselor in Lynchburg at E.C. Glass that she could never do which was, go to college and graduate with honors. After they called her name and she walked across the stage, she sat back down and began to feel nervous and then the thought came, "That's it, what do I do now?" Love' really had no direction. She thought she would teach but she had to take a few more test in order to teach in the state of Virginia. Now, some school system's will allow you teach under the guidelines that you will in fact be working towards taking the required test as well as meeting specific requirements, certification and or licensing mandated by that particular school system within that state.

Love' was just trying to find work and she could not find work for months after she graduated . The gathering of her close friends and family was great but when everyone left, real life began. She finally went on a few job interviews. Neither of the jobs were remotely anything that she wanted to do but she knew she needed something coming in so she began working for a senior home care facility while still working her part time job in a church nursery. Love' began to feel hopeless. She and her mom along with Ziariah moved into an apartment in a decent neighborhood but they were struggling to make ends meet. They just were not making enough. They were about to be evicted. Love' knew that they could not afford the rent but they were in a desperate situation at that time and Rayanna nor Love' did not know what to do. So when they were approved to move in, they moved in. Love' was definitely not making enough money to move out. They did not want to but they would be moving before the lease was up. They just moved into the place less than 6 months ago and would be packing up to move back to Delaware.

Love' was ready to move and so was Rayanna. They had gone through so much after everything had come out regarding Williams. Rayanna was devastated, hurt and angry. She thought she needed to get away. It was not easy leaving but Rayanna had been there for Williams court proceedings along with Love'. Now Williams was in jail and being sent to prison. He had gone to trial and the jury deliberated for less than twenty minutes before determining that he was guilty of performing indecent acts with a minor. He had admitted to doing things with at least 11 other boys. Because D had been in and out of the system, D shared with Rayanna on how he could avoid possibly jail time but he chose to listen to his public defender who according to others was a moron. Love' was angry as well once it became real to her and it wasn't a dream. She loved Williams because she always knew he was a hurting soul but she was angry as well. She was angry for what he had done to d and the other boys. She was angry for what was done to him. she was angry because he was where he was. Love' did not know how to cope with that reality nor did Ziariah because she was at the age where she knew and remembered who Papa was and all of a sudden he had vanished.

Williams had written a letter to Love' during this time. Rayanna was so angry that she told him what Love' had told her about how she did not want to have anything to do with him. So he wrote Love' explaining how he was very sorry and how he was believing and trusting God that he would be leaving there soon. He also explained how he did not care what Love' and her brothers said or felt that he knew in his heart that they were his children. Williams also would send birthday cards for Ziariah. Before Williams was sent to prison Love' and Williams began to develop a pretty pleasant relationship. It was still obvious that he would only allow others to only get but so close but Love' knew that deep down he loved her. She knew that he was a hurting soul. She loved him and was empathetic towards him but still angry. Meanwhile, Love' and Rayanna were facing their own set of challenges.

When Rayanna, Love' and Ziariah arrived in Delaware, they stayed in separate locations. Love' and Ziariah lived with Ron. Rayanna lived with a close friend and her family. This became a major adjustment for them all, especially Ziariah. She did not understand what in the world was going on and why Rayanna was not living with her and Love' anymore. This living arrangement lasted for about five months until Rayanna and her close friend felt that it was best that she left. Rayanna then stayed with one of her brothers until she was no longer welcomed there, which only lasted about a month and then stayed with Ron, Love' and Ziariah. Ron did not want Rayanna to sleep in her car so he offered for her to stay in the guest bedroom temporarily. This lasted for about two weeks and then Ron began asking what the plan was. Love' had not found work. She was applying to 12 jobs a day. She was receiving assistance and in a program called the View Program. This program assisted with childcare while you seek for employment. Love' could not believe that she was in the situation she was in and became very angry towards herself. She tried to have hope and or faith but it was definitely a challenge to do so.

Ron gave Love' and Rayanna a deadline to be out and they took heed and found a place that once again they could not afford. Love' told Rayanna that they would not be able to afford the place but Rayanna was so tired of being in the situation she was in so she decided to take the apartment. Love' and Rayanna stayed there for not quite six months before they were evicted and homeless. Love' asked Ron if they could come back, and he told her no. They ended up living in a hotel for a month which was one of the most humbling experiences. Love' began to reflect on her life. She began to ask herself questions. She wanted to know why couldn't she just land the jobs that others seem to land when they graduate from college? Why couldn't she just have a decent, modest income? Why was she constantly going through these things when she was trying? She simply did not understand why. She finally had an awesome interview for an organization with a decent salary that she was actually hired for in Philadelphia but she needed transportation for that particular position and her car was not legal because of its expired tags and owed property tax. The car needed some minor work done as well as car insurance that had to be verified by the organization by start date. She ended up having to decline the offer and she was devastated. Love' and Rayanna ended up living in a hotel for close to two months along with Ziariah and this broke Love's heart.

Chapter 14

During this time Love' was communicating with Amir a little. She felt a connection to him and they seem to always be there for each other in some way.

Love' never thought she would end up homeless again and especially while being a mother with a Bachelor of Science degree. When Love's longtime sister/friend/cousin heard of her staying in a hotel, she offered for she and Ziariah to come stay with her until she figured out her next move. Love's friend who was more like a play cousin was married with a daughter of her own who was around nine years old and their pit (puppy). They lived in a three bedroom townhouse. Love' and Ziariah slept in Unique's daughter's room. Rayanna was staying with another brother of hers. Love' was constantly thinking of how she was going to get out of this situation until one day the thought came to her to move back to Lynchburg. She spoke with her friend and Ziariah's Godmom, Tina, who offered for her and Ziariah to come stay with her and her two girls temporarily. Love' immediately shut it down but this idea kept ringing in the back of her subconscious. Love' realized a few days later that it was what she was to do. She did not know how she would get there, because her vehicle was still not legal to drive. Virginia does not play when it pertains to tags being expired. So Love' spoke with her dad, Ron and asked if he could help to get them there. Meanwhile, she decided to mention it to her mom. When Love' told Rayanna, she said, "The devil is a lie. I am not going back there." Love' asked her, "Why not? What else is there to do? It just makes sense. The cost of living is cheaper there. I am sure we both would find work, besides you know plenty of people there that I am sure would be willing to help you." Rayanna told Love' that she had to pray about it but Love' did not want to hear anything about praying about anything at this point.

Love' had been attending a gathering that took place on Sunday's known as The House of Re-Awakening Minds (The House of R.A.M.S). Love' loved attending. It was an African-centered place of learning, healing and raising the consciousness and or awareness. They would sing and sometimes dance but most of all honor our ancestors through learning, sharing and studying. There were many people who were of different beliefs or practices attending. The owner of the building was formerly known as a pastor. She is a beautiful person and or soul. Anyway, so Love' did not understand what there was to pray about other than she knew her mom was hoping that the little still voice would tell her to do the opposite of relocating. Rayanna was staying with one of her brothers in Middletown while Love' and Ziariah were in Newark, Delaware with Unique. Rayanna sooner than later realized that she was to move to Lynchburg as well. Rayanna was concerned because she had no idea where she would live. Rayanna's SUV had been repoed during this time as well.

Rayanna decided to call one of her friends who lived in the 'Burg' who she also went to college with. Rayanna explained to her the situation and then Donna offered for her to come stay with her for as long as she needed to. So Rayanna and Love' along with Ziariah were on their way to return to Lynchburg after sixteen years or more of being away from the 'Burg'. It would be two weeks after their decision to return before they actually returned back to the "Burg" (Lynchburg).

Love' told Amir since he still lived there and he couldn't believe it. She didn't want him to think that she was expecting anything from him but he told her that when she got there to let him know because he wanted to hang out. You see a year after Love' had Ziariah, Amir had a son and had gotten someone pregnant right after his son was born. This completely changed the dynamics between Love' and Amir for a moment.

Love' was so excited. For some reason she had expectations of something manifesting while living in the "Burg"; she just did not know what it was. Love' did not expect to make it her permanent place of residence but she definitely felt as though it was where she was supposed to be at that time on her journey. Rayanna was not expecting much initially but once they arrived, things began to happen for Rayanna. She found a decent job and she found a new church home. Love's situation was a little more complicated. She stayed with her friend Tina for about three months. When Love' first arrived she got in touch with her friend Amir and he told her that he would be coming to pick her up to take she and Ziariah out to the park on a Friday. Friday came and left. Saturday came and left. Weeks came and left. She texted him and received no response. She did not understand why. He had disappointed her before but she could not believe he would do this again. When a month had passed and still no response, she decided to block him from her social media page and delete his phone number from out of her phone. She wanted to have nothing to do with him; well at least not for a whole year. Love' would later find out that he had also had two more children on the way, a set of twins and he was going through it but Love' thought that they were close enough for him to feel comfortable to share that information with her. She felt he did not have to stand her up or avoid her but that's what he did.

After three months of living with her friend Tina, Love' moved in with her aunt Kimmie which was Williams brother's ex-wife. She was still having a challenging time finding work. She seemed to be overqualified for some jobs and have not enough experience for other jobs. She wanted to find a job that would afford her the opportunity to move out of her current living situation on the other hand she wanted to be a stay at home mom and homeschool her daughter because most of the childcare facilities were religious based. Love' did not like that and did not want to indoctrinate Ziariah and because she had no job she could not afford some of the better options. She began to feel more stuck than what she felt back at home. She began to ask herself questions about what she was doing and why things were not happening for her the way they seem to happen for others. She knew she was talented, intelligent, and eager to learn and or work but things were not going as she had initially thought they would. Eventually, for convenience, Rayanna moved in with Love's aunt Kimmie as well. While living with family they had the opportunity to go and visit Williams. Love' was a little apprehensive. She could not see herself exposing Ziariah to seeing her Papa behind bars. So the first time that Rayanna went, Love' did not go. On the third visit Love' went and things had definitely taken a turn. Ziariah stayed with a family member, D's youngest daughter, Nyah and her mom Laylah who later became Ziariahs other Godmom.

Williams was very ill and when you are in prison you are definitely not getting the best care. He had been diagnosed with prostate cancer but had shown no signs and looked as though he was healed; however, as soon as he was incarcerated he began to decline quickly. Love' firmly believed that the infirmary treats inmates as guinea pigs and or lab rats testing all kinds of drugs on the inmates. Rayanna was told that they were administering chemo via needle treatment. Love' went to the infirmary with her mom and uncle (Williams brother) and he was on some drug that had him completely not functioning. He had a mild stroke but was definitely able to communicate during the visit that Rayanna made two weeks prior. He was not coherent during the visit when Love' was there. His eyes were glazed and he was making sounds and or grunts. This grieved Love' to see him in this state. He was always a heavy man (overweight) but he had lost a considerable amount of weight. Rayanna prayed with him. His brother prayed with him. Love' told him she loved

246

him and that she would be sending love and positive energy his way and then she kissed his cheek before saying see you later. While that was a lot to deal with Rayanna and Love' still had other things to handle. Williams was about two to two and a half hours away so Rayanna was definitely planning to visit again even if she had to rent a vehicle. Love' and Rayanna had lived at her aunts for about four or five months. Rayanna had desperately looked for a place and she spoke to a few of her co-workers and they put her in contact with someone who was wanting to rent out her home. The woman would eventually be willing to sale. Rayanna decided to be completely honest about her situation. Rayanna and Mrs. Lee connected instantly and she agreed to allow her to move in. Rayanna wanted Love and Ziariah to see the house. Rayanna and Ziariah began to feel excited but Love' began to feel nervous. She was hoping that they did not have a repeat and be evicted again. Love' was determined to find work to help her mom. They moved in August of 2014.

A few months later Rayanna would go back alone for a visit to see Williams. Love' asked Rayanna to relay a message and she did. She told Rayanna to tell Williams that she loved him.

When Rayanna saw him he had lost more weight. His eyes were protruding. He was in a wheelchair due to his muscles being so weak. After that visit Williams wrote Rayanna a letter which was in the month of November of 2014, well; I should say someone wrote the letter for him. He could no longer write. The muscles in his fingers were no longer strong enough. He wrote one word by himself just to show how he could not write and that one word was, "Help." Love' pointed out to Rayanna how symbolic him choosing to write the word help was. Rayanna and Williams family requested for clemency and it was not approved. Rayanna felt so many things during this time and Love' was trying to figure out what her next step should be in the midst of everything.

Love' did not have access to the internet at home so she would go to a local bookstore or anywhere they had free Wi-fi. She began to feel so discouraged and hopeless after filling out application after application having a few interviews but nothing working out. She did not understand why. She had been accepted into the honors society at Norfolk State University. She graduated with honors and to her, it was all for nothing. As time went on she began to really dig deep and search within herself. She began to ask herself what she was supposed to be doing with her life. She had many passions but again, no direction. She wanted her own school, she wanted to teach children but not in a public school setting. She wanted to give back to her community in some way. She wanted her own businesses. She was so tired of running from herself. She also wanted to become a full-time author. She wanted to create music, she entertained the idea of going back to school to obtain her

Master's degree but anyway that list went on and on and on for Love'.

When December came around Love' began to develop a habit of not going to sleep. She would be up thinking about Williams. She felt sad for him. She felt helpless. One night she felt a sense of urgency to write him and she wrote three letters that night to send off in the morning. She was not able to get to the post office in time for a few stamps. The following morning Rayanna's phone rang and it was Williams brother and sister on the phone and they told Rayanna that Williams transitioned at 10:37 a.m. on December 22, 2014. Love' ran out of her bedroom because she heard Rayanna screaming on the phone. Love' knew what it was about and began to weep and then Ziariah began to weep. Rayanna kept repeating while stretched out on the couch, "I don't understand, I don't understand, I don't understand I prayed, Why, Why, Why???" All Love' could think about was the letters she had written but never got a chance to send them off. Love' called her brothers Malik who was living in NewJersey at the time and Ron who was living in North Carolina now with his wife and two daughters. They would definitely be coming to support Rayanna. The pressure became even more real for Rayanna because she knew some of Williams family would not understand why she was making the decisions she would have to make in regards to the service and or arrangements for Williams. She decided on a memorial service in Lynchburg. A lot of his family was not in agreement with this. She had to do what was best financially. In fact, he told Rayanna and his brother about a dream he had regarding his funeral when he was incarcerated and he stated that it was in Lynchburg at one of the bigger churches in the area.

Services took place at his brother's church and it was a beautiful service/ceremony even though the reason why he was incarcerated in the first place was horrible. Malik was not able to attend. Although he tried, things just did not go as planned. Ron Jr. did attend and shared a few words and so did (D's eldest daughter) Melissa and Nyah (his youngest) who were two of Williams five grandchildren. I remember when Love' spoke and the words she shared because she told Rayanna that she was going to be honest about everything. She said, "Daddy and I did not always get along. We bumped heads a lot but over time things began to change. If it wasn't for him I don't know what I would have done after I had gotten pregnant with my daughter. He allowed me to live with him and my mom just so I could finish school after transferring from another school. He allowed me to stay there without paying any rent just so I could focus on school and graduate. He supported me and my daughter. Williams was used to show me how to forgive and to show what unconditional love truly is and I am thankful." Rayanna shared a few words I don't really remember all that she said but she finished with a big bang. She sang a song that the two of them were known to sing together, entitled, "Great is Thy Faithfulness". Everyone was in tears as well as speechless. Rayanna looked like a queen, she was dressed in a beautiful red and gold A-line dress with a head wrap. There were many people there. It was tough because he had impacted many lives in so many ways, good and bad. A shift definitely took place after his transition.

A few close friends and family came over to the home and they had a wonderful time. They laughed and sang. After the weekend Rayanna went back to work. She was trying to be strong but honestly needed time to cope with the reality. Rayanna told Love' it's not so much that he passed it is where and how he passed that hurt more than anything. One night, Rayanna was sitting in the living room and cried out saying, "If I could just have one more time of you holding me, if I could just have one more time of feeling your arms around me." Later on that night she was in her bed and felt a presence get in the bed with her. She literally felt the bed move as if someone had pressed down on the bed and laid beside her. Rayanna jumped up so fast and ran out of her bedroom and ran into the living room with her eyes a bright as the moon. Love' looked at her mom and said, "What?" Rayanna told her what just happened and then Love' told her what had happened to her a few days prior. Love' kept seeing light flashing in her bedroom like orbs. Love' also felt a presence in the room. She also had a few dreams with messages from Williams. Love' would often time feel his presence in the kitchen which was funny due to the fact that he loved food. As time continued on Love' no longer felt the presence as often anymore but sometimes she did and definitely he would still send messages in her dreams. One of the dreams she had was Williams telling her that whenever she would start dating that he would be there with her because there would be things that he would be able to see that she would not be able to see.

Things were becoming a little easier for Love'. She really began reflecting via meditation and exercise. She really began remembering the people she met throughout her journey. She was really focusing on herself, loving her and loving her daughter. Marquis (Ziariah's father) was doing a lot of the blame game. He was angry with Love' but Love' wanted to be friends with Marquis at the bare minimum. It was so important to Love' for Ziariah to always know that she was created by love. Love' and Marquis knew that they would always love each other but it would no longer be able to go back to anything other than them realizing that they were Ziariah's parents.

Around the time that Williams transitioned Amir had reached out to Love's friend, Tina so that she could relay a message to Love' regarding Williams. Amir just wanted Love' to know that he was sorry to hear of his passing. Love' had blocked him from her social media site so he had to relay the message to Tina. Love' decided to contact him on the social media site. She told Amir thank you. Amir began to converse with Love' asking her how she was doing. He then began to apologize and told her how f'd up it was what he had done to her. He wanted to make it up to her. Love' of course forgave him and they were communicating again. Initially, the communication was not so frequent. Love' forgave him but there was a part of her that was just tired of their tango dance. She knew that there would always be a connection but Amir had so much going on and he was always reeling her in and then pushing her away. She was focusing on herself and just wanted to do that for the moment.

She began to reflect and heard these words, "She was a liar, because she told herself over and over and over and over again that she wasn't pretty enough, not good enough, she wasn't worthy not even smart enough but she had not realized she was breaking her own heart. She would grab the popcorn and entertain those thoughts; every thought, thoughts that weren't true until she later realized she was in control of what she knows and what she lets go. She became the truth to herself seeing her worth, honoring her, she was accepting her part; her role to grow was in all she knows; the power of what she thought was in what she knows; she began to tell herself the truth that she was more than physical. She was timeless in all, abundantly magical because she attracted what she thought. How she felt was hidden, the lies and now she realized she was the truth because it was there all along, it was there deep inside."

She realized that she had been living a lie. She had doubted herself for so long due to the physical realm which was based on illusions. She began to see that when you based life on the aspect of who you truly are, life begins to reveal itself in abundance and manifest. Love' spent time on a social media site that really assisted her on her journey with making sense of her spiritual path. She began to attract those who had already been where she was on her journey. She was receiving the answer before the question. In other words, she would receive a message and wonder why she heard what she heard or felt how she felt to only find out in due time.

Love' knew that she was a late bloomer according to society. The things that some youth experienced during their teenage years she experienced during her twenties and thirties. She firmly felt the reason was because growing up she was sheltered in many ways. She learned one of the most important things you can give your seed is communication. Speak to your children about your experiences, answer their questions, honestly. She knew that she was carrying the burdens and memories of her forefathers and foremothers. Love' knew from an early age that life was much more than what she had been taught in church. She spent many moments in deep focus. She was always pondering on life, waiting quietly as she listened for the still voice to speak. Love' told me how from the time she was involved in her first relationship with Amir, that she heard 'let him go', although the voice told her she and Amir would 'reunite again'. This happen when Love' was around 17 or 18 years old when she heard what she referred to at that time in her life as the 'Holy Spirit' say, "let "him go" from that point on that voice would speak to her whenever she was involved either in an unhealthy situation or before it even became an unhealthy relationship. Love' heard this voice guide her but she did not always agree with that voice. As a result, she gained lessons that she later became so thankful for because she had experience and if for some reason her child(ren) ever decided to make some of the same choices she would be able to offer guidance, love and understanding without judgment. She knew she would always remember.

Love' no longer referred to the voice of the Holy Spirit although it was just that to her that voice was known as the higher self/ spirit; it was and still is righteous. She was a part of the source. She realized there was no separation between her and the source. Love' was thankful to have such a strong sense of her spiritual walk. She learned a lot from her mom, Rayanna. While she was ever grateful for internal guidance she did not always take heed to the messages relayed and she longed for the day she would meet someone where she did not hear, "Let him go." It happened with one person years ago. She wondered how he felt or if he wondered about her and remembered their connection or if it was simply a figment of her imagination. She knew she would always have a bond with Amir and yet what she had with Amir was different from what she thought she shared with Mozique. She truly wanted to be able to give her daughter the experience of having a family, a man and woman. She wanted Ziariah to see a man loving her mommy and treating her as a goddess but what Love' was beginning to realize more importantly was that Ziariah needed to see her mommy loving herself as the goddess that she is. This still did not take the thoughts away that would come to Love' regarding the special connection she thought she once shared with Mozique years ago.

Love' became very focused on meditation and unblocking her chakras. She began to see that this was one way to heighten her magnetism. She also began taking the time to focus on her goals, physically, nutritionally, mentally, financially, and unleashing her unlimited potential. She decided she was no longer going to let fear hinder her and she would pursue things that she knew would strengthen her, nurture her and leave a legacy for future generations.

Ziariah was now turning five years old and Love' was really trying to avoid sending Ziariah to school. She truly wanted Ziariah to experience attending an African-centered school where you learned from the African American perspective but there weren't any where they were located. Love' had the experience of being exposed to one back home in Delaware and she saw the benefits. Believe it or not, there were students there attending who were not of African descent. Love' really wanted to have her own school just so Ziariah could attend it. Love' also knew she needed to make money. She still wasn't certain about how just yet.

Chapter 15

Love' and Amir had been in contact a little more frequently than they had been. Most of their interaction were mainly on social media, text and some calls. Amir asked if he and Love' could meet up at one of the local parks and walk the trail. Love' agreed to this, considering she lived so close to the park and the fact that she had been going regularly for exercise. Amir picked Love' up at her house. When they saw each other they did not greet each other with a hug. They greeted each other with smiles. When they pulled up to the park Amir parked in a particular parking space and chuckled. Love' asked him why he was laughing and he told her no reason. Love' knew there was a reason he chuckled. They walked and chatted. It was a nice little visit. As they were headed back to the car after walking the trail. Love' received a phone call from her mom. Her mom told her that she and Ziariah were there at the park on the playground. As soon as Ziariah saw her mommy she ran up to her saying, (with a hug) "Mommy, Mommy!" Love' was a little concern because Ziariah had never met any male friends of Love's in the four in a half years to five years that Ziariah had been on earth. Amir and Rayanna greeted each other. Rayanna and Williams always loved Amir. Rayanna, Amir and Love' watched Ziairah play for a little while. Amir kept saying how smart Ziariah was. They stayed about fifteen to twenty minutes before leaving the park and going there separate ways. Later on that evening Rayanna told Love' that she still saw a connection between her and Amir. Rayanna told Love' that, "he still likes you and still wonders about you and him settling down and how different it may have been if the both of you had made other choices." Love' felt that her mom was a little off. She felt her mom was right about their still being a connection but the latter Love' simply did not believe it.

Eventually, she and Amir began to converse a little more via phone calls. Love' was really trying to understand why they had this connection. It was felt even when they conversed on the phone. You could hear the smiles through the phone. Love' asked Amir one time before, what and why did he think the connection was still there and he responded by saying, "because we still love each other and we will always love each other." Now, Love' of course knew that but she wondered if they were twin flames or soul-mates. Amir told her that they were probably soul-mates. He did not know what a twin flame was. Love' already knew that just because you're soulmates does not mean you are meant to be together. A soul mate to Love' was someone who came into your life to connect with you on a soul level and usually shakes things up a bit in your life to ignite growth. They often times will touch your heart in a way that is just unmatched unless talking about the twin flame. The twin flame is supposedly the other half of your soul. As you work on your personal journey to become balance within yourself you will naturally attract your twin flame often times. The connection is instant and intense. There is only supposedly one twin flame, while one can have many soul mates. Soul mates come from the same soul group liken to a family tree with many branches on the tree but the twin flame is likened to an apple cut in half. They are the same at the core. Sometimes the twin flame does not incarnate on earth with their twin flame at the same time. Anyway, Love' just wanted to understand their connection and she would soon find out what the connection was. She remembered when they first broke up over twenty years ago, that she heard, "let him go" but that they would one day reunite again. This always stayed with her in the back of her mind. Love' wondered if that was just her carnal desires or emotional attachment desires taking precedence. For twenty plus years they did the tango dance, back and forth, ego's being hurt and stepped on and yet unconditional love, undeniably. One night Love' had a dream about both young men. Mozique and Amir. In the dream, both were asking her out on a date. Mozique was telling her that he would pick her up on Saturday night at 8:08. Amir told her that he was going to pick her up on Saturday night at 8:18. In the dream Love' was telling Amir about Mozique and how they were going out and Amir told Love' that she shouldn't go out with him because he did not even respond to your last message you sent him in his inbox on your social media account. One of the many interesting things about the dream was that in her waking life Love' did reach out to Mozique to tell him of a project that she was working on and that she wanted him to know how much he had made an impact in her life. Mozique never responded, oddly. This really made Love' feel that everything she felt or thought in regards to Mozique was definitely just a figment of her imagination. It simply just did not make sense. Anyway, in the dream Amir told Love' she should not go with him for that reason. She also felt within the dream that Amir deep down just did not want her to go with Mozique on the date. When Love' woke up from her dream she became even more puzzled. She wanted to tell Amir about the dream and ask him what he thought. Love' told two of her friends, Calie and Mona about the dream because she knew that those times, 8:08 and 8:18 were significant. She had to research the meanings and or symbolisms with those numbers. The number eight represents manifesting wealth and abundance, also potential, inner wisdom, patience, and personal power, and spiritual law of cause and effect, etc.... Number zero represents universal energies, and magnifies the energies of the number it appears with. Now, 8:18 represents self-confidence and personal power, consistency, giving as well as receiving, manifesting abundance, etc.... Number 1 adds the vibration of happiness, attainment, initiative and creation, new beginnings and insight, etc....

Both numbers 8:08 and 8:18 also have to do with endings and new beginnings and or restoration and healing. By the time Love' had researched those number she was more confused than what she was before researching the symbolism of those numbers. She decided to call Amir and tell him about the dream. As she was telling him and he was listening to her. He told her that sounds about right. He told her that what he said to her in the dream would be something he would definitely say to her in their waking lives. He still didn't understand how Mozique could not want to sleep with Love' when she and Mozique were kicking it and or hanging out. He also told her that if Mozique had not responded that she should definitely not go out with him and go out with him instead. The thing is that Amir had in fact prior to her telling him about the dream planned to take her out of town to a concert. He had mentioned taking her to Maryland for the weekend to visit the harbor and see some of their favorite artists perform but he ended up having to work the same weekend. Many times prior Amir had promised to take her out on several occasions so Love' did not necessarily believe him but then again a part of her did and so she waited to see if it would actually happen. When he told her that he could not take her on the weekend that he had initially planned for, he told her that they would instead go to Richmond just to spend the day together and hang out. Nothing serious. He just wanted to take her out to one of his favorite restaurants and maybe hit the beach. Love' agreed. There was a part of her that just always deep down believed him. They began conversing a little more frequently. One day they talked on the phone for several hours. She finally decided to ask him what his motives or intentions were for asking to take her out. She did not want to believe that he had any ill intentions or motives towards her but to her it just simply did not make sense when they had been living in the same area for a whole year and besides that, he had stood her up when she first arrived in town.

Before arriving in town they had been really communicating quite frequently and then all of sudden it just stopped when she moved to the burg. She felt as though he could talk to her in a flirtatious way because she lived so far away and at the time neither one had no knowledge of her relocating back to Lynchburg. Certainly, when she moved back she had no expectations of rekindling any relationship. So many things had changed in their lives but she thought that because of the bond they shared that at the bare minimum they would be friends. She just wanted to hear from him why he wanted to hang out. Of course in the very back of her thoughts, she had the what if's but not enough to actually consider it ever becoming reality. She honestly did not even think he ever thought or wondered about the same thing.

Later that evening they spoke on the phone and she asked him,

Love': Amir, can I ask you something?

Amir: Yea.

Love': What are your intentions for wanting to hang out, I mean why now?

Amir: That's an understandable question. I just thought it would be something for us to do. I don't do anything but go to work and come home. I was planning on going anyway and thought you may want to go. If you don't want to go I'll understand.

Love': no, it's not that I do not want to go. It's just that I am trying to understand why. It just seems random

Amir: Why do you keep having dreams about me?

Love': I don't know why. I have wondered about that as well.

You see Love' had had two other dreams about Amir prior to the most recent one she told him about. The other two dreams she never really told him in detail what they were about.

Amir: Yea, well I just thought we could go and do something different.

Love': Ok, this makes me feel better knowing what your intentions are.

They continued to converse on the phone a little while longer. The next phone call a few memories from the past would definitely surface. The next phone conversation they talked from the time Amir got off work which was around midnight until four in the morning. During this conversation Love' told Amir how she realized why he chuckled when they pulled up into the specific parking space at the local park the day they walked the trail. The reason being that it was the parking space that they parked in after leaving the movies twenty years ago when they fooled around in the car. The police pulled up and knocked on the window. The windows were foggy due to heavy breathing. They did not have sexual intercourse. They had not even done what they normally did. They were just getting started. The policeman made a comment that Amir looked like he was pretty sweaty. Love' was embarrassed. The policeman told them that the park was closed and that they needed to leave. So they did. She could not believe that he had pulled up in the same parking space that over twenty years ago he had parked in. Amir laughed agreeing that he had done so and that was why he chuckled. Amir randomly asked Love' if she knew the song, 'Do You Remember The Time' by Michael Jackson. Love' told him yes. Love' wanted to know the lyrics to that song and would later google the words to listen to them. A few days later they were having a conversation via text.

Love': Are you mad at me or something, wth?

Love' asked him this because she had not heard from him.

Amir: Lol no I'm not....I know ima taste you one of these days, eventually.

Love': You're a trip.

Amir: Yes Hun.

Love' and Amir had secret nicknames for each other.

Love': Can I ask you a personal question....Do you taste women when you're attracted to them or are you selective?

Amir: Lol???

Love': Huh?

Amir: I wanna taste you!!!

Love': Do you do that to the women you get down with or are you picky?

Amir: Lol no I don't !!! Do you still smell good? Then let me taste you!!!

Love': Lmaaaooooo....You got a little game though...

Amir: Let me taste you Hun?!!??!!???! Until the climax????

Love': Lmaaooo....You're funny. You know dang on well if I were to let you do that we would have sex.

Amir: :(It would be nice for you to sit on my face and ride my face and cum on my face. I would love that. I would rub your back, chest, claws and your booty. With oil. :).

Love': Amir, do you value you? For real? Because you don't know who I've been with. I haven't been with anyone in three years now but that's not the point. The point is that you don't know. Besides you're too fertile. Lol. I knew that this is why you wanted us to hang out. Lol...smh.

Amir: Lol it will be well worth it...

Amir: Lol nooooo we are still going no sex?! We still going....

Love': Ok. When?

Amir: Lol hell we gotta wait until next month hopefully the second weekend.

Love': Lol. Ok.

Amir: third weekend? My daughters birthday is the first weekend.

Love': Oh....ok. We'll aim for the third weekend then.

Amir: Lol we're going Hun....It'll be weird...but let's enjoy.

Love': Lmao.

Amir: Maybe on the seventh? I would go this weekend but I have to work this weened.

Love': Ok. Yup. We can wait until next month then. Why will it be weird?

Amir: Lol do you wanna stay overnight?

Love': Ummm and stay overnight? Ummm you know I am not trying to have sex.

Amir: Yes hun....lol.

Love': Why will it be weird?

Amir: You know I should have brought you back home with me, from the last time I saw you in Portsmouth.

You see the last time Amir saw her in Portsmouth she was struggling to work as a waitress. She could barely afford groceries. Amir went and bought her some groceries and they made love for the first time, seven years later from the time they first met.

Love': Wow. What made you say that?

Amir: Lol I think like that at times. Like the what if's...You know?? Been thinking that. It is what it is now though. But yes it's ok to imagine things like that.

Love': Oh absolutely I understand the what if's!!! Think about things as well. I try not to too much or I'll be depressed.

Amir: Right. Lol! Because it is!!!!

Love': Lol...lol Yeah it could be at times. Now, this all makes sense. Thank you so much. And by the way, I probably would have come back with you and probably would have 5 children by now. Lol.

Amir: Lol yup!!!! Five plus? And a big ole historic home!?!? Lol. I really do think like that at times....smh.

Love': Really? Are you just saying that? Wow. I never knew that but it makes sense and helps me to understand "US" and why all of this time there is still a connection.

Amir: Lol, always!!

Love': Yup!! What's crazy is what my mom told me after we met that day at the park that time.

Amir: What's that o_O ??? lol

Love' was now driving in the car and could not respond as quickly as she had been. So Amir became a little annoyed by that and then responds with

Amir: Oook never mind.

Love': My fault I was driving. She said, she still saw a connection between us and that you liked me, She also said, "He wonders about you and him settling down and how different it would have been if the both of you had made other choices." I believed her as far as the connection part for the most part but when she said he wonders, I did not believe that part one hundred percent.

Amir: Oh my gosh...Your mother is not human cause she hit it on the nail!!!! Wow!!!

Finding this out for Love' was really refreshing. She knew that Amir had children by different women and knew that the chances of them actually being in a relationship probably would not happen but she knew that he would always love her and there was comfort in her knowing that. There was also comfort in knowing that what she felt was not a figment of her imagination unlike the experience she was having in regards to Mozique.

Love' longed for the opportunity to not only meet the "one" but her reason ultimately was so that she could not repeat a generational cycle of settling out of fear of being lonely or not feeling adequate enough to have the best. She wanted Ziariah to experience her mom loving a man who adored her but not only adoring her but also touching Ziariah's heart in a way that would assist her in realizing her healing. She wanted Ziariah to know that she was worthy of everything and anything. Due to the lack of relationship and or affection shown to Love' by her parents because her parents never received some of the same things as well; she began to see how on a subconscious level you could attract the very thing you say you don't want into your life. You can attract it when you don't heal on a subconscious level. It's like your subconscious is rewinding and replaying all of the things felt and heard passed through the bloodline simply for cleansing purposes and or for someone to finally pay attention to the cries within the bloodline.

Love' now saw how she had attracted some men. Some of the young males she attracted simply because she was trying to save the little boy in her dad through the men she chose to be involved with. She saw her dad's potential. She saw a hurting little boy who did not receive the nurturing he deserved from both of his parents. She saw the frustration in her mom because of all that she had inside that she did not use because she married and began having children immediately and while some women are healthy enough to marry young and raise a family without losing themselves in the process, this just had not been the case for Rayanna.

Love' knew the key to cleansing was to take action and go against fear and go with the flow of that still small voice. She was determined to make sure that Ziariah did not repeat the pain that Love' had endured. Yet Love' knew that some of the things she experienced all happened for a reason. She had gained strength, courage and wisdom. She was starting to become aware of all her limitlessness. She had to make those choices to unleash all aspects from within; liken to a rubber band the further you pull the rubber band back and then let it go the further the rubber band soars.

Love' was still uncertain of how to manifest some things but the things that she was aware of she would make it happen via the prayers of her parents, grandparents and her own thoughts and her actions. Her mom's parents were an odd couple. Her grandmother was a feisty, in your face, speak her mind kind of a woman but her grandfather was the complete opposite. He was very quiet and almost afraid to be around groups of large people that he did not know. He was a handsome man and very intelligent, humorous and yet had a hot-headed temper. He was multi-talented and so was her grandmother. They married very young and began having children immediately. They came from some religious dysfunctional families but they managed to remain sane and based on how they presented themselves you would never know all that they endured. It's possible that they learned how to hide it. They learned how to bury it all deep within their souls. Insecurity was the main factor involved in their family and it had managed to remain in the bloodline. Love' was certain that she came to destroy the cycle, someway and somehow.

One day when Love' was working on creating she decided to meditate. During her meditation exercise, she was focusing on unleashing her kundalini which is an energy or force that lives within us all. It means coiled. This energy exists at the base of the spine and is often times symbolic of a snake. Once this energy is awakened there is a level of bliss, peace, intuition and wholeness that takes place. Insight becomes heightened, creativity and the chakras begin to spin and flow after the kundalini is unleashed. Abundance is realized and your magnetism is increased in frequency and or speed. Synchronicity begins to happen on a frequent basis. Love' wanted this to happen for her so much so she began to meditate and do the things required for this experience. As she meditated on a regular basis her dreams became very lucid. She would experience moments of literally being in a different place while knowing she wasn't literally in that place and time. I had stayed the night with Rayanna, Love' and Ziariah. While on my way to sleep in the guest bedroom, I began thinking about James or as Ma Bella called him, Fletch. I missed him and for some reason I felt his presence like never before in that moment Love' was in her bedroom and all of sudden came into the bedroom I was sleeping in and said, "I apologize that I did not stay here with you in the same capacity but I am here with you on your journey and I thank you for being with me on my journey once again it just happens to be in a different way, I'm just in a different role. I sat up on the bed and said, "What?" Love' left out of the guest room. I grabbed my robe and put it on. I opened up the bedroom door and walked down the hall and up the steps and knocked on Love's bedroom door. I called for her and there was no answer. I opened up the door and called her name again and she still did not answer. I walked over to her bed and touched her to try and wake her, she moved turning over and I called her name again. This time she opened up her eyes and began to cry. I asked her what was wrong. She said I saw you in my dream and I was there too. Love' then said, she didn't want to talk about it.

Sadie: Ok, whenever you're ready to talk about it, just let me know.

Love': Ok.

I went back into the guest room. I could not go back to sleep. I cried. I became very anxious. I wanted to know what Love' didn't want to tell me, what was it that she saw? Why did she say those words to me?

I laid in the bed. I began thinking that I made the right decision for now by moving to Lynchburg not long after Love' and her family had moved here. I didn't know why I should move to Lynchburg but I knew that I should, so I did. I was going back for a visit to Wilmington, De; to see my family and maybe Fletch's family and so that my family could spend some time with my son, Jamerson. I wanted to know if Love' and Ziariah wanted to come with us considering Ziariah's dad was there as well along with Love's dad. Love' told me that she would. So that weekend we were on our way to Delaware.

When we arrived in town I dropped Love' off at her dad's house. Love' and Ron had worked out their relationship for the most part. One day she and Ron had discussed some of the things that they had done to one another that were pretty hurtful. Growing up although Love' knew that Ron was a hurting little boy inside this did not negate the fact that Love' was a hurting little girl who longed for her Father's love in a way that he had not been capable of doing for so long. She knew that he loved her but there was a part of him that she nor her brothers had yet to connect with.

Love' was no saint she had disrespected him on several occasions. She often felt rejected by her dad especially when he had remarried. After Love's and her dad's conversation, she and her siblings were standing outside hanging out. Their dad had come out side to join them. Her dad had put his arms around her. He had never done this in her thirty plus years of living with the acceptation of when she was a baby. He later admitted to this and told her, "I thought about something Love' while I had my arms around you that I've never done that and I believe its one of the reasons why you chose who you chose to be involved with regarding some of your relationships." That statement validated what she already knew. He then told her that he would be doing that more often.

The next day which was a Saturday I asked if Love' and Ziariah wanted to hang out. Love' said yes. Love' borrowed her dad's car and met me at the park. I brought a blanket and a basket full of food to have lunch. While Ziariah ran to the playground. I prepared the meal and laid the blanket out on the grass. Love' was pushing Ziariah on the swings. I came over to the swings which were very close to where the blanket was and asked Ziariah if she was hungry and Ziariah said, yes. The three of us began walking towards the blanket and had lunch. Love' knew that I wanted her to tell me what she saw in that dream.

Love': I know you want to know what was in the dream Sadie.

Sadie: Looked up at Love', she smiled. Yes, I do but if you still do not want to discuss it I will understand. We can talk about something else.

Love': I will tell you a little later. I do want to talk about something else though.

Sadie: Ok, Let's talk. What is on your mind?

Love': Do you believe or feel that twin flames are something real? Do you believe in soulmates?

Sadie: I certainly do, why do you ask?

Love': How do you know which is which? I have been doing some research on the subject and it's because there have been two people in my life that I have had a strong connection with. Well, at least I think that is what it is.

Love' continued to explain about Amir and Mozique. Sadie listened and then shared her experiences with three young men. One was a childhood friend named Teddy, then the other was another childhood friend named James whom you know of, who is and or was your cousin and the other is Jamerson's Father. All three played a significant role in my life. I have wondered about the same thing regarding those three individuals. I had and still have a connection with all three. Now, do I know who is who? I have a strong feeling I do. I feel strongly that Teddy was that twin flame and that he sent your cousin James and that he was a soul-mate. Jamerson's Father is also a soul-mate but my connection with James, your cousin also known as Fletch was so magnetic and powerful. Teddy and I did not have the chance to experience some of the things that James and I did because he was just a little boy when he transitioned. So who do you feel is your twin flame?

Love': I am not sure. On one hand, I feel it's Mozique; but on the other hand, I feel it's Amir. How do you know?

Sadie: When you know yourself. When you love yourself. When you honor all that you are. You know when it's real when you are real with you. You know a real connection when you know you are already connected to the divinity within you. The divinity in you will reveal it to you.

Love': I know without a doubt that if neither are my twin flame, then they are definitely soulmates. I have been so fortunate to experience these connections in my lifetime. The connections with both have been so intense. The connections are both so different.

Sadie: What is the difference between the two?

Love': Mozique and I had an instant connection with no hidden agendas. It was pure and the love I had and still have was just there. He made me think, feel, know and understand me but I didn't really realize he did until years later. He left an imprint on my heart. I have never felt that connection I felt with him since that time. It has now been twelve or thirteen years ago. I wish I knew how he felt and what he thought about the connection or if he even felt a connection and then the kiss was magical. We never slept with each other. He never concerned himself with it and considering the fact that he was leaving for boot camp I thought that was really thoughtful and considerate. Now Amir was my high school sweet heart, my first love and you already know about our connection and you know as I am telling you this, I am starting to see much more clearly.

Sadie: Love' you will know if it is meant to be with either one of them, or not. Whenever or whomever he is comes, you will know it. Spend time loving you and having a relationship with yourself.

Anyway, Love' I am considering relocating back to Delaware now. I am really feeling a pull to come back. I am not sure as to why or even when but probably within this year. Love' sat in silence for a moment and then Ziariah finished eating and wanted to go back on the playground. Love' and I walked her to the playground and watched Ziariah play with a few of the other children who were now on the playground. Love' says, "Sadie I think I am ready to talk to you now about my dream." Sadie says, "O.k., I am ready to listen." Love' turns and looks at me and says, "You and I meet again. I told you we've traveled together on our journey's before, just playing different roles. Remember when you heard the words, the touch so subtle without any force; the touch felt like an eternal hug or as if we were surrounded by an ocean submerged in an endless womb of timeless bliss?" I stood there with tears in my eyes, eyes as bright as the moon. Love' began to tell me the dream. "It was you and me right here at this park except for I was James. We were laying out on a blanket. I heard what James was saying. I saw how you two or should I say you and I were up talking one night. I saw different events flashing before me as if I were watching a projector with footage flashing before my eyes." I then asked Love' if she remembered coming into my room after she had the dream and crying when I asked her about it. She said, no. I told her how she came into my bedroom and said, "I apologize that I did not stay here with you in the same capacity but I am here with you on your journey and I thank you for being with me on my journey once again it just happens to be in a different way." Love' did not remember doing that but she remembered her dream in detail. Love' told me how this made so much sense to her and truly resonated with her and the experiences she had on her journey. She always felt old in her soul and growing up she did not know how to describe it.

As far as the connections she was experiencing or felt in regards to Amir and Mozique it began to really intensify. While the connections were definitely different the connections were definitely real, at least for Love'.

Love' had spent the weekend in Delaware and was ready to get back to Lynchburg. She and Amir had been planning to go hang out and spend a Saturday together. Love' was nervous about going. They had not hung out in years other than the walk at the trail in the park. Love' was not interested in having sex with Amir even though it had been almost four years since she last had sex.

She knew what she wanted to attract into her life and she knew her actions would either catapult her or hold her back. She also did not want to take a chance on becoming pregnant and since Amir had recently discussed that he wanted another child she knew she would have to avoid sex with him at all cost. The thing was they had never done the platonic thing but that is what Love' wanted at the time. She was open to the possibility of it turning into something more but it should not take them having to be intimate to determine such.

For a few months after Sadie, Love', Ziariah and lil' Jamerson returned to Lynchburg Love' and Amir had been conversing but for some reason, Love' was not looking at Amir in the same way and it was because she was really observing Amir's actions. She felt as though he was playing with her to see if he would have a chance to be intimate with her again, like a conquest but she wasn't sure because there was a part of her that felt as though he genuinely loved her, in fact she knew he did but she did not want to be sexually intimate with him at this point. Love' entertained him but she could not deny how she was feeling. She was asking for her higher self to reveal to her what the connection was. She thought she was just having a hard time of letting the past go. They were each other's first love's and they were each other's first oral sex experiences. Love' began to realize all the more how some of the men she was attracting was directly associated with the pain, hurt, and rejection she experienced from both parents. It was also a direct reflection of why she would feel the need to save the men she became involved with and yet ignore her self as she had watch her mom due within her marriages. The thing was, is that Love' had been releasing her past and had forgiven her parents, specifically her dad and their relationship was being restored, and or repaired. She loved her dad and began to accept that she did not need to settle for the person who was not fully committed or available in all aspects of their life. She was not looking at Amir as the school crush and googly eyes anymore. She knew she still loved him and still felt a connection but she just wasn't sure if they ultimately wanted the same thing. She did not realize she was keeping the connection charged with her thoughts. You know how powerful thoughts are? Thoughts can have you serving a dead situation. Having you resuscitate it to only have complications.

One evening she and Amir were texting back and forth. Most of the time it was Love' reaching out to him via text. Love' asked him if they were still going to be going out of town just for the day and Amir kept trying to get her to stay the night. This trip to Richmond and or Virginia Beach was supposed to happen for now a month and a half and he kept having to work on the weekend. She wanted to believe him but he had stood her up for various events in times past. Maybe she had become addicted to rejection. He was still making the same promises he made to her back in high school. Promising her to buy her a pair of sneakers, to take her here and there. She still gave him the benefit of the doubt. She wanted to see if he would keep his word this time. When they had one of their many conversations via text while he was at work and he kept bringing up what he wanted to do to her sexually she initially would flirt back with him but this time she was noticing a difference. She noticed the difference after she told him that she has talked to her dad about him.

Love': Yoooo. Just saying hey!!!! Are you still going?

Amir: If I'm off... :/ lol!!! I wasn't going this weekend.

Love': Lol. I know you weren't going this weekend though. Just wanted something to say? Lol.

Amir: Lol awww ummm you miss me? Love': Lol...sure but you never do.

Amir: Lol not true!!!!

Love': Lol. Ok. I believe you.

Amir: Yes baby and I will sink my face in you while telling you I miss you :) ;)

Love': Lmaoooo....wow...ok then you miss my yoni? Ooook. So I don't believe you. Smh.

Amir: Oh? I'm going to say that to your other lips?

Love': Oh wait. Lol. What lips?

Amir: Anyways...

Amir: Lmao don't play...How you been Hun?

Amir: How many lips on a lady?

Love': Two set of lips. I am well. How about you.

Amir: Okay baby.

Love': Who is baby? Lol. That's not my nickname you gave me. You be bull jivin' yo lol...you talk mad ish via text but when we're on the phone we don't talk about things like this, you barely say anything lol. With yo sexy, cool, laid back ass.

Amir: Wtf ??? Ummmm I be on the phone with ya butt till I'm tired AF!?!? Lol!!! Whatever....you're the sexy one!!!

Amir: I wanna chill with you one weekend and spend a day or two? Just a thought...

Love': I would like to but I ain't doing nothing and I know you want to have sex and if I am honest it would be too tempting. I have thought about us chilling and hanging out but just chilling. I don't want to say no but I don't want to say yes. I guess just go with the flow?

Amir: Lol!! Come

Amir: Have fun and enjoy life...

Amir: And sex.

Love': Lmaoo....smh I am not trying to have another child right now. I have been without it for four years. Kind of want to wait until....

Amir: We know what to do.

Love': Lol lol...I knew what to do and still had a child. Lol. Amir: Lmaooo Me too :/

Love': Lol

Love': Wouldn't you be nervous?

Amir: No.

Love': Damn. Ok.

Amir: Baby.

Love': Baby? Wait are you calling me a baby? Lol

Amir: Yes. Baby.

Love': Huh?

Amir: Lol!!!

Love': Why do you think I am a baby?

Love' knew why he called her a baby. It was because she did not want to have sex with him and not know what direction they were going in. Love' knew he did not like that about Love' and yet she knew he did like that about her. She did not want to have sex with him because she wasn't sure if he understood energy and the exchange of it during sex. She was responding to him via text but in her heart, she knew she could not share with him her sacred space at least not just yet.

Amir: Can we spend a day or two?

Love': You came up in conversation with my dad.

Amir: About what dammit lol?

Love': He talked to me about being open but yet be wise. He said he didn't want me to be hurt but that I should hang out with you.

Amir: Lmaooo!! I understand coming from a playa...?

Love': Lol...he put away his card. He's getting older now and ready to settle down again.

Amir: Lol I was joking!!

Love': Lol...no you weren't. Lol.

Amir: I was. I can't speak on him. Look at me....smh.

Love': Lol...at least you're honest about it.

Love' could not believe that he was admitting to the fact that he had been a player, having a few children with a few baby mothers. She was thankful that he was being honest.

Love': Well, if I was sexy like you I'd be a playa too. Lol. j/k.

Amir: Lmfao!!! Me licking you would be so sexy you sexy, YOU!!!

Love': Yo I swear you got some game. You're trying to plant a seed to get me to thinking about it so that I'll think about it so much that I just can't help myself. Lol. I love you though yo. You're a good dude and have a good heart.

Amir must have fallen asleep after Love sent that text because he did not respond until the next evening. Before he responded Love' felt as though for some reason her expressing to him that he was a good dude and had a good heart was assisting him in remembering who she remembered him to be years ago. She felt that he was reflecting back on the exchange of words and specifically on the fact that she had spoken to her dad about him.

The next day his response was

Amir: Lol. I love you too! But damn you putting a nigg down.

Amir: Hi though.

Love': Huh? No, I'm not. You're a good man, Amir!!!

Love' really believed he was a good dude. She just wondered if he could be what she needed and or desired at this point in her life.

Love:' How am I bringing you down?

Amir: Hey baby

Love': Hey...how am I bringing you down?

Amir: I miss you hun...I wanna see you.

Love': Huh? Lol... ooook. I want to see you too but why are we having two different conversations?

Amir: Lol...I wanna squeeze you and peck you on the neck.

Love': Huh? Yooo...what? How am I putting you down???

Amir: I can't wait!!! When can I see you, squeeze you and please you?

Love': Oooook? Huh? Huh? Yoo What? HOW AM I PUTTING YOU DOWN? So you're not trying to hang out now? You're just trying to get it in?

Now of course Love' was knowing exactly what it was now but she did not want to believe that the friendship she thought they had been reduced to a surface, physical nothingness.

286

Amir: Yes hun

Amir: On a cold night at the beach.

Love': Wow.

Amir: Nothing wrong with chilling?!

Love': Ummm no but....

Amir: Yes...your butt

Love': No not that butt.

Love': I think you and I want different things right now in our lives.

Amir: Ok. Take care.

Love': Ooooook...wow. Take care.

Amir: I still love you baby, ALWAYS.

Love': Oooook? Will always love you too!!! Thanks for being a part of my journey.

Amir: Sent a text image of a character bowing.

Love' could not feel anything. She was thankful that he was honest with her. The year prior when he stood her up she was very angry at the fact that he had done that and lied to herself by saying that she was done with him and hurt and wanted nothing to do with him. But she realized that this time she believed she was really Ok to move on from the past. The emotional aspect of their connection hurt some. She went in peace knowing that she had love for him and respect. He was choosing to live in a way that was not complimentary to how she was choosing to live. She knew what she was worth. She knew she did not have to settle by accepting a lie that would go against her truth she had to live. She knew that it was vital to Ziariah to not just accept whomever just because. She was not a trash can where men could dump their loads of frustration into her sacred loving flow of milk and honey. She wanted more and was determined to have more by standing in her own personal constitution without compromise and unwavering or settling and that's pretty empowering. She was beginning to see that she had grown and matured because there was a time where she would have given in for the sake of filling some void that would never be filled by the action of intercourse because instant gratification just does not last. She knew that that portion of this chapter in her book on this journey of having a lack of confidence and no self worth was officially closed. She refused to be a conquest and was so grateful that she stood in her own truth.

Love' really would begin reflecting on the terms and or labels such as twin flame and soul-mates. She began to not particularly care for those terms as much as she enjoyed the experience between souls. She felt that many people were connected to her at some level, some connections just happen to be more intense than others.

She was trying to experience what she had experienced years ago with Mozique with the next soul she was destined to connect with. The connections she thought that she had with him wa intense and less physical than she had ever experienced with anyone. She trusted him instantly. There was just something about him or rather the connection that was so pure and honest. The only thing was that she did not know if this connection existed for him at the same level of energy it had existed at one point in time for her. What she had yet to realize was that she could not or perhaps should not try to recreate the same connection she once had with Mozique because she was in a different place and how can one connect with a completely different person in the same way that one had with someone else?

The words came back to her that she had heard within her soul, "she was a liar because she told herself over and over and over again that she wasn't pretty enough, not good enough, she wasn't worthy enough, not even smart enough, she hadn't realized she was breaking her own heart. She would grab the popcorn and entertain those thoughts. She was believing those thoughts; every thought, thoughts that weren't true; until she later realized she was in control of what she knows and what she lets go. She became the truth to herself, seeing her worth, honor her soul. She was accepting her part, her role to grow was in all she knows. The power of what she thought was in what she knows. She began to tell herself the truth that she was more than physical. She was timeless in all, abundantly magical because she attracted what she thought, how she felt was hidden beneath the lies and now she realized she was the truth because it was there all along; there deep inside." Now she had accepted that she was not a liar but evolving into a being who was accepting her internal truth.

She is all that is inside, is what Love' began to realize. The real connection that she had neglected was with herself.

After Love' and I had come back from Delaware, needless to say, I kept thinking about what Love' told me about her dream and her, in another life, being James. So many things came back to me. I remember when he and I felt a connection with Rayanna and Ron and how they kept staring at James especially Rayanna. I wanted to know if he left here because of me. I knew that I felt such a strong connection to Rayanna and her family but specifically to Love'. I knew that I had to be a support for her as she traveled and returned to earth this time around. I knew I had to be open and honest with her about any and everything. This was my chance to assist in creating a healthy environment so that she can flourish and fulfill all that was and is within her. I was on my way to Rayanna's. I knew that Rayanna would not understand. I just had to be around Love'.

When I arrived at their home. Love' was sitting outside smoking a Capone (a flavored cognac cigar) that she brought back with her from Delaware. I got out of the car and walked up to her. She said, "Hey Sadie!" I told her, "Hey" I did not comment on the fact that she was smoking on an Al Capone simply because I knew she already knew what she knew in regards to that habit and that her mom was probably getting on her about it. I sat down with her in the back yard. I asked her, what was going on and she told me, "Nothing really; I guess I am just tired."

Sadie: Tired of what?

Love': (She sat quietly for a moment before responding) Tired of not accomplishing things. Tired of hurting or being hurt. I don't even feel that what I feel sometimes has anything to do with this life I am living now. I don't know. I am really wanting to experience some things. I really would love to be able to utilize my abilities in order to provide for Ziariah and I. I would love to be able to help out my immediate family financially as well as my extended family.

Sadie: Now that you gave me a list of things that you can actually change, you simply must change then. I can help as much as I can and in any way I can but you must take the initiative and seize every moment.

Love' began to say these words, "you know what, anything is possible; the probability is rooted and grounded and or centered in thought and action. Frequency. What are my frequent thoughts....what are my frequent inner conversations I have with myself....what are my frequent actions....this determines where my frequency is, my altitude...how high can I go...how low can I go...yeah, anything is possible."

Sadie: Yes Love', love on you. Realize your true essence, when you do, you will KNOW your worth.

Love': I feel that I am on the path to realizing.

For the first time, she had put relationships on the back burner, specifically with her "first love" because she was learning to love on her and knew what she wanted and knew what she deserved. How can you have a first love without loving yourself first?

She knew she loved him unconditionally but she knew she was learning exactly how to love herself as well.

Sadie: What is it exactly that you want from a prospective love interest? Have you ever taken the time to write it down?

Love': Yes I have written it down. I even know how I want our lovemaking sessions to be. I know how I want us to communicate. I know how I will be treated. I have given some of this deep thought and some of it is coming to me as I evolve. Like for instance, I envision this mystery man and that one day he and I will be so engaged by each other's essence that we feel each other even now. That we will hear each other even now. In fact, I have heard him. I know it sounds strange but one night as I was dozing off in and out of sleep. I heard a man say, "She is so adorable, she just doesn't know how much I like her yet." I jumped up and said wth?

I also know that when we meet if I haven't already met him that we will connect instantly because our hearts are already in sync.

That we mutually bond on a mental, emotional and spiritual level before we engage in any physical expression of love. That we make each other laugh and feel what the other has already felt inside due to the love we have for ourselves. That we are playful and balanced. I envision that when we finally do create a harmonious atmosphere together to express our love physically that it will already have been revealed via our first kiss of how it would be when he penetrates my loving flow of living waters. I envisioned us looking in each other eye's and connecting so deeply our souls are penetrated before we even physically touch. As we lay in the bed because we are friends first and going with the natural flow we feel and move towards each other as our hearts had already done. We move closer and closer and he grabs my face for a kiss of eternal bliss. The kiss moves us both in such a way because we feel so much energy. We breathe deeply and in sync. Living waters begin to flow as the energy flows and exudes from heart to heart, from each chakra to the other. As we are undressing physically we realize we have been undressed for quite some time through the heart and mind's eye. He saw me and I saw him. Never wanting the kiss to cease as we continue undressing physically. He lays on top of me and before entering he begins to speak to me with his energy without movement of his magical staff that was ready to comfort me as his heart had already done. He whispered with his eyes, kissing my lips in a sensual manner, no lust because we are and have been drawn to each other magnetically having nothing to do with the physical act of sex but everything to do with attraction at a heart level and from the ethers. He saw me, the true me, he saw my kind nature, my pure heart. He saw how I loved and how I thought, he saw how the very thing I longed for had been the very thing I fought against and somehow he knew how to calm that battle within in an instant and I knew I did the same for him. As he laid on me still without movement, no longer kissing, gazing into my eyes as if I were the stars and he saw his reflection in my eyes and with a slight smile that was contagious because he smiled too. He then would say, "There is so much I want to say to you right now but I know you already feel it." He kisses me again and again, the kiss was as if our lips were dancing and our tongues were expressing the vibration of the complimentary energy exchange. The kiss will be as if we are making love and we will not want it to end, his hands caressing my breast, stimulated as if a cool breeze had come and touched them. I begin to feel his magical staff as it was there to comfort and explore my flow of living waters and even exchange of bliss eternal. We begin to flow in movement as the ocean waves, I am feeling transformed with each stroke of magic between us, love knows no end. The ocean waves become more aggressive within in the hour and I have released three times and he has held his for magical purposes so that I can grant him more energy from my living waters as we continue; I slightly move and he knew that I wanted to ride the waves and feel all of his magical staff and he could no longer hold it. He was reaching his peak to release. I instantly and naturally rode him on his journey to climax at the same time and as we did he grabbed me and pulled me close to him and we laid still in silence, resting and reflecting. "There is so much more I want to say right now but I know you already know and feel it." She whispered those words back to him and he caressed her in a warm embrace, resting peacefully together. Yes, I have envisioned this.

Needless to say, I was speechless. I was speechless for a number of reasons. I remembered the night that James and I shared for the very first time and it was similar to what Love' expressed. She literally had written those words down and pulled them out of her handbag. I thought about telling her about what I had once experienced but did not know if that would be too awkward for her or for me for that matter. I still saw her as the little girl I bonded with and now it was obvious she was an adult.

Love': So what did you think?

Sadie: I am speechless. It was magnificent! Honestly, it reminded me of a time and place once shared between James and I.

Love': Really? Now that's interesting. (Chuckling) So what happened? If you don't mind me asking.

Sadie: No I don't mind. I wanted to share. Just didn't know if that would be uncomfortable for you.

Love': No, not at all.

Sadie: James and I were the best of friends as you already know. We connected immediately. The night that he and I made love it was one of the best moments of my life because what we shared was more than physical as well. I remember us kissing for what seemed like hours. He carried me into the bedroom while still kissing me as he laid me on the bed he began undressing me while still kissing. He then said, "before we exchange energy I want you to know what is about to happen with each entrance I give and you receive." I said, "tell me while you're entering." So that is what he did.

As he entered me he said, "Sadie as I enter I want you to know and feel our trust. As I enter in, know that there is healing being realized with each movement. As I enter in we are giving each person permission to see into me, see the real me, see my heart, my soul as we enter and we receive. As I enter in, we look into our souls via our eyes know that love is only connecting with itself in us as us. Know that as I enter in and you receive, I receive and each time we are experiencing the limitlessness in our bond and all of its sacredness. As I enter in, each time healing is being realized in both of us and as I exit hurt is dissipating. As we enter, we receive, knowing we've never left from the omnipresence of this connection being expressed right now. As I enter — trust. As I enter —healing. As I enter —love. As we enter — what we receive is merely realization of what has always been."

As he repeated this I was about to climax with each entrance, each phrase I was releasing hurt, pain, fear, etc.... He had not yet. I think he knew we were not finished. After I released we started again, only I was laying on my side, my back was facing him. He entered me, He was getting ready to repeat but I began to speak, and I said, "James, As you enter my physical body know that we were already connected at the heart. As you enter know that I've always loved and always will. As you enter James, know that I feel so protected especially in this position. As you enter I feel even more connected. As you enter you are experiencing my energy of endless healing power directly connected to all of the inner being that I am. With each moment healing is being realized and so whenever you're ready it is Ok to release. He released and twenty minutes later I began to lay on top of him and began moving on top of him in a circular motion while sitting up. I said, "James, I move on you in a circle because this love will never end. It will always meet, always know this." I began to lay down on him and kept saying, this love will never end, this love will never end... He released only for us to continue one more time. This time we were very quiet and focused. The intent behind our words had been set. The tone had been set, we were tuned in so no words were necessary at this point. As you can see this was a night I will always remember.

Love': Wow!!! I would love to go see his mom. Well, his family, and or my family.

Sadie: I am going back next month for an interview, you're more than welcome to come with me, you and Ziariah.

Love: Ok. I think I may just do that.

After Love' and I had conversed, my son and I went back home. Love' went inside to see what Rayanna and Ziariah were doing. Ziariah was sleep so Love' got on the computer and started applying to places. She was no longer limiting herself to the area that she was residing in. She began applying to places that were anywhere from twenty minutes to and hour and a half away. While she was applying to various places of business she received a text from Amir. Now they had not spoken.

Amir: Damn...

Love': Huh??? What happened?

Amir: Ummm I've been texting and calling you.

Love': No you haven't. I never got one phone call or text from you.

But Love' did remember the strangest thing happened a few nights prior when his name popped up on her phone letting her know that he sent a text but when she went to see what it said there was nothing there.

Amir: Whatever, anyways...Hi

Love': I was like damn...Just like that? Just like that? (in regards to their last convo via text) Anyway, I promise I never saw any text from you.

Amir: Lol noooo I wouldn't do you like that!

Love:' Yea you would. (She didn't say it but she was thinking how he had already done it and repeatedly. He would just stop talking to her for what appeared to be for no reason to Love').

Love': One day your name popped up letting me know that I received a text but when I went to go click on the text to see what you sent nothing was there. So I thought my mind was playing tricks on me.

Amir: Lmao! I'm lost...

Amir: Still lost???

Love': One day your name popped up on my phone and then when I went to see what you sent, nothing was there. Then I reread our last convo via text and was laughing and also like damn at the same time.

Amir: Yes.... text then...lol

Love' did not understand his response.

Love': What ??? Lol...after I reread our convo I wasn't texting you. Lol. Anyway, what were the text that you sent that I never received?

Amir: Lol asking how are ya?? And why you unfriended me on the book of face... Love': Oh I'm good. And you? I didn't unfriend you...

Amir: Ok well you friended me...lol and I'm good.

Love': What?? Lol...I never unfriended you. I wouldn't do that.

Amir: Well I don't know what happened...

Love': Someone made a fake page and was requesting people. It was an imposter.

Amir: Lol. Damn. I was like noooo she didn't!!!!

Love': Lol lol lol...Nope. I wasn't mad. I was a little shocked but then again, not really.

Amir: Ok baby

Love': Here we go with this baby stuff.

Amir: Lol Ok then...Girl

Love': OOOOk ha ha ha, far from a girl.

Amir: Lol

Love' really loved him and somehow she knew that he loved her. She knew what she desired. She knew what she needed and she was finally accepting the possibility that the relationship that was started over twenty years ago, may have to stay in the past at least in this case. She no longer felt like figuring things out, the mind games, the tango dance. She knew she was ready for something more mature. She was not looking to be anyone's bed buddy and that was for sure. She knew she had to be in a place to receive by being what she knew in her heart she needed and or wanted. He contacted her the day after. He was checking in on her quite regularly.

Love' began to see things. She began to reflect on her own thought patterns. She realized she had broken a cycle. The cycle was the deception in believing that all thoughts were her own. She realized some thoughts never belonged to her but were passed down through the bloodline. These thoughts came from external toxic sources.

She realized that those who came into her life that seemed to bring pain often times really came to reveal the pain that was already there. They just came to help bring it up and out. They came to be a catalyst and due to the events that had taken place, she realized that she valued herself enough to wait for the one. The one who would love her unconditionally which was herself. She had to learn how to be patient with herself and take the time to love her. She is the one that needed to love herself unconditionally. She was seeing this so clearly because her eyes were as bright as the moon, sol light shining through. Her heart was releasing the anger that was rarely ever shown outwardly to others but inside is where it had resided. She was feeling a sense of peace. She knew that this was a part of the reason she returned to this earth. She knew she came to become reacquainted with herself, her higher self, the one. She knew she was here to experience life and pain was a part of the process. Almost like a maze and with each turn you experience something that includes an added learning experience. Love' began to see so clearly because her eyes were as bright as the moon even as she diligently sought out work. Her first work was within herself and with her daughter. While Love' was thankful for Ziariah's dad and how they had at one time loved each other and out of that created something so magical. She would forever be grateful for that experience on the journey.

Love' had planned to go with Sadie on her next trip back home and perhaps Marquis would be able to see Ziariah. Love' was especially thrilled about this trip. She just had a great feeling about it and did not know why at the time.

As much as Love' wanted to release Mozique from her memories she wanted to know after some time had passed and she had sent a message to Mozique why he never responded, not a thank you or anything. She waited for so long to hear from him in response to what she wrote him and her exact words were as such: "Hey. Have been up writing and I just wanted you to know how much of an impact you had on my life. I am in the process of completing a book that you are in, of course using a different name. I recently finished the section that you're in and just wanted you to know that you left a positive imprint on my life and taught me valuable lessons and I just wanted to say thank you. I hope this was not too weird. Hope you will get a chance to read it once completed. Peace and blessings to you and yours." She honestly knew how odd it would be after all of these years to share that only after a few mini conversations in an inbox on a social media site but she felt like she should share it even if he never responds. She had nothing to go on other than just a knowing in her heart that he had touched her heart in such a gentle way. He had come into her life with a pure soul, without ill intentions; simply as a sincere friend during a time where she had been hurt repeatedly by those who claimed to love her. She had been betrayed by her love interest and was still not as experienced sexually when she met Mozique. She trusted him instantly. She did not see it fully at the time while they engaged in conversations over a decade ago but she knew he had touched her without a physical touch. He was really used to restore her faith in men. He let her know that there were good men out there who weren't necessarily related by blood but by love. She didn't see to what extent he had touched her because she had to learn other lessons that he could not teach her for his heart was just too pure at the time. She began to know during this time that there are some men who can see you with their hearts, they can pick up on what type of person you are and not be eager to take advantage of a young lady's vulnerable state; where she is naive and yearning to no longer feel rejected by those she loves. She had been searching. She was told that she had searching eyes. She was searching for healing and did not realize that is exactly what she was experiencing the entire time on her journey. The process that she thought was so painful she began seeing how much healing had taken place in her life. Not only healing for her but healing for future generations within her bloodline. She was determined to learn as much as she could to teach her daughter by example and she knew the first place to start was honoring herself through self-love and acceptance. Acceptance of the decisions she had made. One of those decisions that haunted her was losing contact with the person who she wondered about for so long. Love' had many questions to ask that she never got the chance to ask him. She didn't believe she and him would drive off into the sunset but she wanted closure. She wanted to know what it was for him and if it was ever anything. Love' tried to forget about him after a while because he never responded. She knew he had read the message. She tried not to think about him often. She was not feeling rejected but she was feeling as though maybe it was a case of a figment of the imagination for her in regards to the connection she felt they once shared.

Love' really wanted to tell him how she had no expectations only questions of what it was and why he avoided the opportunity to sleep with her, what was his reason? While she was grateful that they did not sleep together at the time she still wondered what his reason were. She remembered him saying, "Let's just go to sleep." Initially, she was grateful and relieved. Later the thoughts began to come and one of those thoughts was, "wait a minute! Was he not attracted to me?" But then the next day she remembered they hung out, he kissed her in a way that said otherwise! That kiss has traveled with her. She tried to unpack it.

It refuses to remove itself on her journey. She remembered other conversations they had years ago that traveled with her.

She wanted to ask but for some reason, she felt as though he would not respond and so she continued reflecting.

It was late and Ziariah was having a hard time falling asleep like most nights. Ziariah was dealing with the same thing that Love' had dealt with along with Rayanna and that was abandonment and or rejection. Ziariah was five at the time. She did not know how to verbalize how she was feeling but she definitely allowed herself naturally to feel the emotions. She was a happy child but there was an inner sadness and anger as well. Love' wanted to make sure that she did not experience what she had experienced most of her life. Ziariah was crying and Love' asked her what she was crying about. Ziariah belted out a hard cry and said, "I WANT MY DADDY AND MY PAPA!!!! Love' did not cry this time but she could relate to the pain. At the time all Love' could do was hold her and say, "I understand Ziariah, I understand." Love' really did not know what to do or say. She comforted her and then Rayanna began to comfort Ziariah. The abandonment they all felt and experienced at one point in their life made it easy for them to connect. After Ziariah became calm, calm enough to fall asleep, Love' went downstairs and began to feel anger. She was angry with herself again, angry with Marquis, and angry with the decisions that she had made. She began to see as bright as the moon that her decisions were a direct reflection of the abandonment she had felt growing up. She felt alone because Love' was already so unique in her thinking. She felt that there weren't many people who understood her on top of the rejection she felt from the abandonment she had experienced. Feelings of abandonment usually lead to not feeling worthy. She began to re-evaluate her life and it was revealed as to why she loved being alone. She could remember while growing up how her family loved having company and how she hated it. She knew it was partly because of the fact that she was an empath but in this moment she realized that it was also because she had become accustomed to being alone. There was a part of her that wanted a space for herself on the inside but that same part was the part that had been stepped on so much; that part of her was sleeping so that it did not have to feel and deal with the reality of that little girl on the inside who was scared to share that part of herself again even with herself. So after a few minutes of being around people especially without her brothers where she felt the safest she would have to retrieve back into her bedroom (literally and figuratively) and go away from the crowd. It was just so much energy for her that she didn't know what to do with. She saw how she had become comfortable in this space. She had not wanted to leave it or expose it. She was no longer blaming her parents because she was well aware of the fact that it was a part of her reason for returning back to earth and she also knew that the abandonment she felt was from many lifetimes. She had to feel abandonment to get to acceptance and love within herself. She had to embrace all of her through the pain of abandonment in order for her to be present to herself to get to her higher self. She had to release this in order to accept who she had always been and who she was but she had to pull back the curtains and undress herself completely. No more spiritual phrasing or pretty words to dress up the pain It all began to become so clear to her. While she did know that there were parts of herself that was likened unto the 99 Neteru's which is within the kemetic culture and according to the Kemetic spiritual system the 99 Neteru is directly correlated to the periodic table of the elements. So the same number connected to your birth month, date and year is the same number directly related to that specific element. In other words, if your birth month is seven you would look for that exact number within the periodic table and the seventh deity within the 99 Neteru. This is determined by your birth date. The 99 Neteru are the aspects or names of nature spirits/deities just as in Christianity, God had several aspects or names for himself and referred by many names for example: Jehovah Jireh, Jehovah Rapha, Jehovah Tsidkenu, etc.... Same deity but when called upon by those names that aspect is believed to be activated. It is the same thing within in the 99 Neteru except it is realized within nature and self, the higher self. The 99 Neteru is of the culture and spiritual principle of Ancient Kemet (Egypt). There are 99 of them but these are the ones directly affiliated with Love's birthdate.

Love's birth date is 7-8-1977 so according to the 99 Neteru and the periodic table she is of the components of:

7. Yaa Keket, Yaa Neter Oh voidness, Oh deity

#7 Nitrogen

8. Yaa Amun, Yaa Neter Oh hidden, Oh deity

8. Oxygen

15. Yaa Aset, Yaa Neter

Oh mighty throne, Oh deity

15. Phosphorus

77. Yaa Duamutet, Yaa Neter

Oh shaper and he who for sees, Oh deity # 77. Iridium

While she knew that she was limitless these key components had revealed to her why she was the way she was and why she had experienced what she had experienced on her journey. You see, she knew that while she felt comfortable in aloneness she knew that it was missing balance and her allowing the flow of all that she was to just be. To just breathe deeply. To just create. To just see through and beyond the physical. To just observe. To just be open. To just accept her value in it all of its limitlessness. She was certainly on that path to just being. She could remember while growing up always being hidden in regards to her presence being felt but yet not seen or heard. She was quiet like oxygen and nitrogen but her presence was missed when she wasn't around. She could see in her life the presence of iridium because there was a hardness there based on the high temperatures of life that brought out and or transformed her into her best self. She could also see and feel the presence of phosphorus using toxic waste to transform herself. Everything that she had experienced and or endured was all for her good. Her eyes were as bright as the moon; sol light shinning through. For she was seeing how everything was being used and she was realizing just how much of an alchemist she was.

Love' was now ready to go full force on her journey. It just did not matter who was staying for the ride and who would be dropped off. She was seeing how to not take things so personally. She was seeing how everyone comes here with their assignments and those assignments are design to teach. She knew it was a choice whether or not who would accept the lessons and grow from them. She could see how there were so many teachers who did not know they were teachers. So many people who she had learned from without them ever knowing and one of them being Mozique. She really wanted him to understand the valuable being that he was and or is. She wanted him to know how he had eventually changed her life after their short period of time of their exchange. She wanted him to know his worth beyond the physical. She wanted him to know it had nothing to do with anything superficial. The question was would she ever have the chance just to tell him. She had no other expectations other than that. She was beginning to think that in general when memories turn into tangled knots don't be afraid to grab the scissors.

Chapter 16

I was going back up north to Delaware and Philly. I asked if Love' and Ziariah wanted to ride. Love' wanted to go. Sometime had passed since their last visit. She was excited. She was looking forward to spending time getting to know Belle, Lois, Ruby and James' dad. She was planning on spending time with

Belle's mom, Ruby. But for some reason, she was really looking forward to spending time with Bella.

When they arrived they went straight to Belle's and James home. They were excited as well. Belle gave Love' the biggest, longest hug. She was very welcoming. No one else was home. She greeted Ziariah and myself. She invited us into their home. I was going to be staying in Philly for a business meeting while Love' would be staying in James's old room, how ironic, she thought. Love' wondered if Sadie had told Belle about who Love' was in her previous life.

I did not stay long and the rest of the family would not be there this weekend. Lois was living in Georgia and Ruby was living in Texas. They were working professionals. Lois had become some sort of University Researcher at one of the schools down there and Ruby was married with a family of her own. She finished school but decided to be a stay at home mom. She had become a lot like her mom as well as like Grandma Tee. She wanted her children to be homeschooled so that she could influence them and instill a level of confidence that in most cases just was not a part of the public school educational experience.

Love' had gone upstairs and was getting situated in the room she was going to be sleeping in. Ziariah had fallen asleep. Belle had come up the stairs and knocked on the bedroom door asking if Love' was hungry. Love' told her yes. Belle told her to come on down. She had already prepared a meal for them. Love' came downstairs and followed the smell of homemade cornbread, homemade fries, fried fish and corn. Love' told Belle that everything smelled so good and everything looked so delicious. Belle smiled and said, "go on ahead and fix yourself something to eat. Where is Ziariah?" Love' told her that she was sleep and then asked her where could she wash her hands? Belle told her that she could wash them right in the kitchen. So Love' did. Then she fixed her plate. Belle had prepared fresh lemonade and poured it into a tall glass and placed it on the table setting where Love' had sat down. Love' had not started eating because she was not sure if Belle would say a prayer or not and she wanted to wait for Belle to sit down with her. After Belle had prepared her plate she sat down across from Love' and they had one of the best conversations. They laughed and just spent time getting to know one other. Belle looked up and was watching Love' finish her last bite of food. Then she asked Love'.

Belle: Love', so what is it that you want to do in this life?

Love': I plan to do many things. I plan to become an author, open up my own school for low-income families and create my own web series. I also would like to become a counselor and plan to go back to school to obtain my masters.

Belle: Do you sing?

Love's eye became bright as the moon; sol light shining through.

Love': Yes, I sing. Can't say that I want to do anything with it but I do sing.

Belle: Hmmmm...Why do you think that you don't want to do anything with it and really what does that mean?

Love': Well, I do not want to do that for a living. I am ok with singing. There really isn't anything distinctive about my vocal ability.

Belle: Would you mind singing me something. If you sing I will share a song with you.

Love' really did not want to but then she thought, well; it's just her and I here so what would be the harm?

Love' began singing a song she wrote years ago

It was love that brought us to this place
It was love that said our love couldn't be erased
Even though it looked as though it was over
When man said no, love said, yes
It was love, It was love, It was love
It was faith, it was love
Instead of looking at what can not be changed
See all that remains
No one has ever been able to touch my heart, my mental or
even look past my scars, some say that memories fade away
but these have decided to stay Years have gone but this love is
strong because it was love that brought us to this place

It was love that said this love couldn't be erased Even though it looked as though it was over When man said no, love said, yes It was love, It was love, It was love,

It was faith....

Belle was in tears. After Love' finished her last note, she opened her eyes and saw Belle grabbing a napkin to wipe the tears from her eyes.

Belle: There was a reason I asked you to sing. Yes, of course I wanted to hear you but more importantly, I wanted to hear your story. You see, while you may not feel or think that there is anything spectacular about your vocal ability there is something unique to your voice, with your story. There is always a touch of all things pure when we express our hearts. You do have a magical gift vocally. A beautiful voice but that is something that you will have to discover on your own. Did you write that song? I don't know why I asked that because the way that song touched me, I am certain that you did write it.

Love': Yes I did.

Love' grabbed a napkin now because Belle's words touched her.

Belle: Why are you crying?

Love':' Because what you said touched my heart.

Belle: See that's what I mean your vocal ability, your voice is magical. We have the power to touch without a physical touch.

Your intention was just to share from a pure place and so reciprocity was in order.

Love' smiled and said, "Thank you." Belle continued on with the conversation.

Belle: Well the writing ability is in you. Our son James was a writer. He published one book before he passed. He was in the middle of working on the second book when he transitioned.

Love' became a little uncomfortable. She did not really know what to say. Her mind was racing. This must have shown on her face because Belle read her accurately.

Belle: Love', are you Ok? You look like you have a lot running through your mind. Love's eyes were as big and bright as the moon, sol shining through.

Love': Yes I am ok.

Belle: Hold on a second, I'll be right back.

Love' could not imagine what Belle was about to do or say. She thought that this lady was so in touch with her higher self. She already adored her and felt such a strong connection towards her. Belle had only gone in the room right next to the kitchen off to the side. Love' was curious to know what was in that room. Belle began to call for Love' to come inside this room. So Love' proceeded to get up from the table and walk towards the room. She slowly opened up the door while Belle was saying, "Come on in." Love' felt so much energy in that room. She began to feel very warm and then she felt a breeze. She began to cry. Her legs became weak and she fell to her knees. Belle began to weep. Belle told Love' that this use to be grandma Tee's meditation room, James's grandmother on his dad side. But what Belle didn't know was that Love' had seen that room before in her dream she just had not told anyone at the time. In the dream, she was with an older very regal looking woman as she was being shown as James in the dream. When she went into the bathroom in the house within the dream she looked in the mirror to confirm that she was herself but after looking in the mirror she could see she was James. Anyway, Grandma Tee and Love' were lighting candles (in the dream) and what appeared to be meditating. Love' wanted to tell Belle but she didn't feel that it was time just yet. Belle pulled out an unfinished book and a couple of journals. She told Love' she could read them. So Love' read them. Love' thought it would be a perfect time that evening to read them because Ziariah was going to spend time with her uncle's. Love's brother Ron was now living in Wilmington,De. He and his wife of twelve-thirteen years had separated and divorced and he had relocated back home. Malik was still living in New Jersey and was coming up to stay with Ron for the weekend so they could hang out with Ziariah and Ron's two daughters, Sanaiya and Rae. They were a lot older than Ziariah but she loved her cousins and they loved her.

That evening Ron and Malik stopped by to pick Ziariah up along with Sanaiya and Rae. Belle was so happy to see everyone.

She wanted them to stay a little while longer but they had plans for the girls. It was Ziariah's only first time spending the night anywhere without her mom and or Nanna. Love' and Ziariah said their goodnights and see you laters and told Ziariah that she would see her the next day.

Love' could not wait to read the journals. She wanted to know what she had to say on her journey as James. Belle told Love' that his first book was based on his life and his second book was as well. Belle began to share various details of her upbringing and the things that she and his family had gone through. As Love' listened, things began to connect in her present life.

Belle: Love', James wrote songs and sung as well. I did not find out until later in his life that he could but when I first heard he and his sisters sing, I cried.

Love': My brothers and I sing as well and write also.

Belle: I am not surprised being though that we come from a musical family. I just wish James was here in the physical form to witness it.

Love': (Thinking to herself, Oh, he is.)

Belle: So tell me, if you don't mind; what is your book about?

Love': No, I don't mind. It's about my journey and the connection between the present, past and future and how they all are equivalent to Now. The now that I live is directly associated with all three aspects.

Belle: So you're not going to tell me specifically (she says so graciously with a smile).

Love': (With a smile) Well, I did tell you what it was about without telling you what it is about.

Belle: So are you seeing anyone? In love?

Love': No and yes. I am not dating anyone but I am in love with those I love. I am becoming more and more aware of the love within me that I am.

Belle: Now that is a great place to be.

Belle held her head down and appear to be in deep thought. Love' asked her if she was Ok and Belle told her she was fine but Love' knew different.

Love': Belle, are you sure?

Belle: Yes. I am just getting sleepy now. Are you going to read tonight?

Love': Yes I am.

Belle: Let me know what you think.

Love': Yes, I will.

That night Love' pick up the journal that had pages and pages of his typed work. She began reading after Belle turned in for the night which was around ten o' clock that night. Love' stayed up reading until five o' clock in the a.m. She experienced many emotions but she felt so inspired to work on her book when she woke up. She was typing on her laptop for about fifteen minutes and for some reason got the urge to write on paper, so she did.

As she was writing she began to feel intensely an overwhelming feeling of gratitude. Her higher self began to speak, she heard so clearly, "All you can do is just say thank you! When you know without a doubt that you've made the best decision that coincides with what you say you want and are ready for. When you no longer are controlled emotionally by what is said or done by someone who used to have that power over you. When your value is speaking to you louder than distractions. That's when you realize you're witnessing evolution within. Stop trying to fit where there's no room for you in that tight, outdated space or place because you are expanding in every area of your life." Love' knew that she had recently let go of Amir or so she thought. She had to because she knew she was not willing to sleep with him and engage in sexual activity without a commitment but even more importantly she was not willing to participate in an exchange of energy with someone who at this particular time was not taking the time to get to know her beyond the person that he once knew while they were in high school dating. Love' had evolved so much. Amir was not used to her not giving in. The other person that had a hold over Love' was Rayanna. They had an interesting dynamic. Growing up, Love' did not remember Rayanna complimenting Love' much. Love' was extremely musical from an early age but it was not cultivated so she at one time felt insecure about her ability. Her mom did not compliment her much on her writing ability. She definitely criticized her often but more than that she just said nothing. So needless to say Love' tried to live her life as the "goody two shoes." She thought she had that. At least her mom was proud of that but when Love' started living her journey without the fear of going to hell or even before that she just allowed herself to experience things in life that Rayanna had never experienced she felt judgement from her mom. Rayanna criticized Love' a lot in regards to Ziariah. Her mom would never compliment her writing ability not until later in life. If her mom thought either one of her brothers wrote a song she would compliment either one of them. This really hurt Love' for some years. It seemed as though even if on a subconscious level Rayanna knew how to get under Love's skin. Love' was feeling so strongly that she had to move not only because of what she was experiencing in regards to their relationship but because the whole entire time she was coming up Love' did not know that it was a co-dependent relationship. As Love' was closing the chapters on her previous relationships she was realizing all the more that she and Rayanna were a lot alike in some ways but extremely opposite in many more ways.

Clarity was speaking to Love' in so many aspects of her life. She knew that Rayanna loved her. Love' could see the feelings she once had about herself at the time during those previous relationships and the connection between the environment she not only grew up in but developed in within the womb. The womb that includes the egg and the semen it took to create her, the things that Rayanna went through while Love' developed inside of her.

Love' began to really reflect all the more. She really began to know the importance of letting those individuals go; the voice that had calmly spoke to her repeatedly the phrase whenever she would get involved with someone that was not for her, "Let him go" with the exception of one person. It wasn't so much about the relationship itself, it was about the relationship she had with herself or the lack thereof, the way she once felt about herself that drew those relationships to her. Those old feelings were being released so the connection would simultaneously be disconnected and besides she had finally learned the repeated lesson that she attracted via those past relationships. Those love ones she was no longer drawn to because she was seeing herself from a different view.

The clarity was also putting the spotlight on the first relationships you establish from birth. She thought that she and her mom had the best relationship and I mean, I guess in comparison to other family members or some of her peers coming up perhaps they did but in order to have a relationship you have to be able to relate and for the most part for a long time they had not been able to relate. Love' was discovering why they had not been able to relate for quite some time. Now, the relationship between them had not always been that way. At some point, it shifted. Love' remembers feeling as though, at one point her mom resented her. One day, Love' decided to take her locs out and wear her hair in an afro and after she had taken them out and was wearing it in an afro her mom told her that she didn't like it. Love' found it odd because she knew that her (Rayanna's) mom at one time had an afro. Rayanna was also wearing her hair in locs at the time and not to mention Rayanna's mom also wore an afro in her latter years. So Love' asked her after her mom told her she didn't like her hair like that...

Love': Mom, why don't you like the afro?

Rayanna: I just don't like it, it's outdated.

Love:' But your mom had it.

Rayanna: I know and I didn't like then either.

Love': I love it.

Rayanna: Ok.

But inside Love' was still a little girl searching for her mother's approval. She was so determined to do her best to make Ziariah aware and confident in her limitlessness.

The most interesting thing was a few years down the road Rayanna began wearing her hair in an afro. Love' told her, "I like your hair." but in that moment she remembered how her mom had told her how she felt about her wearing her hair in an afro so she asked her....

Love': I like your hair.

Rayanna: Thanks, I just want it a little more fuller.

Love' thought for a moment quietly remembering what she had once said.

Love': I thought you said you didn't like the afro when I was wearing my hair in an afro.

Rayanna: I don't know. I don't remember saying that.

Love': Well, you did.

Rayanna: Ok. I am not saying that I never said it. I am just saying that I do not remember saying it.

Love': Oh, well you did but why did you say that?

Rayanna: I don't know.

The dynamic between her and her mother was very interesting. Love' remembered times where she would share different things that she was working on and just like she could remember and count on one hand how many times her dad had ever complimented her and telling her how beautiful she was she could not remember how many times her mom had complimented her on her abilities and talents. But as time went on and Love' began to change her perception of herself and affirm her greatness Love' had forgiven her parents. She was well aware that their behavior was not intentional but it was connected to the pain that they had once faced as children themselves. They had not received some of the same things that they were unable to give. Love' knew the importance of letting it go and forgiving them so that she would not repeat the same cycle with Ziariah and she not only owed that to Ziariah but she owed it to herself. Just as she was evolving so was Rayanna and Ron.

As Love' continued reading James's stories both his published work and the one that he did not get a chance to complete. She began to weep. She saw the connection between his published work and her present life. In the book he was beginning to feel broken-hearted as a result of me (Sadie) not being fully present but yet he was beginning to realize it really had nothing to do with me and everything to do with himself. James had given all of himself and was loving me and I could not reciprocate in the same manner in which he was giving it. I feel a part of me did not feel worthy of such a love because I had yet to give that to myself.

Love' fell asleep a little after five and woke up five hours later. When she woke up she heard voices coming from downstairs. She decided to get up and take a shower. Apparently, Belle had come in the bedroom while she was sleeping. Belle placed a towel and washcloth on the foot of the bed. Love' grabbed the towel and the wash cloth and hopped in the shower. She continued thinking about the relation between her present life and her previous life as James. She had decided that she would talk to me about my relationship with James to find out exactly what I thought happened in regards to our relationship and his transition.

After Love' was dressed she went down stairs, expecting to see where and or who the voices that she was hearing but could not find anyone. She opened up the front door and a young man was standing outside on the corner. He looked at Love' and smiled and started walking towards her. Love' smiled. He approached her. He looked to be about 6 ft and Love' was 4 foot 8 in a half. He stood on the sidewalk while Love' was standing on the front step.

Him: Hey, How are you?

Love': Hello, I am well. How are you?

Him: I am fine. I didn't want anything but to tell you how beautiful you are.

Love' was blushing, her deep dimples showing along with her smiling eyes.

Love': Awww, thank you.

Him: (walking off and then he turned around walking towards her again.) What is your name; if you don't mind me asking?

Love': "L" (was the name she gave when she was drawn to the person but she wasn't sure for what reason.)

Him: Ok. My name is Hasan, not that you asked or anything (with a smile).

While he was standing there and they were conversing, a van drove past and his back was facing the van. The van came back down the street and a woman hopped out of the car and starting yelling and cursing first at him and then at Love'.

Woman: What the hell are you doing Hasan? Who is this bitch?

Love': Standing there speechless.

It had been years since anything like this had happened to Love'. There had been only one incident that had happened before and Love' had promised herself that if something like that had ever happened like that again she would be ready and not caught off guard.

Love': First of all, I do not know you miss and I would appreciate it if you did not refer to me as a bitch. How the hell am I suppose to know that he is your man and secondly we were not doing anything? Third of all he approached me. Now if you're angry or bothered it needs to be with him not with me because I don't know you or owe you anything.

Woman: Not with this bitch though, Hasan, (While pointing towards Love').

Love': Ok you're beyond ignorant and need therapy. I said not to refer to me as a bitch. Who are you really angry with? Me, Hasan or yourself for putting up with foolishness because I am pretty sure this is not the first time you have caught him talking to someone.

Love' began laughing so hard and this pissed the woman off. Love' could not stop laughing and she was trying to stop.

Woman: What the hell is your dumb ass laughing at?

Love': this whole dumb ass scenario. You're mad because your man, I'm assuming because I still don't know who you are, is

TALKING to a woman he just met five minutes ago and I could be a long lost relative, I could be anyone. Then your man Hasan is just standing here watching you act like a fool, I think you're a little off on who the dumb ass is.

Woman: Come down those steps, bitch!

Love': (Was still laughing) Oh yeah, you're a big dummy. Do you really think that I am going to fight you over someone I don't even know? Do you really think I am going to fight someone who is big as their van they are driving? Now if you come for me I will defend myself, but I am not about to fight you for no reason. I don't have a reason. Like I am about to fight for YOUR man TALKING and he initiated it. I don't care if I initiated it. It would then be his responsibility to speak up on your behalf and tell me he has a woman. Girl get back in your van so you can go on a search for an amber alert.

Woman: An amber alert? What the hell you talking about?

Love': Yes an amber alert because your dignity has been kidnapped by your ego or lack of self-esteem. You need to be in search for that, please, quickly, you better hurry up.

Love' realized what she had just said and apparently so did Hasan because he was laughing so hard and now so was Love'. She was not trying to be funny. She was serious but after the fact she realized just how funny it was on one hand but on the other hand it wasn't because this woman was obviously delusional and hurting.

Hasan: Tish, you and I are not together and you need to accept that. This is one of the many reasons we are not together. You have disrespected this young lady and our child is in the van and you are carrying yourself in such an unattractive manner.

Tish: Well, if you had been home when I went to drop Neveah off then I would not have needed to come find you.

Hasan: I was behind time. I apologize. I started my jog later than what I normally start because I was up late last night writing. That is neither here nor there; the point is you were off work today and you should have parked your happy self in front of the house and called me but I have no missed calls from you. You felt like arguing today. It's as if your intention was set out to argue and be the cause of drama.

Tish: (Had tears in her eyes) You are so disrespectful. You are a disrespectful nigga.

Tish began walking towards her van.

Love': (Love' began to feel very compassionate towards her.) Tish, Sometimes it's not about the relationship we once had with those we at one time connected with. Sometimes it is about the connection to the feelings that are missing in regards to how we feel about ourselves. Learn to love you. Focus on you.

Tish was crying. She told Love' that she was right and apologized to her. Love' apologized for saying that she was as big as her van. Hasan was still standing there at the bottom of the step on the sidewalk. Love' watched Tish pull off and was wondering why Hasan was still standing there. Love' was turned off from the fact that he let it go as far as he did before saying anything. He apologized to Love' and she accepted and he walked off. Love' never understood in situations like that how the woman was always upset with the "other" woman even when it would be very apparent that the other woman knew nothing about the person he may or may not be involved with.

Love' decided to go back in the house. Love' walked towards the kitchen and she saw Belle and Sadie. Everyone greeted one another but Love' heard a man's voice and wondered who that was. Belle asked Love' if she was hungry and Love' told her, yes.

Belle: How did you sleep last night? Or should I ask, how did you sleep this morning?

Love': (Smiling) You knew that I was up late huh? How did you know?

Belle: Because I know my son's work and besides I happen to go downstairs in the middle of the night around three o'clock in the morning and noticed that the light was on and figured you were still up reading. So what time did you finally fall asleep?

Love': I fell asleep around five o'clock a.m. His book was so intriguing and I wanted to see what would happen next. I have to read the other book now, the one that he was working on before transitioning.

Belle: Now what was going on outside?

Love' began to tell Belle and Sadie what happened outside. Belle told Love' that she knows Hasan and that he is a real nice young man. She told Love' that he is not only nice but he is extremely gifted in multiple areas of his life.

Belle: He writes and is a published author. He has written screenplays and he is a graduate of Temple University as a double major in African-American studies and psychology. He is also a musician. He has a shyness to him but he is a genius and he is very humorous.

Love': that is funny because my brother Malik says that some of the most ingenious people you'll ever meet are those that are the most humorous.

Love's brothers were extremely humorous and the life of any family gathering or party. Ron Jr. and Malik were very handsome. Ron Jr. looked a lot like Rayanna and Love'. Ron Jr. has very keen features and girly eyes with long eyelashes and dimples. Malik had a mixture in features between his mom and dad, very handsome. He also had dimples and smiled with his eyes, all three looked a lot alike. What was even more strange is how Bianca looked a lot like Love' and mainly like Malik. Bianca was their dad's daughter now their brother by their dad looked more like his mom and really nothing like his dad. When they all got together the humor was evident amongst them.

Ron Jr. and Malik were coming over later for dinner, Belle had invited them. What Love' didn't know was that Belle had also invited Hasan.

Belle: So what did you think of Hasan?

Love': I thought that he was very handsome but I was slightly turned off after he stood there watching myself and his daughter's mom going back and forth.

Belle: So because of that what is your perception of him now?

Love': That he may be easily intimidated. I don't want to call him a punk but just not as secure with handling confrontation and that is not attractive to me because I have dealt with that before within my own life as well as attracting that into my life in regards to the men that I have dated, where I would have to be the one to stand up. Now, some were definitely not like that but the ones who I was so in love with as I became older definitely were.

As Love' listened to her own self-expressing this to Belle and Sadie she began to go deep into thought and realized how important it was for a woman to feel protected and secure with someone she was involved with. A woman must know a man will defend her no matter who it is. If she is a woman of integrity and of a pure heart, with loving energy exuding from her heart chakra, then she should most definitely feel loved by a man who professes his love to her. One of the main areas that a man expresses his love is via protection. He will defend her honor.

He will not believe someone when they have lied on her because he is confident in the woman he has selected to share his life experiences with. These thoughts made her remember Mozique was a reminder of why she trusted him as much as she did at the time. He made her feel safe. He defended her honor. He took his time with trying to get to know her before thinking about sleeping with her. She ultimately felt protected and this was a first for her in her adult life to have experienced such a thing that she just could not seem to remove him or his actions from her heart. She knew that he would forever be a part of her realizing just how valuable she was and is.

Belle began to inquire regarding Hasan.

Belle: So do you feel that Hasan would not be able to demonstrate those attributes?

Love': Usually the first reaction is an honest reaction. I can not say for sure. Perhaps he was caught off guard as I was but a man snaps out of shock usually.

Belle: Did he say anything at all?

Love': Eventually, he did. His daughter's mother eventually apologized to me and got back in her van.

Love' knew that Belle obviously thought highly of Hasan and was hoping for there to be a connection between he and Love'.

Belle told Love' that she was welcomed to some breakfast and that she could fix her plate. She had prepared eggs, homemade waffles and home fries. Everything was delicious. It was about

11 a.m. Love' was ready to go back upstairs and continue reading James's work. She did not want to be rude. I was very quiet and Love' definitely noticed. Belle had gone out in to the back yard.

Love': Sadie is everything Ok?

Sadie: I have a lot on my mind.

Love': Thinking about James?

Sadie: Well; thinking about a lot, I guess.

Love': I have a question for you, if you don't mind me asking.

Sadie: No, go ahead.

Love': What happened to James? I mean of course, I know he transitioned but what exactly happened? You may have already told me a while ago and I just don't remember.

Sadie: (Smiling with tears in her eyes) I would be glad to tell you but I'd rather not talk about it with the chance of Belle being able to walk in on us conversing about the matter. Can we talk about it later?

Love': Of course.

Sadie: Thanks.

Love': Does Belle know yet about me and my dream?

Sadie: Do you mean does she know that you were James in your previous life?

Love': Yes.

Sadie: Not to my knowledge. Why do you want to tell her?

Love': Yes I do, just not sure of when would be a good time to tell someone something like that.

Sadie: If it is for you to tell her, the time will speak clearly to you.

Love': You're right.

Love' excused herself from the table and was headed to the backyard for a moment. When she came back in she told Sadie that she was going to do some more reading before getting ready for tonight's dinner but before she went upstairs she asked Sadie what was up with Belle regarding Hasan.

Love': (With a slight whisper) Why is Belle so intrigued by Hasan? Why is she trying to set us up? I don't live here.

Sadie: (She busted out laughing and responded with a loud tone) Huh?

Love': It's not funny. You see I am whispering! Stop!

Sadie: (In a loud tone again) I DONT KNOW WHY SHE SEEMS TO BE INTERESTED IN CONNECTING YOU WITH HASAN! (Laughing) No, seriously why don't you ask her?

Love': Because I do not want her to think that I am interested.

Sadie: I thought you said he is attractive.

Love': I did say that but that does not mean I am interested in getting to know him on any level.

Sadie: But why not? What will it harm? Are you afraid of it being something real? You have not been involved with anyone for quite some time now. How many years has it been?

Love': A about five years.

Sadie: Damn and you're not interested in at least getting to know him on a friendship level?

Love:' No. I really want to close the chapter with someone from my past even if they already have but I will be ready soon.

Sadie: How will you be ready soon? How do you know that you are not ready now?

Love': Because I just know.

Sadie: How do you plan on closing that chapter if the person who is in the chapter with you doesn't even know they're even in the chapter or that it is open?

Love' did not know how to respond to that. She did not have an answer. She could not make him respond. Love' really wanted to converse about a few things that happened. She wanted to ask him questions but did not know how to ask him. She thought it was just too awkward.

Sadie: Ummm, HELLO? Earth to Love'!?

Love': I am here. Just thinking, maybe you're right. I should be open to possibilities.

Love' was extremely proud of herself regarding Amir. She felt that Amir was just looking for that bed buddy and Love' was waiting for something of more substance. She did not know what would come of the connection or even if there was connection with Hasan and maybe a part of her was a little apprehensive.

Love' really enjoyed talking to me because although I was old enough to be her mom she would tell me how I was so young at heart having a youthful look.

Love': Ok. I will definitely be open to a new friendship.

Love' went upstairs to read James's work. When she was finished it was about four o'clock. Love' was speechless. She saw a lot of similarities to her present work and to her present life and yet she realized how it was all related.

She did not know what time dinner was but she decided to wash up and change clothes. The first guest arrived around five o'clock. When she heard the doorbell she decided to get ready to go downstairs. She had been laying down contemplating. Love' was always contemplating.

As soon as she went down stairs she realized who it was. It was Hasan, his daughter and Hasan's mom and dad. His mom and dad were no longer married but they were still very good friends. Love' walked into the family room and Belle introduced Love'. Hasan's mom greeted Love' with a genuine hug and a big, warm, inviting smile. She said, "I am so pleased to meet you, finally." Love' thought, "finally?" His dad was laid back a lot like Hasan seemed to be. His daughter's name is Neveah. She is a beautiful girl. Thick head full of hair and a round face. The same complexion as Love'. She is a golden, honey, graham cracker brown complexion. She has big bright eyes. She is four. Only a year younger than Ziariah. Hasan greeted Love' with a hug also and everyone was silent in that moment, so Love' said, "ooook, why is everyone so quiet all of a sudden?" Hasan busted out laughing and then so did everyone else. Love' sat down in the family room with everyone waiting for the rest of the guest to arrive. Shortly after the doorbell rang again. It was Ron Jr., his girls and Malik and Ziariah. Love' was so excited to see Ziariah. They never spent time apart, especially overnight. Everyone was introduced to one another. Belle asked everyone to go wash their hands in the bathroom and then wanted everyone to come to the table and sit down. She asked if she could say a few words before eating by repeating after her.

May the nutrients bless every organ with high levels of energy of love.

May the nutrients exude gratitude in which the hands that have prepared it be made aware in the body that partakes of it.

We are thankful for family and we commune with one another in peace, harmony, love, truth and abundance. Ase'.

Everyone began passing the food around. Everything looked so tasty. Belle had prepared baked chicken, mash potatoes, string beans, salad, fried turkey, quinoa and gravy with homemade rolls. Our beverages consisted of Sweet Tea, wine, water, apple juice and Jamaican peach rum.

Everyone was so quiet at the dinner table until someone noticed that it was too quiet.

Belle: Your silence can say one or two things. Either it is so good you don't want to stop eating. Or it is so horrible and you don't want to lie.

Love': Awww stop, you know this food is delicious. We give thanks to the hands that prepared it.

Everyone agreed. Belle was laughing and she said, "thank you, it was truly an honor."

After dinner Love' and Sadie offered to help clean up, of course Belle said no that she would handle it but Love' and Sadie insisted. Belle told Sadie for her to help with setting something up downstairs for her and she said on second thought, "Love' would you mind helping me in the kitchen?" Love' told her no and so she went to the kitchen and started washing the dishes. Love' had the water running and could not hear what they were laughing about in the other room but when she went to put the dishes in the dish drain she realized someone was standing there. It was Hasan.

Hasan: So because I have already noticed how observant you are I am pretty sure you know that some of them are trying to play matchmaker.

Love': Yes, I have definitely noticed that. (smiling)

Hasan: Belle asked if I would come in here and help you in the kitchen. So show me what you want me to do.

Love': Ok. I'll wash and you dry.

Hasan grabbed the towel and began drying and since he had been over Belle's several times he knew where to put the dishes they were moving pretty quickly.

Hasan: I want to apologize for the other day. I was so embarrassed that Tish was acting like that and it was as though you said everything that I was going to say so eloquently.

Love': Oh it's Ok.

Hasan: You were really hilarious. I know you made her think. She and I usually argue every day and now she has been very agreeable. So, thank you because something you said touched her in a way that made a difference.

Love': How do you know it was what I said?

Hasan: I just know. So how long are you here for? Aunt Belle told my mom that you no longer live here and have not lived here for a while.

Love': We are leaving some time next week.

Hasan: Would you like to hang out at the park? We can bring our daughters.

Love': Well, Ziariah will be going with her Uncles again tonight and will not be back until tomorrow night at some time point but I can go.

Hasan: (Smiling) Ok. What time is a good time for you?

Love': one o'clock.

Hasan: Ok. I can pick you up then.

Love': Ok.

Hasan and Love' continued conversing and laughing. Love' was actually enjoying his company. He had a very contagious smile, just like Love'. It did not seem to take them long washing the dishes. When they finished; Belle wanted everyone to come downstairs in the basement. It was a huge basement and it was a finished basement.

Everyone began heading towards the steps and Love' became so nervous because of how it was set up. Sadie was looking directly at Love' because Sadie knew she was nervous and that she would know exactly why Belle had set it up the way; it was set up like a nightclub. There was a microphone, keyboard and a few other instruments in the corner. Belle asked everyone to have a seat. Belle went up to the microphone and said, " I set this up so that we may honor one another, so that we may honor the divinity within through our gifts and abilities." Belle went on to say that she was waiting on a few more people to arrive before starting. Love' was nervous as hell because she knew that Belle would be calling on her. She did not want to sing but she knew that Belle would definitely be expecting that. Love' would rather do a poem rather than a song. Everyone heard the door bell and then footsteps as if some people had come in. So Belle told them that she would be right back. We all heard voices and no one knew who was coming. We all heard the footsteps coming closer to the steps. It was Belle's husband

James, and her children Lois and Ruby. Everyone was being introduced and greeted one another.

Belle: Ok, everyone, Let's get started. I have everyone's name in this here hat. We're only going to select seven people this time. I am going to pick from the hat and who's ever name I pick is the one who is going first and everyone has to have a turn, even the babies if their names are selected.

Belle drew from the hat and the first name to come out was Hasan's. Love' had a facial expression of relief on her. Hasan got on the keyboard and sang a beautiful song entitled 'Tomorrow Is Now', an original song.

"Waiting patiently when you can do what you can do now Decisions and direction and seem to be going nowhere, growing nowhere slowly quickly. I was telling me I was waiting on life and life was telling me it was waiting on me because tomorrow is now...."

Many of us were tearing up because it was something that we all had experienced or were experiencing. After Hasan finished singing his song. Belle called for the next person to come up. The next person was Ziariah. She did not want to go up at all but her mom made her and she sang a song that had everyone in tears. The third name that was called was Love'. Love' was nervous as hell. She got up and did an original poem/song entitled, In The Twinkling of an Eye.

In the twinkling of an eye, souls magically intertwined
a sudden glance in her direction an erection, the heart standing
up at attention touching her soul without a hand, she felt
protected and instantly connected. She began to feel what she
had never felt before and when their lips touched... she was
changed forever, nothing physical but all eternal,
In the twinkling of an eye she had been changed from the
interaction an orgasmic feeling of eternal bliss, in the twinkling
of an eye her heart yearned to repeat the moment of magic
where in an instance with the sudden glance in her direction,
connected not through an exchange of words, but with
complimenting uniqueness in oneness of frequency; intimately
aware of the other's heart from the very start. There was no
beginning and no end. It was eternal and she was made aware.
A sudden glance in her direction an erection, the heart standing
up at attention touching her soul without a hand, she felt
protected and instantly connected in the twinkling
of an eye, she finally realized she loved him.
This was no ordinary love. It just always was even if the
opportunity was never presented to express the love she never
knew she was feeling until the time, until now; place and space
had passed in the distance. She knew that love was standing
still and yet moving for her to be aware of what and why she
was feeling the way she felt, for so many years
had passed and the magic was still the same.

In the twinkling of an eye her life had changed, she would only hope that he felt the same way. Even if they never crossed paths again, love would always remain. In the twinkling of an eye, she began to see what he had done for her. He helped her to accept just who she was without a physical touch, he saw her heart. He felt who she was from the very start and in her heart she knew who she was but she thought how could this be? How did he know me oh so well? They had only known each other for a short time. But she heard the answer because love knows not time and in an instant... in the twinkling of an eye where there was no space, place nor time. Magic and eternal bliss command the heart to stand up at attention, even in silence they spoke, she heard and felt the voices of angels touch her soul. This is why it had been a challenge to let him go; but then she realized it was not that she had to let the love go and the fact is, in the twinkling of an eye she had been changed. That triumph would never fade away, even if not in the physical they would ever reunite again. They were of love so that would stay forever in her heart, she would remember he was a part of her change that had come. He saw her, how she had always viewed herself even if for a moment she'd forget. But he was the first one outside of herself who would honor it.

In the twinkling of an eye, souls magically intertwined.
A sudden glance in her direction an erection, the heart standing up at attention touching her soul without a hand. She felt

protected and instantly connected. In the twinkling of an eye, she learned to cherish every precious moment, for they always come and quickly go. She knew that she would forever be grateful for the experience of change in the twinkling of an eye.

Love' had memorized that piece and was shedding a few tears. It obviously came from a real place and touched all those who were listening, including Hasan.

The next name was called. There were three names written on one sheet of paper and that was Love', Malik and Ron Jr. The three of them had not sung in ages. Malik was singing in shows in Philadelphia, NY and New Jersey. He was writing and building in regards to his music career. Ron Jr. was writing as well and Love' and Malik along with their mom was trying to encourage Ron to perform his music as well. The three of them sang that evening and everyone was in tears. They sang from a place that they had not sung from, together in a very long time. After they sung; Lois, Ruby and Belle sang in honor of James. They sang one of the many songs he had written. After they sung, Sadie looked over at Love' and her eyes were filled with tears. Sadie's eyes began to flow like rivers of living water. Sadie knew why Love' was touched. The song they sung touched a part of her soul that her soul had not forgotten.

We had a lovely evening and enjoyed getting to know one another and for some of us getting reacquainted. Everyone began leaving around midnight. Ziariah left with her uncles and she had a ball with Neveah that night. Love' told her brothers that she was going to hang out with Hasan and that they could just call her when they were ready to bring Ziariah back to Belle's. They agreed and told her that she needed to go out and have a nice time.

The next day she rose early from bed even though she stayed up late again the night before because she was still reading James's work. She went to the bathroom, washed her face and brushed her teeth and then went downstairs for breakfast. It was about nine a.m. When she got downstairs she noticed that Belle was not home. So she poured herself something to drink and went back upstairs. She realized she really wasn't hungry. She was slightly nervous about going out even if it was just to the park but she was excited to finally get to hang out with a man who she may actually have things in common with beyond surface things.

Love' decided to read at least for another hour and a half or two. She really wanted to finish reading both of his books before Ziairah came back. She finally finished both pieces of writings and it was just about twelve o'clock in the afternoon. She had lost track of time, especially when reading his second book. She knew she needed to have that conversation with Sadie. She was looking forward to that.

When Love' noticed the time, she jumped up and took a quick shower. She picked her outfit out and began getting dressed. It was now thirty minutes after twelve. She styled her locs and put a little lip color on. She put on essential oil, frankincense and myrrh and waited downstairs for him to arrive. While sitting downstairs she remembered she had not eaten and went into the kitchen. She noticed the clock on the wall and realized it was quarter till one. She opened up the fridge and pulled out leftovers from the night before and looked for the microwave and saw there was none, no microwave? she thought, wow! That's actually a good thing. She would have to take the time to warm everything up. Then she decided to make a turkey sandwich instead. Love' was trying her best to hurry and wolf down that sandwich before that doorbell rang. She managed to finish eating the sandwich before the door bell started ringing. Hasan was ten minutes late now. She finally heard the doorbell and it was him. Love' thought that he was even more handsome than the day before. Hasan had long locs, they were longer than Love's and not as neat which Love' loved. Hasan has a very distinguished look. Very handsome. He greeted Love' with a hug asking her if she was ready; immediately Love' remembered she didn't have a key to lock up the house. She told Hasan. He said, "You don't have to have a key to lock up, just lock the bottom lock and I know where Aunt Belle keeps the spare key if we happen to get back before she gets back." Love' said, "Ok.

Thanks." Hasan opened up the car door for her to get in and then closed the door and then he got in.

Hasan: (Smiling) Are you nervous?

Love': I was but for some reason, I'm not now.

Hasan: (Still smiling) That's a good thing.

Love': (Looking over at him smiling) Yes it is.

Hasan: Are you hungry?

Love': No, I just ate a turkey sandwich before you came and quite frankly I wolfed it down because I didn't want to take a chance on my stomach growling.

Hasan: I would have taken you out to eat. I honestly want to take you to one of my favorite spots but it is in Philly.

Love': Okay.

Hasan: We can eat at the park.

Love': Okay.

They had a ball together. They laughed so hard. Love' thought that Hasan was hysterically funny. It's funny because she thought that he was shy or quiet but he wasn't. They really seemed to be enjoying each other's company. When they arrived at the shop Hasan asked if she wanted to come in to order the food and Love' told him no that she would wait in the car and that he could order for her. She told him no pork or beef, please. He agreed. He comes back about fifteen minutes later to the car.

Hasan: Okay, we're off to the park.

Love': Okay.

They both glanced at each other with a smile. Hasan had his music turned down really low in the car and he heard a song that sounded like one of his favorite throwback songs and it was, Shalimar's 'Get Ready'. That was Love's cut too. They were both grooving in the car. They were singing and harmonizing.

They arrived at the park about thirty minutes later and were back in Wilmington. Hasan pulled a huge, heavy quilt out and they went to the biggest tree and laid under it. Love' wasn't really hungry but she was very thirsty and he had bought her some homemade lemonade from that restaurant shop in Philly. So Love' nibbled a little but she was now intrigued by Hasan. She wanted to get to know him. It was obvious he wanted to get to know her because he could not stop asking her questions. Love' was not used to this. It was new to her because most of the men she had been in serious relationships with never really communicated. They were very limited in what they shared as well as what they would ask her.

Hasan: So what is that you want to do with yourself?

Love': I am working on a book. I want to eventually have my own school for African- American youth. An African-centered curriculum; from pre-school to middle school. I also want my own business and or non-profit organization for young girls to show them how to create the life they want to live starting with self-love and having a positive, healthy self-image.

Hasan: Wow, I like that. That's dope.

Love': (Smiling) Thanks.

Hasan: So the poem that you performed last night, who was it about if you don't mind me asking?

Love': No, I do not mind. It is about a young man that I met years ago who changed my life. He met me during a rough time in my life. I was living with my roommate after being put out of my mom and stepdad's home and kicked out of the church which is a long story. Anyway, I felt rejected to say the least. I had been hurt by a few men. I was so tired of being hurt. At the time I was not aware that I was attracting that sort of behavior into my life. One of my homegirls at the time had just graduated from college and was coming from Lynchburg, Virginia into town (Portsmouth, Virginia) to go to the club. We were going to a club called Picasso's. I remember as if it were yesterday. When we arrived we went to the bar and got our drinks. I remember there was some space in between she and I. She wanted to appear that she was there by herself, I guess. There was a guy who had approached her and the next thing I knew he had come over asking me for my number and my name. I was a little tipsy so to me, it appeared that he was handsome. Looking back on it I think he was trying to talk to Naseeya and she told me something alluding to the fact that he was trying to talk to her, but that she let me have him. She also said it was because I lived in the area. While most would have felt some type of way, I didn't. Even back then I knew that everything happens for a reason. It was not an accident that he and I met that night. He would come over from time to time. We developed a friendship and I instantly trusted him and that had never happened to me before. The connection for me was just natural. Somehow I felt or thought he would never intentionally hurt me. I remember when I first met him. I thought he was so handsome and then when I found out that he was from here we were both shocked about that. Anyway, he had come over to hang out on a few occasions and we seemed to vibe but one night on a Friday night around two in the a.m. he called and asked if he could come over. I told him yes. I wanted him to come over but I thought he must want some ass. I did not want to do anything with him. By this time, I had just lost my virginity only three or four years prior and still was very inexperienced but I wasn't so inexperienced that I didn't think that I knew what he wanted. When he came over I took him back into my bedroom where a blow-up mattress laid. I told him to come on with no desire whatsoever. He must have felt that from me because he ended up going soft and said, let's just fall asleep. I was relieved because although I was attracted to him I did not want to sleep with him so soon. The next morning he told me that he would be back over either later that day or the following day. I said ok and he left. He kept his word though. He came back over the following day. I remember the day prior telling my homegirl Cali about it and began thinking, "Oh my goodness, he is not attracted to me!!!!" I later realized it was not that he wasn't attracted to me. He just did not want to have sex, I guess. He just did not want to have to drive back to Virginia Beach after leaving the club that night after having a few drinks. He needed a place to crash but at the time I didn't realize that. When he came over the following day one of the most magical experiences took place. He was sitting on the sofa across from me and he got up and laid down on the floor beside me as I sat on the sofa, he reached his hand out and wanted me to take his hand and I did, even though I was puzzled. He slightly pulled me towards him to lay on him and he pulled me in for a kiss. The kiss was supremely magical and it lasted for about twenty minutes or so. No wandering hands. Just an intimate kiss. We never spoke of this kiss. When we finished kissing, we got up and went back to talking like nothing ever happened. We continued conversing for a few more hours and then he left. I asked him to call me when he got home. He did. We talked and I learned more about him. I found out that night that he was joining the military. He was joining the the navy to be exact and would soon be leaving for basic training. I was so sad. I had never trusted anyone so quickly. Right before he left, he came over for the last time. A few months later I relocated to Georgia.

Before he left, he told me that he would have the same number. My friend Cali would always ask if I tried calling him to see if he could receive calls yet. I would call from time to time but his phone was off. When I finally got an answer I was so excited to hear his voice. He seemed to be excited to hear from me as well. His boys were in the background saying, "Oh! He talking to a bitch." He told them, "Nah yo, she ain't like that, don't call her that either." I was grinning from ear to ear. I felt so protected. He said something else in defense of me but I don't remember what it was but he kept touching me without physically entering me. Anyway; he had to get off the phone and he told me he would call me back and he did. The next conversation we had he was singing the song by Amerie called 'Why Don't We Fall In Love'. I told him I did not like her vocal ability and I only liked a few of her songs. He said, "Listen to those words though." I told him that I knew I would have fallen in love with him if he had not left. He asked, "what makes you say that?" I said, "Because I would have. It's the truth." I also told him how he and I reminded me of the movie Brown Sugar. He asked, "Why?" My response was, "because of the type of relationship that they had." He and I talked for a few minutes longer and then he had to go. He told me that when he called again he would be calling to give me his new number. He would be stationed out in California. I told him, that he was probably going to fall in love with an Amerie type. He said why do you think that?" My response was, "because I can see that happening." Sure enough, years later that is exactly what happened. Anyway; he did call me just as he said he would when he moved to California and received a new phone number. He told me to write it down and I told him that it was on the caller ID but what I didn't know was that a few weeks later unknowingly I would be relocating and have no access to the caller ID and the number would be erased. I was distracted due to a psychotic relationship I had gotten involved with even though I didn't know that is what it was at the time. So I lost contact with him until I found him on a popular social media site and still could not tell if it was him for a whole year. Once I realized it was him I was thrilled but that's when I realized he had a child and was involved. Of course, I was not trying to be with him. I just wanted to reconnect with him. So much time had passed but I thought we would eventually reconnect. I sent him a few messages and he responded a few times. About three or four years after our last interaction on social media and a eleven to twelve maybe even thirteen years now after we were last in communication via phone and in person I finally got up enough nerve to tell him how he had left an imprint in my life and messaged him how I was working on a book that he would be in. He never responded. But anyway that was a summary I just gave you (laughing) of who or what the twinkling of an eye was about.

Hasan: Wow, it makes sense to me.

Love': What makes sense to you?

Hasan: How you still feel a connection towards him.

Love': It does? I mean it makes sense for me even though it may not make sense to him.

Hasan: Oh it makes sense to him.

Love': What doesn't make sense is how it makes sense to you. I have felt so odd, weird even; to still feel this way after thirteen years has passed. Wait; how do you know it makes sense to him?

Hasan: I know someone who had a similar situation.

Love' became slightly nervous thinking he may know Mozique.

Love': Who?

Hasan: Myself.

Love': Really? Ok. Your turn.

Hasan: Well, about nine years ago I met someone named Alexandria, her nickname was Dria. She was beautiful. We met through a mutual friend, Mason. Mason was feeling her but she wasn't feeling him in that way. All three of us were really good friends. It was an innocent platonic friendship initially. I tell people all of the time when you start off as friends is when you will know if it has the potential to ever become anything beyond that, well; at least in my experience.

Love': That makes sense.

Hasan: We started hanging out as a threesome but sooner than later it turned into just she and I hanging out. Everyone assumed that she and I were together but we were really just friends. We just loved being around each other. In fact, we were dating other people at the time. Neither one of our significant others could handle being involved with someone who was as close as Dria and I were especially being though that we are of the opposite sex. Her boyfriend broke up with her first. What was funny is that she didn't care. When my then girlfriend broke up with me it was because I would not abide by her ultimatum which consisted of me getting rid of Dria. She literally wanted me to stop being her friend completely. When we met our then significant others Dria and I had been friends already for about three years. There was no way we were going to stop being friends especially when we knew there was nothing going on between us at that time.

One night we were hanging out at her apartment. We were watching movies. We watched her favorite movie first. Her favorite is Love Jones. One of my favorite movies is Brown Sugar. We watched both of those movies. After the movies went off. We were just chillin' and listening to music. She was sitting under the hair dryer with a glass of wine. After she finished drying her hair I was about to leave. She said, "Ok." I left and went to go unlock the door and realized that I did not have my keys so I had to go back in her place. When I knocked on the door, she asked who was it. I told her it was me. She opened the door. She said, "What happened? Are you alright?" I told her, "Yeah, I am fine." Then our song came on, Love of my Life by Erykah Badu. We were dancing. I mean we were going hard on the floor. After that song went off, the next song was by R.L and Deborah Cox, called 'We Can't Be Friends'. I glanced at her and she glanced at me, we both awkwardly looked away and then I grabbed Dria and pulled her to me, thinking I would just hug to let her know that I know we both have the same thoughts but we were both thinking that we did not want to mess up our friendship, our bond. So, I thought hugging her would affirm that. I understood already what she was thinking and or feeling. When I grabbed her to hug her it just naturally happened and we kissed for what seemed like all of eternity. I didn't want to understand what was going on. We did not go any further than that kiss. After we kissed I told her that I needed to get back home to Neveah, which was true but I also knew that I still wanted us to be sure before engaging in that type of activity. Dria told me, Ok. She told me to call her when I got in and I did. When she answered the phone our conversation began.

Dria: Hello

Hasan: Hey

Dria: Ok, so what the hell happened?

Hasan: (Laughing) I don't know. I just went with the flow.

Dria: No you didn't because you stopped.

Hasan: I know I stopped but so did you. Why did we stop it?

Dria: I don't know, maybe I was following your lead.

Hasan: What did it mean to you?

Dria: What did it mean to you?

Hasan: (Laughing) I asked you but I will tell you. It was as if we were touching each other's soul. It felt as though we were making love with our lips and our hearts.

Dria: Ok. Damn. Come back over.

Hasan: (Laughing) It will happen.

Dria: (Laughing) I felt the same exact way and you're right, it will happen. (Laughing) When? You a "boss" Hasan. Let me be your employee (laughing).

Hasan: (Laughing).

We continued to chat the rest of the night. The sun was up when we finally hung up the phone which was nothing unusual for us. The only difference was the fact that we had just expressed our love for each other in a different way for the first time.

Love': Sooooo what happened? I mean are you guys still in touch with each other?

Hasan: No. She moved to Atlanta to pursue a career as a musician. I just never heard from her after she left and now your story makes me feel a lot better knowing that it could be many reasons as to why she never called.

Love': Yes. I am sure she has a legitimate reason for not calling. I am certain she wonders about you and how you are doing.

Hasan: So do you think the reason you didn't call Mozique was because of your new relationship that you had just started when he had given you his new number?

Love: I guess, maybe; I was distracted. About a week later I realized that I didn't have his number. I was so disgusted with myself.

Hasan: Every relationship teaches us something. So what did you learn from that relationship? It had to be an important lesson, considering you ignored homeboy (Laughing).

Love': I did not intentionally ignore him but I did learn valuable lessons as a result of that toxic relationship. Lessons that I am sure that I would not have been able to learn from Mozique because he was so kind to me.

Hasan: Ok, what lesson's did you learn from that toxic relationship?

Love': I learned how crazy I was, how crazy and weird my dysfunctional family was. I also learned that there are many people hurting in ways unimaginable. I learned that you can think that you had it bad until you hear someone else's story. With each relationship, I realized that it was uncovering and or unraveling me to get to the depths of my inner womb. I remember while living in Georgia a woman coming through my line when I was working at a Super store and she was staring at me. She told me that I was divine and that I had searching eyes. I would never forget that. At the time I really did not know why she said that exactly even though I certainly knew what it meant. I went home and googled it to see if me reading the definition would give me the insight I needed. It did not but my experiences did.

Love' and Hasan really had a wonderful time that day. They exchanged numbers. He told her, "add my number to your contact list now, dammit!" (Love' laughed).

When they arrived back at Belle's they noticed that she still was not home. They sat on the porch and talked some more. Love' called her brothers to see where they were. Love' and Hasan sat there for another hour. Hasan received a call letting him know that something had happened to Belle and that she was in the hospital. So Hasan relayed the message to Love' and asked her if she wanted him to take her to the hospital and of course, Love' said, "yes." They were walking towards the car when they noticed Belle pulling up. So Hasan and Love' stood there perplexed.

Love': Ok. Who was that that told you that nonsense?

Hasan: My mom.

Love': Oh, oops.

Hasan: (Smiling)

Love' and Hasan began walking towards Belle's car. Belle got out of her car, holding her arm close to her as if she were in pain.

Love': Are you Ok?

Hasan: What is wrong with your arm?

Belle: I banged it up a little. I was in a fender-bender.

When they looked at her car they realized it appeared to be a little more than a fender bender.

Belle: Can you guys help me into the house, please?

Love' and Hasan helped her into the house and then Hasan asked her, "why did I receive a phone call that you were in the hospital?

Belle: That's probably because I was but I wasn't staying there. No sir. I told them clones I'm going home. They wanted to keep me so I could be there guinea pigs and try to make me sick. I am going to soak in the tub and do some deep breathing and stretching. I going to rub some of grandma Tee's special ointment and I will be just fine.

Love': Well, I can not argue with you there. I'd rather not go to the hospital myself.

Hasan: I just don't want it to be anything serious.

Belle: Goodnight Hasan. You guys do the smoochity and or call each other on the phone so you can get back home to that beautiful baby girl of yours.

Chapter 17

The following two days Hasan and Love' spent a lot of time together. Their children adored each other. Love' was enjoying the interaction with masculine energy but she was ready to go back home now. She wanted the opportunity to talk to Belle before heading back and they had already stayed a day longer than what she and Sadie had originally planned for.

Love' was helping Belle out around the house. One of the things that Love' found so odd was how James, her husband, had not been there as much so Love' was going to talk to her about this. It was the perfect time to do so because Ziariah was napping. Belle was sitting in the living room looking out of the window. Love' asked her if she could speak with her for a moment. Belle told her to have a seat.

Love': What is on your mind Belle?

Belle: Just thinking about the life I have lived.

Love': I have a question for you; Where is James?

Belle: (She looked over at Love') When little James transitioned things changed a lot, in a twinkling of an eye. James became very angry. Our girls became so focused on living that they forgot that a part of living is experiencing and sharing with those you are connected to. And to those that have the same blood running through their veins. James is in and out of the house. He comes for about a month and then leaves again. It was just too painful for him. The girls check on me often but they do not spend much time here. I think they feel so much pain when they visit that they would just rather avoid visiting. I visit them as often as I can. Sometimes I feel so lonely until I remind myself that I am connected to my heart and all things loved are with me.

Love': (Feeling a tad bit emotional) Do you feel that reincarnation is real?

Belle: (Her eyes were as bright as the moon, sol light shining through) What made you ask this question?

Love': Why does it look you have seen a ghost?

Belle: (Chuckling) To answer your question, yes. I have seen ghost or energy.

Love': Really? Who?

Belle: Grandma Tee and her husband and my Aunt Elizabeth. I have felt other's presence and smelled other's fragrances that reminded me of them. I always hoped that I would see my son again (Smiling).

Love': But you haven't?

Belle: I feel that I have, now (Smiling).

Love' looked as though she had seen a ghost. She became slightly nervous and uncertain of her next question or response. She began looking down at the floor. It was something about the floor that helped her to feel grounded, from grounded to confident, from confident to decisive, from decisive to gratitude and love, from love to power in her words, from power in her words, to insight she could see beyond any words. It literally flashed right before her. It was as if Love' was watching Belle see into her. Love' began to weep and so did Belle. They had yet to say a word. Belle got up and walked over to Love' and laid her head in Love's lap and cried. Love' placed her hand on Belle's hair and began combing it with her fingers. This moment lasted for what seemed like an hour or so. When Belle sat up and looked into Love's eyes, she smiled and Love' smiled back.

Belle: Tell me what is you want to say now.

Love' began to tell her about her dream and how she knew she was James in her previous life. She began to share things with Belle regarding the encounter she had with Sadie when she went into Sadie's bedroom in the middle of the night only to make her aware that she was once James.

Love': How did you know? Or when did you know?

Belle: I knew that we had a connection when you were first born but I can't say that I knew until you came to visit this weekend.

Love' and Belle continued to converse and enjoy the moment.

Love': It's easy to see when you're looking through the eyes of the heart and or soul. You saw into me. I love you, Belle.

Belle: (Weeping) I love you too. Yea, energy is borrowed. It just transitions. We all just switch roles or travel to other worlds and or dimensions.

Love' was looking out of the window now. Belle noticed it and asked her what she was thinking about. Love' answered.

Love': What do you think about Hasan?

Belle: (Busted out into a hearty laugh) I think someone is having a change of heart. You already know what I think about him. Is there someone else you have in my mind?

Love': No, not really. There is just someone that has crossed my mind over the last thirteen or fourteen years.

Love' began telling Belle about Mozique. She explained to her how the piece entitled, In the twinkling of an eye was about him.

Belle: Wow, it definitely seems as though there was a connection between you two.

Love': Yes.

Belle: Did you and Hasan kiss?

Love': No. We had a really great time. There is definitely chemistry there. Anyway, I am just going to focus on myself and Ziariah.

Belle: Was Mozique your first love? for lack of a better term.

Love': No. I will always love my first love though. Amir and I are in two different places of our lives. He wants to be "buddies" because he has so much going on. I don't. I want and deserve more than physical affection and therefore I am not willing to compromise. Although if I meet someone and their energy is high and loving, healthy and functioning on a colorful level then, maybe I would be open to an exchange of some loving, mutual respect sex, it has been 5 years since I have....oh, anyway...

Belle: Sometimes, what we want is staring us in the face.

Love': Who? Hasan?

Belle: No, you. You can give yourself the unconditional consistent love, until you are ready for whomever you meet or connect with in that way.

Love': I have realized throughout my experiences that I was naive and or unaware and my actions began to exude that I truly did not feel good about myself. Of course at the time I was unaware of what takes place when a person, specifically a woman, engages in sexual intercourse.

Belle: What do you feel takes place?

Love': An exchange of energy. If you think about the word inter-course. A woman is typically open even if she isn't aware that she is. Her body and make-up are naturally open on a conscious level and subconscious level. Enter course. The energy flows throughout all of our systems and it can either be healthy or toxic. While all things lead to the path of self-love and discovery if I can avoid toxicity as much as possible, I will. Love' and Belle continued their conversation.

The following day Love' and Sadie were heading back home. Love' was so grateful for the opportunity she had to come visit. She and Hasan had exchanged numbers and he told her to call him once she got back to Virginia.

Chapter 18

Love' was looking forward to heading back home. She was definitely motivated to get busy working on some things and completing some of the things that she had already started. We left around four o' clock in the a.m. Ziariah was sleep. Love' began telling me about her outing with Hasan. She then began telling me about her and Belle's conversation. After she finished talking she became very quiet. I knew she was ready to talk about James. She was ready to talk about things that I was not ready for but I had made it up in my mind that if she brought it up I would share.

Love': So do you mind telling me about what happened with James?

Sadie: No, I don't mind. I need to talk about it but first I want to know why you want to know. Was it something you read in one of his books?

Love': Yes and just a feeling I have. He really loved you but you became pregnant with someone else's child. It seemed as though you loved him as well.

Sadie: Yes I loved him and I took him for granted. He had always been there for me. I did not know how to receive his love. I was scared also. I was there the night he transitioned. I noticed he kept holding his chest area where his heart was. He was so hurt that I was pregnant by someone other than him. I feel as though he transitioned due to a heart torn or broken. I dealt with guilt and shame for years.

I began crying as I shared this story with her. While at a stop light I happened to glance over at Love' and her eyes were as bright as the moon, sol light shining through.

Sadie: What are you thinking about.

Love': I see the relationship between this life and the other. My heart must remain open to all and any of the limitless possibilities. Life is infinite. I was holding onto the past because my heart has been afraid due to the past painful experiences. So the one experience that I had where I was not hurt I held on to it and refused to open up completely. If that friendship with Mozique was truly what I have been saying then I will be open to opportunities. I have been afraid to live, to experience even in the expansion regarding my ability to create and manifest the divine vision for my journey. The bottom line is that I have a choice. I can either hold on to things that I can not control or be aware of the things that I can control. I can be free to live, even if I begin to have feelings of fear I can shift those feelings just like when a child needs to redirect their energy. I can shift. I can be afraid of pain which is a part of life or I can be bold and courageous and enjoy life or learn and grow from the cosmic lessons.

Love' began to cry. She was extremely thankful. I cried with her. We continued to converse until Ziariah woke up and then we were entertained by Ziariah and her beautiful personality.

We arrived back in Virginia around ten o' clock in the a.m. I thanked them both for coming and dropped them off at home.

Over the next month Love' was working on her book entitled, Our Eyes; Bright As The Moon (Sol light shining through). I was excited for her. She was also working on getting into a career as well.

She has applied to an organization that went into the low-income schools and taught. She had been offered the position and was excited. This would require her relocating to a different state and although she was a little nervous, she was ready. The position would not officially begin until the summer. So over the next six months, she would be working an "in the meantime" job. Another one of Love's jobs consisted of working hard to get her book published. She had no idea where to begin. She did not want to self-publish and she began realizing how costly it was if you did not sign with a major publishing company. Love' wanted to own the rights to her work but on the other hand, she wanted a nice check. She became very frustrated because nothing seem to be working out at the time for her book getting published. She did not know who to ask initially.

Over the next month, she and Amir had been in communication again. She wanted to tell him how she appreciated his honesty regarding what he was looking for or not looking for. Amir missed them communicating. He asked if they could go hang out and Love' agreed to but she really did not believe that he was going to follow through with it. Love' knew that they would always have their connection.

Love' began to voice her concerns regarding her book not being published and I made the suggestion of speaking with Belle and a friend of the family who had helped publish James' work. So

Love' did and she submitted a copy and it was protected under copyright laws so no one could steal her work.

One day about two and a half months later after she submitted her work and our visit to Delaware, Love' and I were on the phone. Someone was beeping in on the other line. She asked me to hold on and I did. When she clicked back over, she was crying and I could barely understand what she way saying. I told her to calm down so I could understand her. She did.

Love': It was the publishing company. They want to meet with me. They want to do a deal with me. Needless to say, we were both ecstatic. I felt like this time James would thrive as an author. Well, the soul living through James as now Love' would. Her book was published two months later. I remember when Love' made the announcement on her social media outlets and how she had wanted to do that for so long.

Another six months had passed and Love' had been communicating with Hasan quite frequently. She really had a connection with Hasan. They had never been physically intimate. He loved talking to her. They had many conversations that went beyond the typical "getting to know you" conversations. Hasan loved her and although Love' had not admitted to it I knew she loved Hasan too. Whenever anyone mentioned him, her eyes were as bright as the moon, sol light shining through. They were planning for Hasan to come for a visit. She was relocating to North Carolina and he wanted to help her move in. He told her after he helped with her moving in he would then stay for another week. He was bringing Neveah as well. The move to North Carolina would be taking place in a few weeks because she had been asked to do a book signing and a conference for aspiring African American writers on the west coast. She and Hasan had already spent time together one weekend in New York a few weeks ago and nothing happened sexually. This just made their bond so much more intense. Ziariah loved Hasan and Neveah. They still had not labeled this connection but I felt strongly that the time for that would soon be manifesting. Anyway, She was planning for the trip to California for the book signing and conference.

Hasan was now working for an independent production company as a writer that was located in a few cities on the coast and was going to be in San Francisco at one of the offices during that time which was about six hours away driving from where Love' would be which was Los angles. He really wanted to see her and come and support her.

The closer it became time to traveling, the more nervous Love' became and she did not know why. Rayanna, Ziariah and myself would be traveling with her. It would be Ziariah's first time on a plane. They would be leaving for California in two weeks.

The day that they were leaving they had to be at the airport by five in the morning. While on the plane Love' began reflecting and one of the thoughts that came to her. "When you were thankful, it didn't go as you planned. When you were trying to force it and it just wouldn't work. When you were trying to understand and asked, 'Why me?', the mindset at the time just wasn't big enough for where you are going and who you are. Couldn't force it because you had to expand, continuously expanding."

She became overwhelmed with gratitude. She knew that she had to grow through; in the process there was clarity. Everything she had ever been through she was thankful for it all.

When we arrived they went to the car rental place and drove to the hotel. Love' went straight to sleep. Rayanna and Ziariah were up and excited. Rayanna and Ziariah would not be attending the book signing on Saturday, I was going to that one but they were planning to attend the conference on Sunday.

The next day Love' woke up ready to start her day. She meditated and did a ritual in remembrance of her ancestors. The ritual consisted of lighting a candle and visualizing her ancestors, specifically her immediate ancestors. She poured libations out as well. She wore a very sacred, ancient and powerful fragranced oil.

Her book signing was at three o'clock. Rayanna and Ziariah were up and were ready to go get something to eat. The time was 7 a.m. They all showered and got dressed to get something to eat. Love' wanted to be back no later than ten o'clock. The three of them had a great time at breakfast. I stayed behind and slept some more. After eating they headed back to the room. Love' did not start getting ready until noon and hour later we were on our way to the book signing. She was wearing a yellow and white fitted dress with camel colored heels. She looked and felt amazing. I was so proud and honored to be there with her. We were only forty-five minutes early. It was a really nice crowd. Her agent who ultimately became Love's friend greeted Love' and I. Her agent's name is Paula. Paula introduced her and explained to the audience that Love' would answer a few questions and then have a ten to fifteen intermission before answering a few more questions and proceeding with signing books.

I could see that Love' was nervous. I looked at her and we smiled. I was sitting in the front row and I mouthed to her to take a deep breath and I did the same with her. She smiled again. When she was standing in front of me talking about the process for writing and some of her experiences she told the people, "While this is not all that I have experienced in this book. This is nowhere near the journeys I have lived in this life or the next. What was shared was chosen for healing purposes not just for me but for those who took the time to read it. I can remember while writing and typing focusing on healing energy. I prayed that those who read it would experience healing of some sort. That they would find something that they could relate to." Love' shared a few more words and then It was time for the crowd to ask questions. There was a microphone in the middle of the aisle and a line of people ready to ask her questions. I could see that Love' became teary eyed. I imagined she was feeling as though it was surreal. She often said, "I just want to help people. I just want people to be healed."

Love' had looked down for a moment to take a sip out of her cup of lemon/lime water with mint and when she looked up; eyes were as bright as the moon, the brightest I had ever seen them, sol light shining through. I looked back to see who she saw and then I looked back up at her, I didn't know whether she was going to cry or run but she had the most beautiful smile on her face and in her soul. Her eyes lit up. Yeah, eyes were bright as the moon, sol light shining through. There was a mirror and I noticed that she was looking directly into it and smiling but then she kept looking in the direction of a young man. I turned towards my right and noticed that Hasan had come and was grinning from ear to ear with deep interest in everything that Love' was saying.

The first person's question was, "What was the overall message you received from your book?"

Love': (Smiled) A tear falling down from her eye and she said, "I was just looking in that mirror right there and realized that James's mother, Belle was right, the thing that you need and want is staring you right in the face. I don't think that for me there was an overall message that was gained. I gained multiple. One being, no matter how deep, spiritual or knowledgable one may be, always ride with your gut intuition. It has directions and knows where it's leading you. For me, the 'connection' had more to do with me being connected to myself, the highest self, force, and or God source. If I am not connecting within then no connection will be functioning at its highest potential, which is really limitless. Listening, observing and reflecting and becoming aware of my thoughts and actions is another vital nugget. Love is a force that has a way of assisting with clarity and patience in order for one to learn how to stay present in the moment, it's a force that just always is. In this moment clarity was speaking as rain drops falling on a warm beautiful sunny day with flowers in full bloom and the melodies of nature whispering sweet tunes. For Mozique merely introduced me to the love within myself I just had to live more and or travel more on this journey to remember and realize this internal awareness of self-acceptance and appreciation had always been there laying dormant to only awaken. In fact in some way most if not all connections have done that, of course not with the same touch of magnetism" Her eyes were as bright as the moon sol light shining through....

As Love' continued answering questions I noticed a slight reaction from her; one that she was trying to not be obvious with but one that was noticeable if you knew her as I do. She began smiling. I turned around once again to see if I would recognize who it was. I knew that Hasan was there but he was on the opposite side and it did not appear that Love' had even noticed that he was there, or at least not just yet. She was looking in the direction of where the people were lined up asking questions. Her eyes lit up so bright. Her eyes were bright as the moon. She looked as if she saw something or someone. Love' began to smile. It was the most brilliant smile. Paula walked up to the microphone after the seventh question and Love's reply and once Paula announced that the intermission would begin Love' immediately rushed off to the bathroom.

Love' stands in the bathroom waiting to get to the mirror. The bathroom somehow managed to be already filled with a lady in each stall and many in the mirror. These women must have left way before the last question was answered. It turned out to be more people in the audience than Love' had expected.

Love' was standing near the bathroom door and realized she should move, as she was turning her back away from the door so that her back would face the wall she was once standing in front of she noticed out of her peripheral vision a small to mid-size circular mirror standing off away from everyone. Not too far away from where she was already standing. She took about seven steps and stood in front of that mirror and saw a light, a glow shining from within and in that moment it truly hit her and then a mature woman, short, dark skin complected woman with long gray hair and glasses tapped Love' on the shoulder with the most brilliant smile, beautiful physique, beautiful face and her high cheek bones, big, brown eyes and said, "There's a light. You have a glow shining from inside and I can see it." She then grabbed Love's left hand and said, "You know there are always two reasons that people believe when a woman has a natural glow 1. She is in love with her man or 2. She's with child; but they just don't realize that sometimes that glow is a love you realized on the inside. Yes, divine one; you are in love with you and it's shining. I've seen that glow before and I've still got it." Love' held the lady so tight and thanked her because that is what she realized standing in that mirror. Mozique had come into her life to show her, guide her back to herself many years ago and in that moment she accepted years later that everything she had been through was simply for her to return to herself, love and honor herself. All of those years prior while enduring many things she felt as though she was watching herself outside of herself going through and now she was within herself, feeling and knowing she is so connected to that divine source, the source, the highest, her higher self. The divine source would speak through her love ones but during that time she could only hear it; not listen to it. Depending on what the situation was and or what was happening in her life at the time. She ultimately had to learn to practice the art of listening to the divine source within herself before she could accept it from others as often as she does now.

Something within Mozique saw what she needed and desired even if he wasn't consciously aware. She was thankful for the experience and now she knew love within herself in such a way that no matter if they never crossed paths again, she was who she was waiting for and she had everything inside of her to attract opportunities and or experiences that would always remind her how to love herself first and others. She had herself to remind her of love and to love as well as to listen. She had accepted that divine love would always exist with or without acknowledgment from anyone outside of herself. She glowed because she knows. She is divine Love'. She was ready for the next phase.

I saw her coming out of the bathroom with the brightest smile. The audience clapped. I looked at her in awe of how poised and confident she was. I watched her intensely as she was walking and I noticed she began waving to someone with so much joy in her eye, eyes as the bright as the moon sol light shining through and a tear fell from her eye.... For a moment, I wondered if it was Amir. For the most part; throughout the years he'd always supported her, always been there for many pivotal moments and or experiences of her life and they supported each other. She knew as well as I did she would always love him; no matter what happened or where they were or end up on their personal journey's because the love was unconditional.

I knew that she had already glanced over at Hasan but perhaps she saw him for the first time in a different light.

She had one of the most brilliant smiles and this smile was different. I just kept rehearsing that wave she did emphatically, her eyes were just as brilliant as her smile, her eyes were as bright as the moon, sol light shining through and that tear that fell from her eye and then another tear.... What or whom did she see? Was it him? Mozique? the connection she felt years ago towards him would always be a valuable memory for her, always!!! Her heart would always feel that endless touch and or kiss of bliss.

Love' remembered hearing often how society would say men did not listen and how women have to repeat themselves to them, over and over again. As she had grown on her journey she realized that there were women who did not listen too well either; including herself at one point and time in her life. She realized on her journey that when a man tells you by his actions and often times he will even tell you verbally who he is and who he is not. Instead of listening sometimes women try to change him. He will often times tell whether he's looking for commitment or if he is not. He will often times tell if he is or is not 'feeling' you. Some women turn their listening ear off and hear the pain of their fatherless past. Since they could not "save" their fathers from the pain their fathers may have faced, they could not "feel" their fathers love. So they continually invite the same cycle of chasing after someone who is not truly "feeling" them or they search for a boy they can control since they could not control their fathers being in and out of their lives. Some times it is the pain carried through the DNA due to the experience of a motherless childhood or fatherless. Sometimes the parents are physically present but are not mentally, emotionally or spiritually in tune (present). No matter what, when "he's" not feeling you accept this as a great sign. He may be telling you there is no connection and that he is not capable of loving you the way you have yet to love yourself and or incapable of being a vessel in a healthy relationship. Love' was thankful for many realizations. She then began to truly experience giving and living thanks by not allowing anyone or anything including herself to deceive her via mistreatment or thought into thinking she was anything less than what she is or who she is....

Love' was thankful for her family. She loved her parents dearly and would ever be grateful. She learned so much through the ups and downs how to live and release. The relationship she had with her family she was finally able to appreciate and love as it was continually evolving just as she and the journey she was on and still is on. She was accepting her authentic self. She realized it was not about the labels of soul mate or twin flames. It was about an honest genuine connection that ignites awareness and healThy growth!!!! Her eyes were just as brilliant as her smile, her eyes were as bright as the moon, sol light shining through and that tear that fell from her eye and then another tear....It seemed as though she was seeing someone other than Hasan or was it Hasan? What or whom did she see?

James began staring out of the window after typing the last line wondering what he would write about next; perhaps something entitled Dragonfly Magic Sun....

Allegiance

I pledge allegiance to the divine laws of nature to the divine within to the light codes within my DNA. Giving eternal thanks to the ancestors from which I stand and the cosmos from which I am. To the ancestors who have come before and are running through these veins - no grave are they in, they are alive, even looking through my eyes - Feeling their presence - seen and unseen. Allegiance to balance - love - nature, the supreme within.

Answering the call, here to learn, to share and gather - to cherish and remember love is nature.

Sol Light Shining Through
About The Author

I am so mysterious; I am unexplainable even to myself at certain moments yet it always makes sense in hindsight.

Some call them psychics, others call them prophets, seers, those with intuitiveness, knowledge & insight. Love' heard a conversation one night through her gift of intuitiveness. The question she heard was, "What did you see in her?" and her reply while in deep thought within after hearing the question asked so clear: "What he saw was more than, having nothing to do with the physical; for what he saw could never be erased. For what he saw was within. It just so happened to shine in the midst of the adversity as Love' traveled on a soul's journey."

Love' began to see, love and experience the love within. As she accepted this truth, her life would forever change. He helped her to see beyond. Not so much in those moments, but it would be many years before she would be ready to accept love so deep within. It wasn't him. It was love, a soul's journey; eyes as bright as the moon, sol light shining through.

At one time all of the philosophies, teachings, and truths that were unveiling and being revealed had her head spinning. If it were not for those things she was remembering and learning, she would not have seen the inward path. Those philosophies, teachings and/or truths, revealed levels of an innate awareness of unique sequences and tailored patterns that connect ever-evolving truths that are for a specific trip ~~ the journey she was on.

Love' was on a path to discovering and rediscovering. Where soul traveled, would be exactly where she needed to be in order to accept her truest self. Through heartache and love, she realizes now that she gained a higher level of awareness. What she imagined actually turned out to be real. Eyes as bright as the moon, sol light shining through.